Sustainable Management, Wertschöpfung und Effizienz

Reihe herausgegeben von
Gregor Weber, Breunigweiler, Deutschland
Markus Bodemann, Warburg, Deutschland
René Schmidpeter, Köln, Deutschland

In dieser Schriftenreihe stehen insbesondere empirische und praxisnahe Studien zu nachhaltigem Wirtschaften und Effizienz im Mittelpunkt. Energie-, Umwelt-, Nachhaltigkeits-, CSR-, Innovations-, Risiko- und integrierte Managementsysteme sind nur einige Beispiele, die Sie hier wiederfinden. Ein besonderer Fokus liegt dabei auf dem Nutzen, den solche Systeme für die Anwendung in der Praxis bieten, um zu helfen die globalen Nachhaltigkeitsziele (SDGs) umzusetzen. Publiziert werden nationale und internationale wissenschaftliche Arbeiten.

This series is focusing on empirical and practical research in the fields of sustainable management and efficiency. Management systems in the context of energy, environment, sustainability, CSR, innovation, risk as well as integrated management systems are just a few examples which can be found here. A special focus is on the value such systems can offer for the application in practice supporting the implementation of the global sustainable development goals, the SDGs. National and international scientific publications are published (English and German).

Weitere Bände in der Reihe http://www.springer.com/series/15909

Vanessa Just

Sustainable Business Processes in Global Companies

Current Perspectives and Future Trends in Regard to Efficiency and Risk Management

Springer Gabler

Vanessa Just
Bucharest, Romania

THE BUCHAREST UNIVERSITY OF ECONOMIC STUDIES SUSTAINABLE BUSINESS PROCESSES IN GLOBAL COMPANIES. CURRENT PERSPECTIVES AND FUTURE TRENDS

Scientific supervisor: Prof. univ. dr. Bogdan Christian ONETE

ISSN 2523-8620 ISSN 2523-8639 (electronic)
Sustainable Management, Wertschöpfung und Effizienz
ISBN 978-3-658-28195-3 ISBN 978-3-658-28196-0 (eBook)
https://doi.org/10.1007/978-3-658-28196-0

Springer Gabler

This Springer Gabler imprint is published by the registered company Springer Fachmedien Wiesbaden GmbH part of Springer Nature.
The registered company address is: Abraham-Lincoln-Str. 46, 65189 Wiesbaden, Germany

Table of Contents

List of Abreviations

Ad	Amortisation duration
AD	Anno Domini
BM	Business Model
BPM	Business Process Management
BSC	Balanced Scorecard
CFROI	Cash flow Return on Investment
CMD –CU	Customer Master Data
CMMI	Capability Maturity Model Integration
COSO	Committee of Sponsoring Organizations
CRM	Customer Relationship Management
CRO	Chief Risk Officer
DHG	Developing Health Globally
DJSI	Dow Jones Sustainability Index
DJSIC	Dow Jones Sustainability Index Committee
EBIT	Earnings Before Interest and Taxes
ECV	Expected commercial value
EFQM	European Foundation for Quality Management
ERM	Enterprise risk management
EU	European Union
EVA	Economic Value Added
GDP	Gross Domestic Product
GPM	Business Process Management
GPM	Global Precipitation Measurement
GPS	Global Positioning System
GRI	Global Reporting Initiative
IAA	Insurance Auto Auction
IFRS	International Financial Reporting Standards
IPMA	International Project Management Association
ISO	International Organization for Standardization
IT	Information Technology
KPI	Key Performance Indicators
MPM	Multi-Project-Management
OEMs	Original equipment manufacturers
OPM3	Organization Project Management Model
PESTEL	Political, Economic, Social, Technological, Environmental, and Legal
SSCM	Sustainable Supply Chain Management

UNEP	United Nations Environment Programme
PMO	Project Management Office
PPM	Project-Portfolio-Management
PSC	Project Scorecard
PwC	PricewaterhouseCoopers
R&D	Research and Development
ROCE	Return on Capital Employed
ROI	Return on Investment
SLA	Service Level Agreement
SMEs	Small and Medium-sized Enterprises
SMR	Sustainability Management and Reporting
SWOT	Strengths, Weaknesses, Opportunities, and Threats
TQM	Total Quality Management
UNEP	United Nations Environment Programme
VDI	Virtual Desktop Infrastructure
WC	Working Capital

List of Figures

List of Tables

1.a Introduction

Lately, the idea of sustainable advancement has faced an increased interest from scholars, policymakers and businessmen. However, for most business officials, the idea remains hypothetical. In many cases, this is due to the fact that, if sustainable advancement is about to reach its real potential, this must be holistically approached in all business processes developed in a company; an exercise quite hard to be accomplished.

For any company, sustainable improvement means embracing all business procedures and exercises implied by both the company and its partners in the present, while securing, maintaining and upgrading all types of assets that will be required in the future. The core of this approach reflects the one initially proposed by the World Commission on Environment and Development and outlines that sustainable improvement must address the issues of a business and of its stakeholders. The latter may refer to investors, moneylenders, clients, representatives, providers, and other groups who are directly influenced by the company's activity. Likewise, it features businesses' reliance on human and normal assets, notwithstanding physical and monetary capital. Nevertheless, the financial aspects should not be totally excluded.

This definition is expected to enable business executives to apply the idea of sustainable improvement in their organization. However, it is worth emphasising that sustainable advancement cannot be accomplished by a solitary endeavour – either a company, or a whole business group. Sustainable advancement is an extremely complex phenomenon, which requires the involvement of each member in the worldwide economy – taking into consideration customers and governments – where all present issues need to be addressed in a proper way, considering their implications for future generations as well.

Achieving such a goal is quite a task in an economy governed by continuous changes. This refers to the reconsideration and re-examination of how businesses develop their activity in a framework strongly characterised by pronounced innovation. Businesses have constantly changed within various circumstances. However, high technological advances – for example, cloud, social, and Big Data examination – have quickened the pace at which present businesses are developing and how much they change the way they work, approach and serve customers. The intense usage of information is changing business models, encouraging new products and services development, creating new procedures, producing usefulness, and introducing innovative management cultures. Digitalization leads to changes in almost every industry.

V. Just, *Sustainable Business Processes in Global Companies*,
Sustainable Management, Wertschöpfung und Effizienz,
https://doi.org/10.1007/978-3-658-28196-0_1

By changing the focal point of development from equipment to programming, IT has significantly quickened the procedure of new business-model creation.

This thesis casts an innovative light upon how business processes can be improved in global companies in a sustainable context. The thesis approaches the development of sustainable business processes in global companies in a challenging environment, focusing on how these companies change when applying Business Process Management procedures in developing sustainable activities.

The thesis is based on an extremely comprehensive literature review process and on field and desk pieces of research. The literature review process outlines a personal contribution and, at the same time, an innovative approach through the methods and techniques implied; comparative and critical analysis were developed. In addition to a complex theoretical approach to sustainability, business processes, project management, risk management and business models, the thesis outlines important case studies in the research area. Referring only to the latter aspects, the thesis puts forward a series of trends in performant business models within a sustainable framework, in the transport industry, supporting and promoting the idea of self-driving cars, in the particular case of Germany. The innovative contribution of the thesis in the research area consists in developing a complex case study research about the improvement of business processes in global companies. The research focuses on revealing insight into the structure and difficulties related to sustainable business processes development, keeping in mind the end goal of generating a system for supporting directors in enhancing their business models. Developing a model for increasing process efficiency, quality and agility in business processes, by following the example of sales support processes in various countries, was one of the objectives set by the main case study. Another important objective of the case study was to ensure quick adaptability of processes through standardization and further automation, that shall support the sustainability of processes. In order to design such a model, features of the project excellence model were introduced into the project management processes. With the project excellence model, the success of project management can be increased on the long-term. The continuous improvement process and optimization of the processes themselves lead to success. The first recommended step for any company is to carry out a self-assessment process, that offers the possibility to uncover initial weaknesses. Furthermore, projects can be internally compared, and successful projects may be identified. This leads to an internal exchange of particularly good methods and approaches for project management, whereby the project excellence model combines all the enablers and results of all success factors of project management, in terms of both quantity and quality.

The thesis approaches an up-to-date issue, of high importance for scholars, entrepreneurs and managers. Developing sustainable business processes in global companies in a changing environment raises many questions for entrepreneurs and managers. Through its fundamental pieces of research, this thesis aims to provide proper answers to these questions, raising awareness among entrepreneurs and managers, not only about developing sustainable business processes and models, but also about continuously improving them. The thesis may represent an important guideline for entrepreneurs and managers in their activity. Apart from its high practical impact, the thesis brings an important contribution to the diversification of the scientific literature in the area of sustainability, especially by approaching this subject through the lens of global companies and their specific business processes.

Both its theoretical and practical impacts are an outcome of the thesis content and structure, briefly illustrated in figure 1.

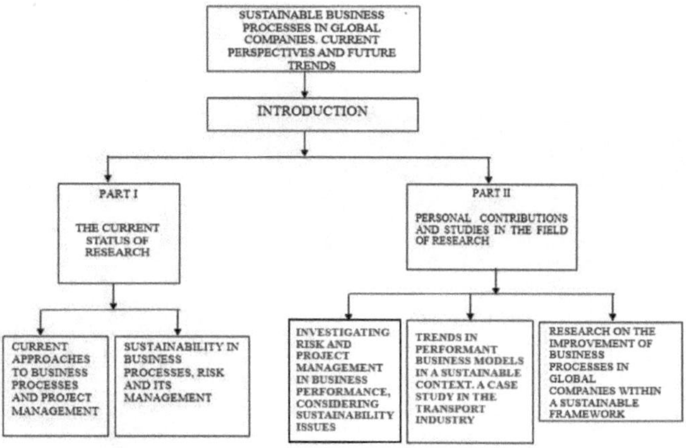

Figure 1: Thesis structure

Source: own representation

The thesis is composed of two main parts. The first one details the current status of research in the area of investigation and sustainability. It is mainly theoretical and comprises two specific chapters. Chapter one approaches business processes and project management, while chapter two tapps the ideas of sustainability in business processes, corelated with risk management issues. The second part of the thesis highlights the main personal contributions and studies developed in the research area. This part, of high theoretical and practical impact, is composed of three chapters, all based on innovative pieces of research and contributions. The third chapter of the thesis opens this section with fresh approaches to risk and project management in assessing business performance, taking into consideration sustainability issues. This chapter makes the connection and transition from the theoretical to the practical part of the thesis, generating a comprehensive introduction for the following two chapters. The fourth chapter outlines a novel study in the transport industry, focusing on performant business models within a sustainable context. Chapter five closes the second part of the thesis with a complex and comprehensive case study research, aiming to outline a model for improving business processes in global companies within a sustainable framework. The thesis ends up with a series of final considerations.

Part I: The Current Status Of Research

1 Current Approaches To Business Processes And Project Management

1.1 General Aspects Regarding Business Processes

Throughout the 1990s, organizations started to expand their attention towards business structure and association. The accomplishment of process changes or advancement goals was improved with approaches such as the Business Process reengineering (Song & Choi, 2011).

So far, there is no broad material approach for organizations to actualize sustainable business forms. However, various surveys outlined in scientific literature and/or reports, as well as the experience of different organizations, may represent an important starting point in enhancing business procedures and making them sustainable.

This chapter aims to show the similarity and impact of business process administration and sustainability, taking into consideration various kinds of organization forms, economic sustainability and sustainability for business association and procedures. Within such a framework, the chapter aims to prove, support and promote the idea that sustainability in business process administration may enhance the company's success in all areas.

Lately, sustainability faced and still faces an increasing significance and consideration in the professional workplace. The main determinants may be related to social viewpoints, administrative perspectives, client prerequisites, among others. Numerous organizations are embracing sustainability in all their hierarchical levels, activities and business forms overall. However, there are still many organizations that have not achieved the sustainability level as targeted in the initiation phase of their company. One cause may be the fact that most sustainability-related activities are focused on one particular division, or territory of the association, instead of approaching them in a more holistic manner. The organization, in its entirety, should focus on the same goal, respectively achieving a high level of sustainability through its activities. In such a context, a more refined examination is necessary, and this should take into consideration the entire communication procedure, to assess the full status of the sustainability execution.

The concept of sustainability is an ancient and widespread principle of human thought and action. Ever since ancient times, humans were guided by this principle and lived in harmony with nature, in a way in which resources were conserved. The

V. Just, *Sustainable Business Processes in Global Companies*,
Sustainable Management, Wertschöpfung und Effizienz,
https://doi.org/10.1007/978-3-658-28196-0_2

term "sustainability" was first used in this context at the beginning of the 18th century in forestry and, since then, it has been subject to constant changes.

Regarding companies, when entrepreneurs understood their impact on the environment, and the responsibility they have towards it and the communities they belong to, sustainability became a major issue. Furthermore, since its direct correlation with profitability became incontestable, this turned into a subject of high importance on entrepreneurs' agendas. This process has been going on for several decades.

The subject of sustainability is highly approached in the Information Systems Research (ISR), Business Process Management (BPM) being the topic that catches all the attention in this field. Guided by the principle that "making processes more sustainable will ultimately lead to making organisations more sustainable" (Pernici, et al., 2012), "BPM experts develop tools and metrics that are aimed at integrating sustainability aspects into the process analysis and (re)design" (Levina, 2015).

1.1.1 Types and elements of business processes

The term "process" frequently alludes to advance, methodology or improvement. However, this is not always portrayed in the same way, not outlining an unanimously accepted definition in the scientific literature. However, the term may be defined as a "sequence of steps developed in a logical order, having a well-defined starting and finishing point, which leads to a desired result or outcome. Thus, each process can be divided into individual activities, which do not exclusively extend in a row" (Just, 2016*)*.

According to EN ISO 8402, a process is defined as a "set of interrelated resources and related activities". Resources include, for example, personnel, finance, facilities, as well as techniques and methods (Haubrock & Schär, 2016).

The process may also be described as a sequence or an array of individual activities, which start at a specific time and end with a measurable result.

The core of any organizational objective is a number of business processes that determine the success rate of the corporation's goals (Mateescu, et al., 2015). Processes exist in every company and its departments and they are not implied only for developing physical goods. (Harvard Business School, 2010)

Processes are complexly approached by Porter (1985): "Every company is a collection of activities designed by the product, manufactured, distributed, delivered and supported. All these activities can be represented in a value chain."

Vital components of procedures are inputs, throughputs and outputs. Inputs are accessible components as articles as well as data, which are provided during the start or amid the procedure, from the outside – in this way, the usage and execution of the procedure is conceivable. Affecting conditions and attributes of the procedure are incorporated with throughputs. The value adding exercises upgrade or prompt the outcome as the output of procedures. Outputs are questions or administrations which are created and accessible before the ending of the procedure (Becker, et al., 1995). All sorts of inputs (as raw materials, data, information, duties, and status) are changed into outputs (Burlton, 2001).

Distinctive sorts of procedures exist inside the organization, contingent upon the degree of combination in the development of client esteem or the association's structure (Karavul, 2015). A business procedure gets a starting input and finishes with the accomplishment of the procedure objective (Bejinariu, et al., 2016).

There are two sorts of business forms: essential and strong/auxiliary procedures. The order relies upon whether a procedure is directly engaged with the formation of client esteem or worried about the association's inner exercises. Essential procedures of ventures are, generally, related to logistics, marketing and selling. Essential procedures inside the value chain are those directly associated with the formation of significant value by delivering products or services; essential business forms are mainly aiming to provide benefits specifically for their clients (Porter, 1985). The remaining processes, usually referred to as secondary processes in the specific scientific literature, have a supportive function. Procuring, controlling, or human resources are just a few examples in this sense. Generally, these are important as they support the proper development of the primary business processes.

1.1.2 Distinction between primary processes and supportive processes in organizations and their classification

Support and enabling processes make available the input factors – such as services, resources and facilities – which are needed for the management and core processes. Accounting, technical support and human resources may represent proper examples of supporting processes.

In order to identify whether a process is a primary or a support one, the level of involvement in the procedure for value performance can be distinguished. This depends on whether a process is directly involved in the creation of customer value.

In accordance with the highly acknowledged value chain model of M. Porter, a classification of business procedures can be determined. In this model, primary activities of enterprises are, for example, logistics, marketing and sales. Generally, it can be stated that primary processes in the value chain are those directly involved in value creation, by producing goods or services. The remaining processes – supportive processes - have a supportive function and may refer to procuring, controlling and human resources, for example.

Thusly, Porter's value chain model, which forms on a division of primary and secondary activities, bears direct relation to business processes. Business processes might be cross-functional and therefore range above several business purposes but are embedded in the overall value chain, implicitly in the organizational structure (Rummler & Brache, 1995). Thusly, it can be stated that the value chain model of Porter seeks a distinction of primary and secondary activities, according to the degree of integration. This differentiation will be elaborated further on in the chapter, three essential types of processes being thoroughly described.

The degree of formality is another way for process classification. "*Informal*" means that the enterprise does not document its processes as a set of steps which should be executed under certain conditions. Procedures ought to be (exceptionally) formalized to pick up mindfulness and learning, and additionally to upgrade a typical comprehension. Procedures may be envisioned as an arrangement of exercises. Occasionally, processes might be an informal procedure, before the enterprise increases the degree of formality by documentation and/or description (Harvard Business School, 2010).

Processes classification is based on process-oriented thinking and on an analytical approach. Orientation towards processes may facilitate the reduction of costs and achievement of goals (Fischer, et al., 2006). Regardless of the process type, the objectives should be clear, consistent and deductible for the executive levels (Moews, 2002).

The classification of various process types may be synthetically illustrated as a pyramid (Figure 2). The development of corporate strategies is part of the top level, while the conceptual orientation of processes is classified at the management level.

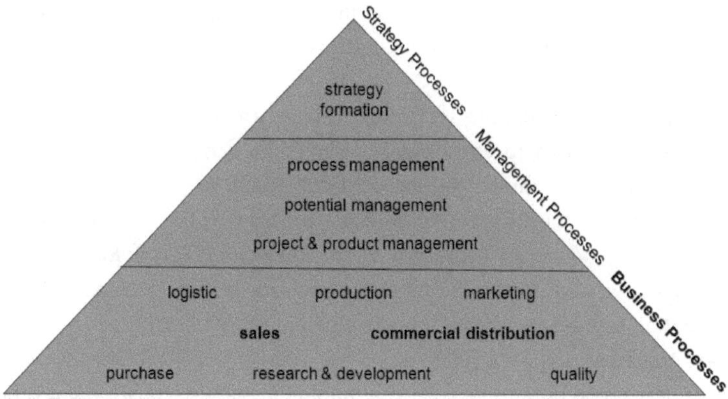

Figure 2: Classification of process types

Source: Fischer, et. al., 2006

Strategy processes

Strategy processes are those which oversee the process of a system, or enterprise, being placed at the top of the pyramid. Strategy management processes determine the overall strategic orientation, planning and management for derived processes – the core, operational (Hammer, 2014).

Management processes

Generally, management includes planning, organization, implementation, and control, which enable the achievement of targets. Thereby, corporate strategies are developed and transferred to overall (governance) processes. Example of typical management processes include "corporate governance" or "strategic management". As such, they are the basis for the definition of (detailed) business processes and facilitate the derivation of subsequent, operational processes. It should be mentioned that changes in the market might lead to changes regarding the strategy and management processes. In such a context, these processes should allow a continuous, iterative adjustment or optimization.

Business processes

A business process entails a cross-functional sequence of value-adding activities, that generate services expected by the customer and meet the process objectives derived from the business strategy and goals (Schmechel, 2013). It can be deduced that the focus of a business process lays in the achievement of defined goals and in providing the services expected by the customers.

Business processes link people, technology and information to create valuable outputs, enabling enterprises to carry out their mission, achieve their goals and measure their performance (Harvard Business School, 2010). As an element of processes, people carry out process activities, which are based on the received inputs, while their skills and knowledge represent additional inputs. Technology can be named as a further element often used by people, to facilitate process tasks. Additionally, information represents a main process element, as a relevant input or output of business processes.

Business processes contain the core, operational processes, consisting of various fields of operations, which convert and effectuate the predefined management processes. Core, operational processes can be characterized by the direct involvement in the creation of value for the enterprise and (internal, as well as external) customers. Core, operational processes constitute the primary business and generate the primary value stream. Thereby, these processes are incorporated in the business' vision and mission; as a result, these have strategic significance.

Business processes add value for (internal) customers. Therefore, the process outcome of a well-designed business process should increase effectiveness – in terms of customer value – and enhance efficiency through cost-reduction, for the enterprise. Business processes provide answers to the following basic questions (Springer, 2013):

- What input is supplied to the company?
- Which resources (money, people, raw materials) are processed in the company?
- Which customer-specific output is generated?

The meaning of business processes is innovatively outlined by Brocke & Rosemann (2014), taking into consideration two distinctive dimensions - "model vs. real world". (Table 1)

Table 1:Meanings of Business Process in different contexts

	Model	Reality
Types / Schemata	Graphical perception, (in)formal portrayal of a succession for execution in business setting; normally speaks to a process case in reality, yet may exist autonomously as a business process in reality.	Execution steps/exercises as a major aspect of processes for creation in organizations; is not really recorded by methods for a process display.
Tokens / Instances	Novel graphical portrayal of an arrangement, e.g. EPC diagram; mostly contained in a SAP reference show.	Extraordinary/uniquely occurring of undertakings for execution/as system in business setting; free of the presence of a process demonstrate.

Source: Brocke & Rosemann, 2014

Reasons for classifying business processes include the creation of value, complexity, function of the procedure, as well as the importance and / or immediacy of involvement in the product growth procedure. Every organization exists to produce and deliver value.

The effective and efficient performance to deliver goods and add value (for the customer), represents a general requirement for an internal system of processes and resources within the value creation process. Thereby, processes should manage work effectively and enhance the organization to afford a competitive benefit.

Relevant levels of the value creation system are summarized and described below, especially to gain consistent understanding about the subject (Brocke & Rosemann, 2014):

- ***Enterprise Level***: At the top level, the organization should be seen as a system with business units for generating revenues. Every enterprise is depicted in the context of marketplace, resources and its competitors. These represent the general environment in which the enterprise, implicitly all its business processes, operate. Enterprises also contain the depiction of the value creation, outlining distinctive features in terms of created, sold and delivered products. Thus, every (individual) business process is contained in the enterprise system and may be derived from the enterprise level.
- ***Process Level***: contains processes for launching (e.g. research, product development and product extensions to make new products available), selling and marketing, as well as delivering procedures to transport products and /or services to the customer. Impacts are typically market or customer inputs, such as orders or product ideas. The processes usually end with an outcome for (internal) customers or at a specified stage of the value chain.

- ***Sub-Process/Task Level***: decomposition of a given process into sub-processes – respectively tasks – which contain even greater details about procedures, and operative performance becomes visible.

For a detailed and precise description of business processes, the following criteria should be identified (Brocke & Rosemann, 2014):

- requirements of (internal) customers;
- inputs and (demanded) results;
- service production and creation of value;
- process owner and persons involved;
- objectives and measurements to control and improve the process performance.

A business process receives an initiating input and ends with achieving the process objective. Processes exist detached from the enterprise organization, whereby process orientation might cross barriers of structural departments. Independently of classification, business processes can be demonstrated over a large number of approaches and techniques. The modelling of business processes may be correctly tapped as an asset of the organization and this may and should be sustainable.

Therefore, sustainable business processes and process management can be approached as important elements for achieving the companies' goals. Process management has a great impact on sustainability of business processes. It is indisputable that process management and its sustainability are essential to business success. Continuous observing and optimization of processes are vital elements, necessary to survive, resist and to succeed in an extremely competitive markets.

The term *"sustainable"*, with specific impact for this thesis, is defined in rational connection to business process (Burlton, 2017).

"Sustainability means to meet the requirements of the current without bargaining the ability of future generations to meet their own needs" (World Summit on Social Development, 2005).

In 2005, during the World Summit on Social Development, objectives for practical advancement, with respect to monetary and social improvement, and in addition ecological security, were defined. Improvement reasonably implies the harmonization of essential human needs, social and monetary necessities and the safeguarding of the common habitat for the present and for who and what is to come (Costanza & Patten, 2015). As a rule, sustainability is characterized as a change in the nature of human life and, subsequently, it covers ecological perspectives, as well as political and financial measures to look at (The Earth Charter Initiative, 2017).

1.2 Project Management For Business Process Improvement In A Sustainable Framework

Project management implies starting, arranging, executing, controlling, and achieving a particular objective in a predetermined time. Strategic company plans are regularly realised in the projects procedure. Project management is closely related to sustainable business performance. The evaluation of strategic projects and the final monetary and social results, correlated with project management for enterprise success, considering sustainability issues, gain increasing importance in present times (Scheiblich, et al., 2016).

1.2.1 The concepts of project management and project scorecard for measuring the contribution to business performance

In business practice, objectives are increasingly planned and accomplished in project programs. Referring only to the evaluation of strategic projects – and their impact to the planned business goals – project portfolio management is a fresh approach for a lot of businesses. To measure the monetary contribution of inputs for these projects, a new controlling approach is specified and operationalized for small and medium-sized companies: the project scorecard (Campana, et al., 2005). The current status of research in the area outlines two directions: one is based on the maturity of processes (e.g. OPM3 or CMMI), while the other focuses on the output-calculation, in relation to the project inputs.

1.2.2 Ideas of Project Portfolio Management in regard of sustainability

Multi Project Management (MPM) aims to achieve trans-sectoral and cross-company management for various concurrent projects of an organization. Its tasks are related to comprehensive planning, organisation, steering, and supervision of the projects and all organizational methods that are essential to MPM.

Project Portfolio Management (PPM) is a very important component of MPM (Dammer, et al., 2005), which becomes a key prerequisite of an effective PPM. PPM ideally observes all the company's projects and programmes and analyses them, considering their strategic contributions in achieving current goals (e.g. strategic contribution, profitability and benefits). All these relationships are briefly illustrated in figure 3.

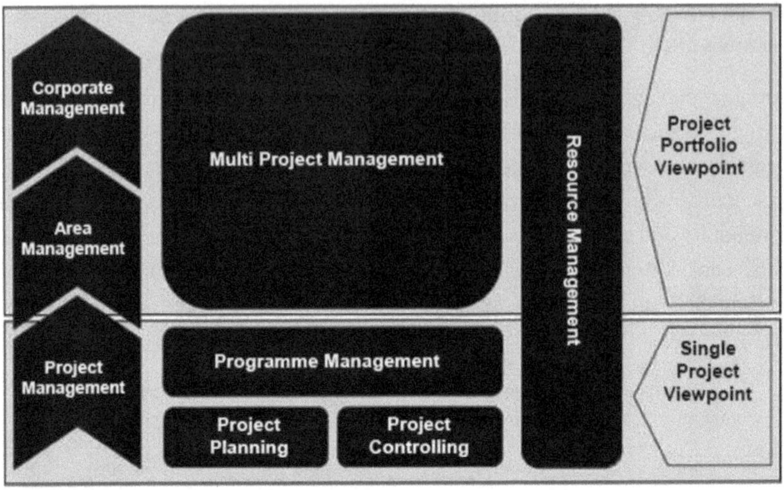

Figure 3: Relationship between the concepts

Source: Campana et al, 2005: 115

Based on an empiric study on MPM, Dammer, et al., (2005) developed a generic process model which covers the whole project portfolio cycle. This is explained and depicted – in a slightly modified manner – in the following figure.

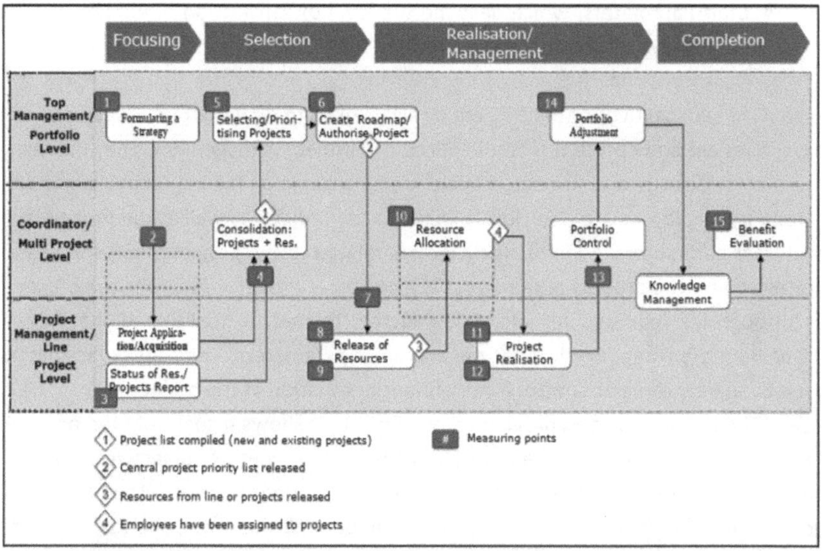

Figure 4: Project Portfolio Management as a continuous process
Source: Adapted after Dammer, 2008

Project portfolio controlling is an important part of PPM, as it allows the link between business strategy and the progress of the projects during its development (Dammer, et al., 2005). PPM needs controlling methods and indices in order to comprehensively plan, steer, supervise, evaluate, and control the portfolio.

Further on, the Project Scorecard (PSC) will be derived from the Balanced Scorecard (BSC), which was developed in the 1990s by R. S. Kaplan and D. P. Norton to improve the measuring of business performance. The objective of the PSC is to find an approach to illustrate the evaluation of project-spanning influences on the overall result. The PSC serves as a tool to link the strategic project level with the operative level. The parameters differ slightly, when compared to the general BSC, and are adapted to the project, programme and portfolio management. They are divided into:

- Classic Parameters, which describe how performance, costs, time, and quality relate to one another.
- Customer Parameters, which describe the level of satisfaction of the stakeholders and how the project environment is developing.
- Process Parameters, which describe how the project processes develop and how processes are improved by continuous improvement measures.

- Staff Parameters, which describe the level of satisfaction of employees and what they give to the project.

The perspectives of the PSC are directly linked to one another. Employees and executives are an important factor of success in project management. They influence the project directly and are responsible for its success or failure. Financial impacts caused by employees are also closely linked to the project, as well as the process and customer parameters. All influencing factors related to the project process are categorized under the process parameters. The customer directly influences the processes through his requests. All influencing factors related to quality and the project framework are categorized under the customer parameters. The classic parameters thereby merely serve as control for the financial situation of the project.

The PSC is meant to provide an overview that shows a goal-oriented and uniform direction of the project and to allow the measurement of objectives, using indexes. The measures of the PSC are not exclusively numeric values. They are partly descriptive information used for project evaluation. Furthermore, the PSC is an important steering tool for the project manager, supporting him in planning, steering and controlling, especially in complex and comprehensive projects and programmes (Kunz, 2007).

The PSC helps especially to:

- reach a consensus among the stakeholders about the project objectives, right at the beginning of a project;
- connect strategic projects with the business and department strategy;
- clarify the question of 'What is the project (result) meant to be accomplished'?

The PSC is meant to provide an overview of what processes directly or indirectly impact the value contribution of project management.

2 Sustainability In Business Processes, Risk And Its Management

2.1 Sustainability - Conceptual Framework

The concept of sustainability is an ancient and widespread principle of human thought and action. Ever since ancient times, humans were guided by this principle and lived in harmony with nature, in a way that led to the preservation of resources.

Sustainability is characterized as a change in the nature of human life, covering various perspectives such as ecological, political and monetary (The Earth Charter Initiative, 2000).

Considering the business environment, sustainability can be approached as a goal, value or instruction for responsible and proactive decision-making behaviour, in order to gain "balance between ecological resilience, economic prosperity, political justice and cultural vibrancy" (Kates, et al., 2005). For business forms, sustainability implies a continuous advancement without critical disintegration of assets inside the value, including change (Blewitt, 2008).

Development in a sustainable way means the harmonization of basic human needs, social and economic requirements and the preservation of the natural environment for the present and future generations (Costanza, et al., 1995). It is mandatory for a sustainable development to meet "the needs of the present" (World Commission on Environment and Development, 1987).

"Sustainable" is categorized by (Just, 2016):

- consistence;
- efficiency and effectiveness, especially in terms of costs;
- goal orientation.

2.1.1 The importance of sustainability for business performance

In an extremely dynamic and changing environment, businesses have to quickly react and adapt, in order to ensure their survival and success on the market. International companies, but also local ones, have started to use new management tools and methods and to focus on differentiating themselves from competitors, by adapting to the customers' needs and providing high quality services (Mateescu, et al., 2015). In such a context, the requirements for sustainable business processes increased tremendously. Consequently, companies have to be able to create integrated business processes, flexible and adaptable to all changes (internal or external) (Müller, 2011).

V. Just, *Sustainable Business Processes in Global Companies*,
Sustainable Management, Wertschöpfung und Effizienz,
https://doi.org/10.1007/978-3-658-28196-0_3

Due to the cumulative impact of social and environmental issues on business success, companies are more oriented towards sustainability (Just, 2016). This is generally based on economic, ecological and social pillars (Srebotnjak, 2011). The economic dimension reflects how sustainable management affects costs, revenues and thus the profitability of a company (Nina, et al., 2017). In environmental terms, the orientation focuses on how (natural) resources are used. From a social perspective, it is important how people in the company, consumers, suppliers and other stakeholders are treated. Therefore, the sustainable development of enterprises can be considered as a process of continuous improvement regarding ecological, economic and social performance (Dyllick & Hockerts, 2002).

Business processes sustainability means a continuous development without significant deterioration of resources within the value-adding transformation (Hillman, et al., 1998). Therefore, sustainability should also be incorporated in management, risk methods and practices (Zu, 2013).

Companies increasingly align their products and processes to the idea of sustainable development. Measurement represents an essential precondition for improved sustainability. The appropriate key performance indicators to make the sustainability performance of companies assessable and controllable, should be measured, monitored and adjusted to achieve sustainable development and processes (Lexikon, 2015).

Indicators are major tools to determine the achievement of targets and the identification of needs for optimization, being also an essential basis for reporting (Kompas, 2017). Indicators are common to measure, predict, plan, and manage. Sustainability not only has various dimensions (economic, environmental and social) but it can also be seen in different contexts (historical development-development paths, role of the state vs. individual). So far, no general approach for direct measurement of sustainability is defined, but concepts of different approaches, frames and measurement methods exist.

The way the world is changing puts human resource management in the spotlight, human resource professionals facing a wide range of changes in workforce demographics, technology and competitiveness (Losey, et al., 2005).

People involved in the business are crucial for its success; human resources are the most valuable asset in an organization. They must be carefully chosen, to be suited for the tasks they need to perform, in order to ensure a proper achievement of the company's goals. For instance, employee satisfaction is an essential element to the success of any business, a high rate of employee contentedness being directly related to the turnover rate. The responsibilities of human resources management have to include executive and leadership development, performance management, compensation, and labour relations. Furthermore, keeping employees satisfied with their careers should be a priority for companies, in order to develop durable and sustainable activities (Storey, 1989).

2.1.2 Description of sustainability dimensions and sustainable processes

The substantiation of sustainable development is based on a three-dimensional approach. The concept of sustainability is therefore divided into the following areas:

- ***Ecological sustainability***. The ecological dimension of sustainability requires politicians, private sector and households to treat natural resources considering a long-term approach, in order to preserve them for future generations. This is best known to the public, due to the worldwide discussions on topics such as global warming and climate protection, but it also includes many other topics, such as the preservation of biodiversity, the worldwide protection of resources or the minimisation of hazardous substances in the production of goods (Liese & Zapke, 2011). Due to the increasing concerns about environmental protection, companies are required to minimise the direct and indirect impact of their processes, products, services and actions on the environment. Companies can contribute to this process with an increased usage of renewable energies and raw materials and relying on environmentally friendly products and manufacturing processes, in order to reduce risks to people and the environment, as far as possible (Hauff & Kleine, 2014).
- ***Social sustainability***. In addition to *ecological sustainability*, the demand for *social sustainability* is becoming increasingly significant. This defines its objective in the preservation or increase of a company's social and human capital. Social capital encompasses the social relations of all the players in a company and social services such as the number and creation of training places. The motivation and expertise of the individual employees result in human capital (Gunner, 2011). Companies are therefore compelled to deal with interest groups and employees in a respectful and fair manner and to be aware of their responsibility towards society. They should operate in such a way that future generations can also be guaranteed a basis for a stable and fair working environment (Schaltegger, 2002). These include, for example, decent working conditions, fair pay and equal opportunities. In the long term, social problems such as youth unemployment or the gap between rich and poor are to be combated.

- ***Economic sustainability*** aims at preserving and, if necessary, expanding economic capital. This includes not only the economic production capital in the form of non-monetary and knowledge capital, but also the classical financial capital that is brought into the economy (Gunner, 2011). This allows companies to be able to act economically sustainable if they can always generate above-average returns for the owners and, at the same time, guarantee sufficient liquidity. Therefore, one aim of the economic dimension is to secure and maintain the long-term existence of a company and, if necessary, increase its competitiveness. In the long term, however, this goal can only be achieved if ecological and social factors are taken into account in the overall sustainability management process (Wilkens, 2007).

The result of a company's economic sustainability creates the monetary basis for investments in social and ecological sustainability measures (Figge, 2001). Long-term sustainable competitiveness can only be ensured if the ecological and social sustainability goals are also economically viable and generate added value for the company. If they merely generate costs and do not lead to economic success on the long run, they are often not taken into account in practice (Steinke, 2014).

The performance of the processes depends on the efficiency and effectiveness of each process, with direct effects on the economy. However, performance cannot be sustained if processes are not properly defined and controlled. All processes are designed for resistance. Sustainability plays a vital role in achieving a company's goals (Mocan, et al., 2015).

A sustainable process involves a detailed and precise description of business processes, by identifying the following criteria for each process (Brocke & Rosemann, 2014): requirements of (internal) customers, inputs and (demanded) results, service production and creation of value, process owner and persons involved, objectives and measurements to control and improve the process performance (Bejinariu, et al., 2016).

The degree of formality can be one of the aspects that affects process performance over time. "*Informal*" means that the enterprise has not documented its processes as a set of steps which should be executed under certain conditions. To achieve sustainability, processes should be (highly) formalized to gain responsiveness and facts. Processes might be envisioned with a flowchart as a categorization of events with incorporated decision points. The process matrix, as a categorization of events with significance rules based on data in the process, might be another form of representation of formality in business processes. Occasionally, processes might be an informal procedure, before the enterprise increases the degree of formality by documentation and / or description (Harvard Business School, 2010).

Other characteristics refer to the distinction according to the level of association in the procedure and transmission of information. The responsibility and knowledge of the process owners, access to information for all involved parties, but also communication can be factors that influence process performance and determine its sustainability.

Business processes might be cross-functional and therefore range over several business functions but are embedded in the overall value chain, implicitly in the organizational structure (Rummler & Brache, 1995). Thus, it can be stated that one of the main criteria that determines the degree of sustainability is risk management at each process junction: interaction between two processes, between two steps of a process or between two parties involved in the process.

Process monitoring, control and optimization are highly important for ensuring its sustainability. Process owners and other assigned responsible employees have to constantly observe any deviation from the process protocol, including all activities, time frames, involved parties, and outputs (results).

2.2 Tapping Sustainability For Business Organizations And Processes

There is a strong connection between companies' processes and sustainability. There are also a lot of dependencies between the governance framework of a company and its sustainability. The execution of an organization's procedures is closely connected to achieving the business goals.

2.2.1 Outline of process management phases, considering sustainability aspects

Process management refers to the organization, planning, management, and control of a company's value or value chain, considering individual business goals (Wirtschaftslexikon24, 2015).

Process management implies different phases which are illustrated in the figure 5 and thoroughly outlined in the next paragraphs.

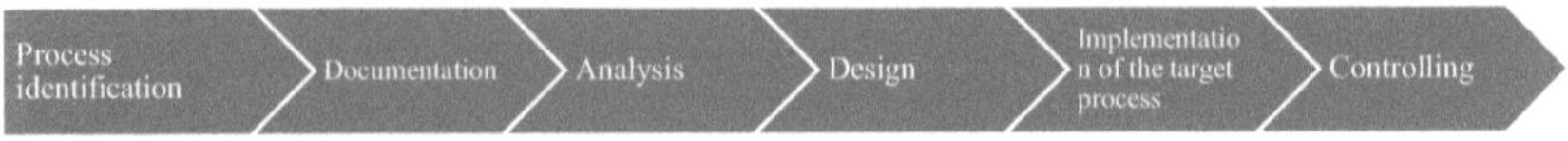

Figure 5: Phases of Process Management

Source: Rosemann & Schwegmann, 2002

Process identification

The first step in process administration is represented by distinguishing the proofs of existing procedures. With a specific end goal, to demonstrate a recognized proof of the procedures, first, these must be plainly recognized from each other. In addition, after distinguishing the pertinent procedures, the start and end of each procedure ought to be clearly specified/characterized (Technische Universität Kaiserslautern, 2015). Each procedure chain must have a start and an end (Rosemann & Schwegmann, 2002).

In recognizing a process, the accompanying questions ought to be obviously characterized:

- Who oversees undertaking the procedure displaying, appointing an appointee, and propelling the outcomes?
- Which life cycle status is allocated to the models? Possibilities may refer to: "at work", "draft", "draft, professionally confirmed", "propelled" and in addition "not substantial".
- Which correspondence channels are to be picked?
- How will the interpretation activity happen? In time, will the models or protests be changed, erased or chronicled?

Documentation

Process documentation is crucial when dealing with processes. To enable an effective and efficient workflow, process documentation is extremely important. The visualization and the documentation of a process build the foundation for a professional discussion and for the following optimization of a process. By the documentation of the process, transparency shall be created. Additionally, the documentation helps to teach new employees and serves as a basis for certification, according to quality management standards.

The aim of process documentation is to create transparency regarding the processes, and to fulfill an important requirement for process analysis, process steering and process optimization.

After distinguishing the individual procedures, is fundamental to have them appropriately documented. This infers the individual procedure proprietors must be incorporated (Technische Universität Kaiserslautern, 2015).

The "procedure proprietor" is recognized from different capacities or assignments of process administration. The "procedure fashioner" underpins the documentation of procedures through information of the current demonstrating instruments and traditions. The "key user" coordinates the discharge and distributing methodology of process models, with step by step learning of the procedure displaying apparatuses.

Conversely, the "process owner" is approached in this chapter as a procedure part, which is in charge of the persistent financial plan, documentation, direction, and advancement inside his procedure and for accomplishing his procedure targets (Figure 6). When all tasks are accomplished, a procedure proprietor acts with uncommon learning as a supporter in the interest of the procedure, assumes liability for the performance and starts change, while alternate process parts particularly upgrade the (specialized) demonstrating and execution (Burlton, 2001).

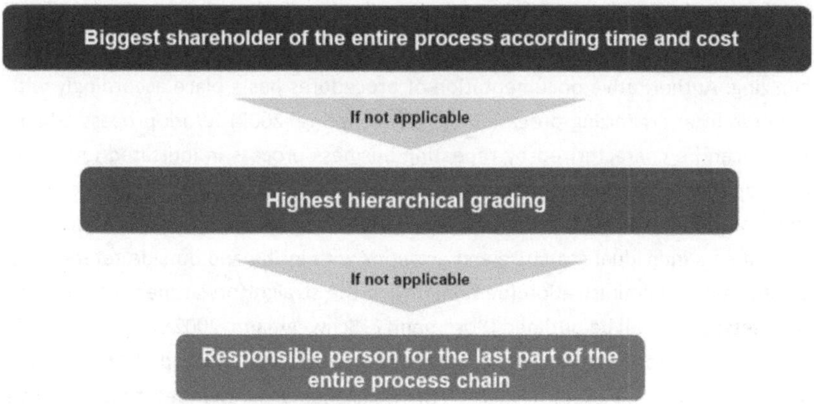

Figure 6: Criteria for process owner definition

Source: Burlton, 2001

The procedure proprietor is responsible for coordinating the whole procedure, which incorporates upstream and downstream procedures inside the formation of the procedure and the privilege of utilization for monetary assets.

As credited undertakings, the procedure proprietor:

- defines the procedure with its members and guarantees the procedure documentation, refresh and filing;
- defines the procedure focuses considering the current vital system;

- defines process markers with regards to the procedure targets;
- plans and applies the required budgetary assets and other assets for achieving satisfaction;
- implements the procedure and guarantees the required know-how of the procedure members;
- initiates and completes process enhancements.

Subsequently, the procedure proprietor may be a man or an advisory group, specifically engaged with the procedure.

No matter the procedure proprietor, workshops with the procedure members should be developed, especially to guarantee that all procedure features were approached, and a procedure display has succeeded (Technische Universität Kaiserslautern, 2015). This outlines a vital part of the procedure administration. The general point of the planning is to make a displaying standard, which serves to demonstrate the procedure (Rosemann, et al., 2002); this is a conclusive part of institutionalization and sustainability.

The proposed application should be characterized by a specific end goal to decide the displaying reason. There are eleven purposes to be shown, which can be separated into the classification hierarchical organizing and framework application organizing. Authoritative documentation of procedures has a place accordingly with the hierarchical organizing process (Kugeler & Vieting, 2002). Work process administration can be characterized by repeating business process in indicated undertakings, preparing units and connections (Schewe, 2015). Accreditation (whereby the documentation is conclusive), benchmarking (which portrays the examination of an organization's individual structure and activities with inside and outside references), and information administration (demonstrating the straightforwardness of the business assets) should all be outlined (Rosemann & Schwegmann, 2002).

However, to adopt the most appropriate displaying philosophy, the demonstrating purposes and prerequisites of the user should be analysed together. This process is frequently labelled as multi-point of view data demonstrating (Rosemann & Green, 2000). Furthermore, the sustainability setting ought to be thought about; the same number of procedures must be connected for longer time span.

After characterizing the displaying reason, individual correspondence channels can be recognized. Different choices are available. One alternative is to make plots as vast notices on office dividers. On these, the models can be replicated, and the exchange of data can be ensured. This correspondence frame is prescribed amid the improvement and result introduction stage, as it does not imply high info costs. Another option is a handbook, which can be utilized for a far-reaching dissemination.

The last option refers to the utilization of the organization's intranet. Along these lines, current procedures can be seen and changed immediately. Other than being exceptional, the intranet can permit a high level of sustainability. This is a consequence of the way that all information and archives are added to the framework, stay open whenever, and stay unaltered on account of an adjustment in work force. Information misfortune will be counteracted accordingly.

Other than picking the displaying model, the demonstrating tradition is additionally dictated by the format, the utilization, the level of detail, the name, or the database organization (Rosemann & Schwegmann, 2002). The displaying apparatus and its necessities likewise, decide the demonstrating tradition. These necessities incorporate, for instance, the ease of use for various clients, utilization of interfaces, utilization of models in a database etc. (Fank, 1998).

The making of layouts for singular content records and introductions are important, if these are not produced by the device being utilized. Moreover, an acknowledgment test in genuine situations must be generated, keeping in mind the end goal of looking at whether the representations have been completely comprehended by the clients and if they have a long-haul legitimacy (Hansmann & Neumann, 2002).

Various types of models for process demonstrating, supported by a short description and a graphical illustration, are outlined in the table below.

Table 2: Main types of process modelling

Modelling Type	Purpose of Use	Graphical Illustration
Value Chain Diagram	Representation of a series of functions, which add value to the product. It is used for representing highly aggregated processes or functions. This modelling type cannot give a detailed description of processes. (Porter, 2015)	

Event-Oriented Process Chain	Since it can be applied without prior knowledge of modelling, this way of modelling is widely used (Scheer, 2011; Keller, 2015). This approach gives a representation of the control flow, using three basic elements: the function, the event and the connector (or a combination of both).	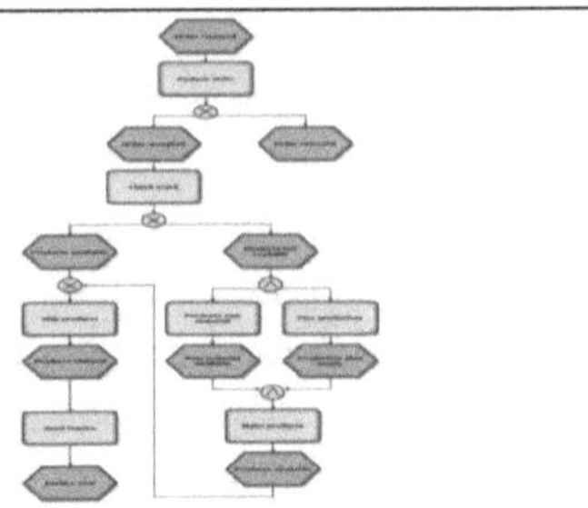
Event-based Process Chain in Column Form	This is derived from the Event-Oriented Process Chain. In this modelling, each symbol is assigned a specific column to increase the readability. Apart from the control flow column, each column can be chosen as required. Generally, organizational units, input and output objects and system application columns are applied.	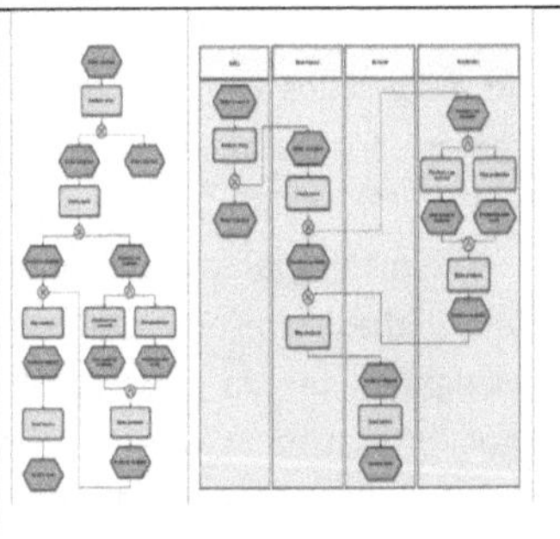
Swim Lane Process Mapping Diagram	This is a modification of the Event-based Process Chain in Column Form. Here, a column will be opened for each competent authority, in which all process steps are entered and executed from this point of responsibility. (Harvard Computing Group Inc., 2017)	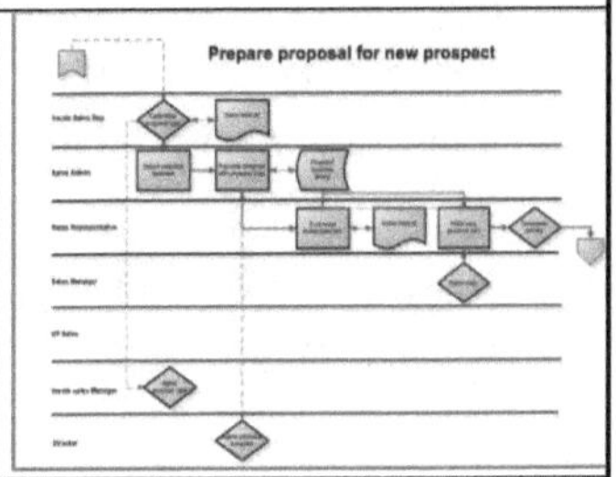
Term-based Models	Information models with only one object type – the technical term. Amounts and examples are representable in this model.	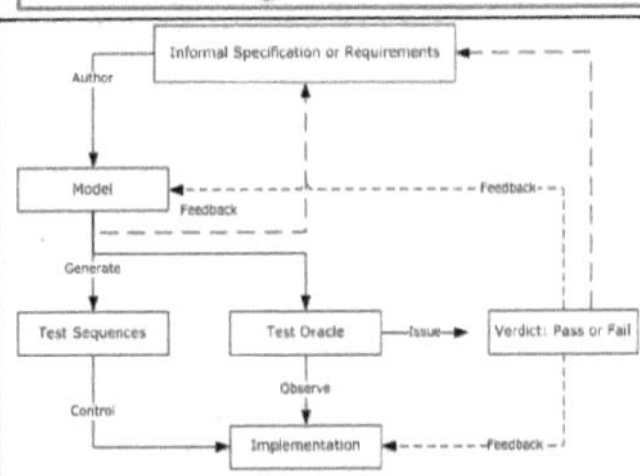

Business Process Modelling Notation (BPMN)	This widespread modelling style represents an easy understandable form of presentation for processes, no matter the type of user (Stiehl, 2017; Object Management Group, 2017). This could be achieved through a new standard that has been set. For this, it is only necessary to fix the elements (Guodys and Tietjien, 2011), such as flow blocks, connection objects or swim lanes for the uniform design of a process. (Buchholz, 2015)	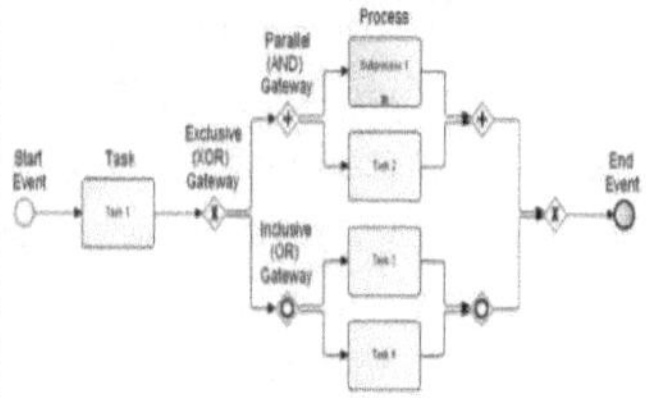

Source: Rosemann & Schwegmann, 2002

Besides choosing the modelling type, the modelling convention is also determined by the layout, the usage, the degree of detail, the name, or the structure of the database. The modelling tool and its requirements also determine the modelling convention. For example, such requirements may include the usability for multiple users, use of interfaces, use of models in a database, or a user-friendly interface. In the last stages, rules must be defined. This way, the modelling will also succeed, from an organizational perspective. The creation of templates for individual text documents and presentations is necessary, if these are not created by the used tool. Also, organizational rules after model creation, need to be examined by reports. Additionally, an acceptance test in real scenarios must be undertaken, in order to examine whether the models have been fully understood by the users and possess a long-term validity (Rosemann & Schwegmann, 2015).

Analysis

In the process analysis stage, the feeble focuses must be recognized first. In this sense, an assessment of the data and correspondence frameworks, the operational and hierarchical structure, ought to be completed (Schwegmann, 2002).

Reference models and benchmarking can be utilized to open data about existing weak points. This documentation can be situated on a specialized or business level. In both cases, this is a combination of existing models, master feeling and documentation of the framework application, which restricts the weak focuses (Schwegmann & Laske, 2002). The term benchmarking describes a continual comparison of key figures of different company branches or between different businesses, to infer statements about the competitive ability (Horvath & Gleich, 1998). Using benchmarking, possible weak points of a corporation can be identified.

Experts from various specialty fields and methodology experts will then analyse the list of weak points (Schwegmann & Laske, 2002). Considering the identified weak points, potential for optimization can be deduced and clearly defined. Besides, quality indicators must be set up so that the quality requirements for the optimized process are well-defined (Technische Universität Kaiserslautern, 2015). This avoids indifferences and ambivalences at other stages of the process management, at a later point in time.

Design

For developing a target process, the following requirement is necessary: the processes must be fully optimized, and the target process has to be modelled on this basis. To undertake this properly, criteria for the structure of the hierarchy, the generation of other variants, as well as the differentiation between the target and ideal model, need to be considered. Target models are models which remain unchanged for approximately six months and serve to reach the project aims. Ideal models, on the contrary, can be seen as a distant aim (Speck & Schnetgöke, 2002).

According to this modelling technique, developed processes must be reanalysed. To this aim, the model is examined for deficits with respect to its quality and consistency, by the modelling team, usually through process simulation or against reference models. This allows the avoidance of any unintended change in the commercial area and can guarantee sustainability.

Implementation of the target process

After the target processes have been launched, all the participants can be informed, and if needed, training units can be implemented (Technische Universität Kaiserslautern, 2015). To this aim, consistent and permanent process management requires stable accountability. People responsible for individual tasks are those responsible for processes, process owners and process managers. The person responsible for the process has to provide an efficient and effective sequence. This means that one must assure the pursuance of the process aims and the measures for improvement (Schwarzer & Krcmar, 1995).

The process owner is situated at the top-management level of the corporate hierarchy and determines the process aims. Furthermore, he assigns the responsibilities for individual sub-processes to the responsible persons, according to their field of process expertise (Krahn, 1998). The process manager coordinates all the activities in the company aimed at modelling and improving. Additionally, processes can be implemented in the daily business activity (Technische Universität Kaiserslautern, 2015).

Controlling

Controlling is the last phase of process management. In this stage, the application of the process in a real situation and the quality indicators are tested, while the pre-defined quality indicators are measured. These results will also be documented.

All aspects of process management influence sustainability. A high level of process orientation is an important element to gain sustainability, too. Process orientation implies the support of the company vision and derived strategies, as well as emphasizing the core competences. It also strengthens the customer orientation within the company and leads to continuous improvement of processes and performance.

Sustainability for process management is an important factor for corporate success; sustainability cannot be generalized but gained by matching the company's individual process needs with generally accepted aspects specific to process management. In order to create a sustainable process, all specific characteristics must be clearly defined and marked, all steps of the process management must be documented and shared with all involved parties, and all risks related to the process must be identified and analysed.

Business Process Management (BPM) is responsible with designing and aligning the processes within a company, in such a way that strategic corporate goals can be achieved in the long term. The BPM defines "the external influence of a company". The sustainability of business processes is an important sub-task. The main objective of sustainable business processes is the long-term optimization of ecological and social efficiency, in a successful market environment.

Long-term sustainable business processes require efficient sustainability management and regular monitoring of the defined sustainability goals. Sustainability performance measurement offers many advantages to the company, such as satisfying the information needs of stakeholders. Only in such a framework, companies will be able to maintain or increase their competitiveness in the long term (Tachkov, 2011).

Sustainability is not only a common term in politics and business today, but it is also becoming increasingly important on the stock market. More and more private and institutional investors are considering the sustainability performance of listed companies in their investment decisions. They are convinced that companies which operate in a sustainable manner have a much higher value-added potential than ordinary companies (Fichter & Schneidewind, 2013).

The Dow Jones Sustainability Index (DJSI) is the world's leading index in the area of sustainability. This was established in 1999 as a joint project of the American Dow Jones publishing house and Zurich-based investment advisory firm, Robeco Sustainable Asset Management (RobecoSAM). The index is subdivided into a European (DJSI STOXX), a North American (DJSI North America) and a global sub-index (DJSI World).

The index is regarded as a globally recognized seal of approval and motivates companies to pursue sustainable business practices. In addition, it offers investors a relatively reliable selection criterion for investment decisions in sustainable companies.

Dow Jones Sustainability Index is used by several global companies in order to track and monitor the financial and environmental performance. The index covers social, economic and environmental factors with the final purpose to maximize long-term shareholder value. The following main criteria are used to assess companies' sustainability (Robecosam, 2015):

- corporate governance;
- risk and crisis management;
- customer relationship management;
- innovation management;
- operational efficiency;
- talent attraction and retention;
- environmental policy/management system.

The Dow Jones Global Index (DJGI) contains 2500 companies with the world's largest market capitalization. The best of these companies is selected according to the so-called "best-in-class" principle, i. e. the best (about 10%) of each sector in terms of their sustainability performance for the DJSI. Each year, the Dow Jones Sustainability Index Committee (DJSIC) reviews all the companies based on the obtained results in different areas, and decides upon the companies that shall be part of the ranking; some of the companies remain in the ranking, while others may be excluded. For example, in October 2015, the worldwide known leader in the automobile industry Volkswagen AG was removed from the Dow Jones Sustainability Indices (DJSI), because of to quality failure in the emissions tests. Some of the industries leaders in terms of their DJSI, between 2012-2015 are outlined in the table below.

Table 3: Dow Jones Sustainability Indices for industry leaders

Company	Dow Jones Sustainability Indices (Robecosam yearbook)	Environment	Corporate Responsibility
General Electrics	Industry Leader 2012	• reduce freshwater usage • reduce energy usage • reduce greenhouse gases • reduce carbon footprint	• Developing Health Globally (DHG) program • Ecomagination program: renewable energy alternatives for seawater desalination; technology development for gas reduction
J. Sainsbury	Industry Leader 2013	• reduce waste • reduce energy consumption • reduce carbon emissions • reduce packaging	• support the milk farmers through the Dairy Development Group • reduce sugar levels from juices and drinks • invest in customers to reduce household food waste
Unilever	Industry Leader 2015 (Unilever Netherlands)	• eliminate deforestation • reduce energy and water usage • waste and CO2 emissions reduction	• advanced packaging technology • Dove's Self-Esteem program • 100% renewable power for all U.S sites
JP Morgan	Sustainability Member 2014	• preserve natural ecosystems (Nature Vest Program) • restore land and	• support small business development • jobs offered to U.S. veterans

		water ecosystems	• Financial Solution Lab Program

Source: own development based on Dow Jones data and corporate responsibility programs for each company

Individual companies, as well as the global economy face major challenges. Companies need to replace the previous economic system with a sustainable long-term economy, while respecting the natural limits of earth and mankind. If this change does not take place in time and it is not comprehensively enough, the consequential costs of global warming alone will make it impossible to manage the economy in the future, as it has been the case to date (Rogall, 2013).

When assessing the performance of an organization, the obtained profit and the return of investment are the key metrics that are considered by shareholders. However, the social responsibility and the environmental factors should also play a decisive role when considering a sustainable development of the company. In addition to success-oriented economic corporate goals, sustainable criteria are becoming increasingly important (Meyer & Teuteberg, 2012). Critical investors, sustainable competition and internal factors such as the ethical attitudes of employees, shareholders and owners, may mean/reflect that companies attach greater importance to sustainable actions, implicitly to sustainable business processes (Münzing, 2001).

Processes are part of the infrastructure of every company and are an essential component in the analysis of corporate performance when it comes to business sustainability.

2.2.2 Dealing with complexity related to risk management and sustainability

Projects are becoming increasingly complex. The resulting bottlenecks in projects create an increasing demand for methods and other solutions to control this complexity (Lange, 2015). The impact of complexity on organisations is not a new topic. This has been approached by scholars since the 19th century (Burns, 1961; Lawrence, 1967; Perrow, 1967; Thompson, 1967; Mintzberg, 1979). On the other hand, complexity in project management research is considered less frequently (Rapoport, 1986; Baccarini, 1996; Payne, 1996; Shenhar, 1996; Kallinkos, 1998; William, 2002; Turner, et al., 2006; Vidal, 2008; Hanisch, 2011; Hanisch, et al., 2011).

Measures to deal with complexity should be identified and evaluated. The focus is on the complexity created by classical management. Subsequently, recommendations for action are formulated for a future procedure to deal with complexity in project management.

The term "complexity" is autologous, i. e. applicable to itself or even complex (Luhmann, 2014), and the scientific literature outlines various definitions for its meaning. For example, Edmonds and Bruce (1999) define complexity as "the property of a model that makes it difficult to formulate the entire behaviour in a given language, even if adequately complete information about the atomic constituents and their interrelationship is given". Contrary to Edmonds and Bruce (1999) definition, Lange and Sabrina (2015) explain complexity based on six characteristics in the project context. These were developed based on Cilliers and Paul (1998) premises and refer to (Lange & Sabrina, 2015):

- *History.* Projects change over time. This historical development cannot be fully recorded retrospectively. People can design highly complex systems that an expert, or the developer, can barely understand. If even the developer no longer understands the system, because this has changed over time, then the framework is no longer complicated, but complex. The property history can also be relevant in the project or organizational context.
- *Non-linearity.* The development and behaviour of a system cannot be predicted with certainty. Systems with this characteristic, both social and technical, do not behave linearly. A doubling of "x" does not necessarily lead to a doubling of "y". An example applied on teams may refer to the following: A team of 3 people completes a task in 10 days. If the team is doubled to 6 people, then the task will not necessarily be completed twice as fast, meaning in 5 instead of 10 days.

- *Delay.* The effect of an action is not immediately obvious in association with the delay over time and varies greatly in its manifestation, in the short and long term. Delays pose a complex challenge.
- *Feedback.* Apparently obvious interventions lead to non-obvious consequences. For example, in the manufacturing industry, to offer products at a lower price, a supplier is changed, and costs can be saved when purchasing materials. However, it turns out that the cheaper material does not meet the agreed quality requirements and is therefore unsuitable. This leads to weak points and problems in the system and a shorter service life. The associated effort to remedy the weak points and problems was not planned in this way. The new product also reduces customer satisfaction, which has a negative impact on the company; consequently, it decreases sales and, most likely, profits. This situation describes an important aspect of complex systems: complex systems cannot be described in their behaviour in its entirety, otherwise they would only be "complicated". Feedback of this kind is also referred to as multi-causal contexts, and it is very difficult to estimate the full extent of this feedback.
- *Accumulation.* Accumulation is when many variables are networked with every other. For example, the calculation of health insurance premiums can consist of: age, gender, place of residence, street, marital status, occupation, etc. In addition, the amount of the premium can be influenced by whether other family members are already insured with the insurance company, etc. In this respect, insurance companies have an unlimited decision-making space. Due to the numerous variables intertwined with each other, it is almost impossible to comprehend their direct and indirect influence. This condition creates a self-dynamic framework with a certain unpredictability.
- *Efficiency.* Value creation and complexity are not linearly related. If many tools and procedures are being installed in a system that is suitable and increasingly complex, it does not mean that its added value – i.e. the benefit of the system – is increasing at the same rate. However, this may still be true at the beginning.

Complexity is not a new challenge, just one that is more effective than ever. The main reason for this aspect lays in the fact that increasingly data, signals and information can be produced, transmitted and experienced faster and faster. On one hand, this leads to a remarkable acceleration of processes. On the other hand, it leads to a flood of stimuli and messages. This makes it increasingly difficult to filter out the relevant information and process it sensibly (Pruckner & Maria, 2005).

Complexity is not a property that can be avoided; it occurs in different forms, strengths and weights. Frequent causes may refer to increasing demands; the environment becomes more demanding due to international projects, globalization, all-in-one solutions, the Internet, which shapes the behaviour of customers. All these contribute to making projects more challenging and complex (Lange & Sabrina, 2015). This fact is inevitable, and businesses encounter these conditions in every environment (Vester & Frederic, 2015).

A high degree of complexity places great demands on businesses that have to deal with it. Information must be collected, integrated and transformed into actions. It is not necessary to overstep the processing capacity of each business. If this is the case, information must be reduced to the minimum necessary, to avoid the "complexity trap". In Pruckner and Maria (2005) view, this refers to the lack of relevant information, which leads to more complications through an overdose of irrelevant information.

Since businesses can't escape the complexity, there is only one alternative: to face the complexity. Further on, the complexity will be examined and delineated in more detail, before examining the forms in which complexity occurs in the project environment. However, before proceeding, the misleading, colloquially synonymous use of the terms "complex" and "complicated" must be clarified.

An explanation for the difference between "complicated" and "complex" is given by the Latin origin of the respective terms. The word "complicated" comes from "complicare" which refers to complexity, but also to something familiar. "Complex" originates in "cum plecere" (Latin) which points to the opaque or unknown aspect that constitutes complex systems. The Cynefin framework offers a further approach to differentiating between the two terms. This is a knowledge management model which helps to describe and classify problems, situations and systems (Snowden & Dave, 2017). The classification through the Cynefin framework is primarily intended to create a clearer distinction between the different terms. This is relevant because projects move in or between the complicated and the complex environment (Pilcher & Martin, 2013). However, according to Lange and Sabrina (2015), there are four main types of environments/systems in which entities, either individual or companies, may act:

- *Simple*. The "simple" environment is characterized by repeatable patterns and unambiguous results. Dependencies and relationships are clear, and the cause and consequences can be described and assessed without difficulty. Problems can be clearly answered. In this framework, "best practice" is often spoken of. The procedure is based solely on knowledge. This knowledge allows entities to give clear instructions, while the actions and results can be controlled. The danger in this environment is perceived to be a false sense of security.

- *Complicated*. If a system cannot be written linearly, this is a complicated system or environment. Causes and effects are still evident but cannot be understood by everyone. The system is predictable, but usually only by experts. These experts must be aware of the fact that one's own knowledge is limited. They should also know at what point they need support or to give up their own tasks. Therefore, the expertise of experts is indispensable in a complicated environment. Instead of taking an obvious solution for a problem like in a linear system, it is important to analyse the situation and the system, because, depending on the perspective, different answers are possible and lead to a goal-oriented solution. Therefore, in a complicated environment, the idea of "best practice" is no longer approached, but that of "good practice". Known procedures must be adapted to current situations. The relationships between cause and effect must be analysed.
- *Complex*. The complex system or environment is known for its constant changing. Behaviour is no longer predictable, and interrelationships are no longer directly apparent to experts. There is no longer an answer; even thinking about it does not generate a solution. There are many unknown aspects, areas etc. and there is no knowledge to uncover them. The meaning of the overall context is also unknown. In such a framework, the most common term is "unknown ignorance". To move forward, creative and innovative approaches, as well as many unbiased ideas that can be contradictory, are needed. To this end, an environment that offers room for new ideas and learning, must be created. Experimenting, as well as observing the results, make possible a continuous progress. The words that characterise this type of environment are "trial and error". It is important to work in teams to generate creative and innovative solutions. It is important to not disturb teams, they have to organize themselves and find solutions on their own responsibility.
- *Chaotic*. There are situations which cannot be estimated in any way, e.g. in their causes, effects, relationships. The number of unknown factors and variables is too large, so that too many decisions have to be made in a short time. Thus, the probability of wrong decisions is high. The situation can be described as "unknowable", circumstances cannot be predicted nor estimated. Decisions have to be taken according to the "Wild West Principle": first

decide, then ask what circumstances exist. This is justified by the fact that immediate action is unremitting. In these situations, long deliberation is wrong. Every form of action involves risk and opportunity. It is important to rely on intuition.

Business process complexity is defined in the scientific literature referring to its high diversity, high lack of routine, high degree of difficulty, high uncertainty, and interdependence of activities in the business process (Mani, 2010). High business process complexity makes it difficult to define rules and standard operating procedures and to respond to potential problems (Daft, et al., 1981; Karimi, et al., 2007; Mani, 2010).

As complexity increases, the amount of facts that has to be processed in order to maintain the business process performance and quality, increases. If process activities are insecure and highly dependent on each other, the complexity of the business process increases (Melville, 2008; Fredendall, et al., 2009). This means that process managers or executors face a high degree of uncertainty and a high diversity and interdependence of process activities (Karimi, 2007; Niranjan, 2007; Mani, 2010). Business process complexity complicates the standardization of processes and causes considerable workload (Sobek, 1998; Barki, 2005; Hanseth, 2006; Hall, 2009; Mani, 2010). The nature and characteristics of an individual business process make it possible to associate it with one of the three classes proposed by Lillrank (2003): Standard, Routine and Non-routine, as outlined in table 4.

Table 4: Properties of standard, routine and non-routine processes

	Standard	**Routine**	**Non-routine**
Acceptance criteria	one option	limited number of choices	open quantity of inputs
Evaluation	site acceptance test	categorisation	interpretation
Conversion rules	switch, algorithm	algorithm, grammar, habits	heuristics
Repetition	identic	similar, but not identical	unique, non-repeating
Logic	binary	fuzzy	interpretative

Source: Lillrank, 2003

The main difference between these classes is that each class represents a different level of business process complexity: a standard process has the lowest level of complexity and is more of a purely complex challenge, whereas a non-routine process is the most complex (Schäfermeyer, 2012).

A standard process has a pre-defined input, produces a pre-specified output and is always repeated identically. There is no diversity of content; each activity is carried out in the same optimal way, every time (Lillrank, 2003). A predictable process is characterized by greater diversity both in the sequence of work events and by two or more different types of alternate outputs (Mason, 1978; Lillrank, 2003). The input of a routine process must be understood and categorized before a limited number of actions or algorithms can be selected (Lillrank, 2003, 2004). The goal is usually clear, but it can be achieved by different means, which is due to the diversity or variety in the sequence of events and actions (Pentland, 2003). A non-routine process is characterized by vague or unknown inputs and outputs (Lillrank, 2004). The unknown input cannot be directly associated with certain actions or algorithms. The variety of possible input quantities is greater than the amount of experience that is used in process execution (Lillrank, 2004). This uncertainty regarding the input can only be counteracted by highly qualified and knowledgeable employees (experts) who cultivate new knowledge during the process (Schäfermeyer, 2012).

The more complex a process is, the less it can be standardized. This indicates that when projects are understood as a process or non-routine process, they cannot be fully standardized nor standardized by sub-processes (Schäfermeyer, 2012). It should also be noted that complex processes are often combinations of sub-processes, which in turn are standard, routine or non-routine processes (Lillrank & Paul, 2003). A non-routine process is so complex and varied that employees have to use implicit knowledge, most of the time (Schäfermeyer, 2012). This knowledge cannot be documented, and, therefore, it would not make economic sense to try to codify it in the form of standard operating measures or process documentation (Davenport, 1998).

The relationship between the structure and variability of a process is also complex. There is a higher tendency to achieve a high degree of structuring over time in processes with low variability. On the other hand, with high variability (or high complexity of a process), there is a tendency towards low structuring (Schäfermeyer, 2012). Therefore, it can make sense to first describe a comprehensive business process on a high level of abstraction and only then to detail individual components step by step, this way reducing the complexity.

From various perspectives, processes determine many challenges within projects. The main issue is that many complex aspects are treated like complicated ones by the company, this way generating disruptions. Frequently, processes take up freedom and do not offer the flexibility required in complex challenges such as projects.

Often, processes or tools cause additional time pressure. If, for example, results are delayed, this may lead to a lack of trust in senior management, which, in turn, may result in additional processes developed to monitor the employees. The added effort and time pressure reduce the value added and motivation of the employees and the complexity, due to the connections between the management, the employees and their tasks. In addition, it must be considered that the introduction of new tools and processes results in a new, additional effort for the employees, and that they need to get acquainted with the new topic.

An introduction of processes and tools only leads to a small increase in value added, but a strong increase in complexity, until an optimum is reached. At this point, any further "optimization" in the form of additional processes or tools only contributes to an increase in complexity and a reduction in added value. Thus, a slimming down of the system – i.e. focusing exclusively on value-adding tasks – will help until just the essence of value creation is left, and all complexity has been removed from the system.

This fact shows the negative influence that complicated elements can have in complex systems. Similarly, the lack of flexibility of the waterfall or V-model has a negative effect on the added value of projects. These models are designed especially for complex challenges, since they are linear in nature and complexity in projects is characterised by their non-linearity (Long, 2015). Another difficulty that is emerging in such a context is the separation of experts, which requires heterogeneous teams to solve complex challenges. However, if a simple transfer of an activity from expert to expert is carried out, as in classic process models such as the Waterfall or V-Model, the separation of experts is promoted; this can be particularly observed in matrix organisations.

As a final consideration, it can be highlighted that, the complexity of processes outcomes from a network of many processes and that they have different relationships with each other (Scherr, 1993). On the other hand, the challenge consists in the increasing number and variety of elements and dependencies within business relationships and, therefore, the complexity of the business processes is estimated to increase (Blecker, 2005; Schäfermeyer, 2012). Consequently, the amount of information that has to be processed by processes is also increasing (Melville, et al., 2008; Fredendall, et al., 2009). A standardization of processes is not possible in a complex environment or, it possible only at a very high cost and expense, without the guarantee of success, and, therefore, not suitable. Another insight is that complexity is, more or less, proportional to the variability of a process (Schwickert, 1996). In a complex environment, processes are not conducive and even reduce added value, having a discouraging effect on the employees who have to follow the processes (Lange & Sabrina, 2015). Furthermore, additional introduction of processes and tools increase complexity. In the end, classic process models, such as the waterfall or V-model, fail in a complex environment.

Part II: Personal Contributions And Studies In The Field Of Research

3 Investigating Risk And Project Management In Business Performance, Considering Sustainability Issues

There are changing expectations for sustainability, coupled with demands for efficiency, in planning, constructing and maintaining the environment. Balancing factors within the social, economical and ecological dimensions and properly handling trade-offs in time (the long and short term) and space (local, regional and global effects) is at the core of sustainability thinking.

Risk is seen as a condition that could unfavourably influence the accomplishment of business goals (Anderson, 2005). Every day, organizations face different risks. Accordingly, it is essential to distinguish and oversee risks, to limit their dangers and enhance their potential (Institute of Risk Management, 2006).

Organizations need to confront different risks which may have an exceptional effect on the business achievement, as well as on their hierarchical procedures. Managing risks and openings is an important part of organizations' exercises, especially when sustainability is aimed. At whatever point, organizations manage misfortunes for their business and consider and oversee risks.

Organizations success is determined by the way risks and opportunities are managed (Global Corporate and Specialty SE, 2016). Associations need to manage different risks and their related vulnerabilities to obtain results. In this way, the management of risks and openings ought to be a key player in organizations' exercises. To distinguish conceivable risks which may happen, a feasible risk management system – as to proficiency, viability and ampleness – ought to be actualized inside the organizations' structures (Paul, 2014).

V. Just, *Sustainable Business Processes in Global Companies*,
Sustainable Management, Wertschöpfung und Effizienz,
https://doi.org/10.1007/978-3-658-28196-0_4

3.1 Risk Management And Project Management – Main Coordinates

Risk and project management are essential elements that need to be considered when assessing the business performance, especially when sustainability aspects are approached.

Organizations have different levels of maturity. According to the Capability Maturity Model (CMM) developed by the Software Engineering Institute, there are five such levels:

- *Maturity level 1 – Initial*. No requirements are needed. All organisations automatically have this maturity level. Projects are being carried out, but processes are not recognizable. The environment is chaotic and unstable.
- *Maturity level 2 – Repeatable*. It is possible to plan, and control projects and they can be repeated. Maturity level 2 requires defined processes and a documented project culture. Project management practices and processes have been implemented (Jenny, 2015).
- *Maturity level 3 – Defined*. Projects are carried out according to an adjusted standard process, and an organization-spanning improvement process exists. Standards and project plans exist, and those responsible ensure that the standards of the process flows are observed (Thyssen, 2010). Processes are defined, documented and consistent with one another and are applied by trained employees.
- *Maturity level 4 – Managed*. Statistical process control is carried out with exact procedures and measurements of quality and costs. Metrics and indexes are used to establish an improved decision-making basis for further process optimization.
- *Maturity level 5 – Optimizing*. Work and methods of operation are continuously improved. Processes are precisely analysed with respect to problems, and improvements are applied to other projects.

The requirements are distinguished by specific and generic goals. Specific goals only apply for the process area and describe the specific requirements related to the process area (Thyssen, 2010). Generic goals describe the so-called "institutionalisation" of the process area, i.e. everything that needs to be done so that the specific goals are regularly, continuously and efficiently implemented. Every generic goal is assigned to a capability level:

- Capability level 0 = Incomplete
- Capability level 1 = Performed

- Capability level 2 = Managed
- Capability level 3 = Defined
- Capability level 4 = Quantitatively managed
- Capability level 5 = Optimizing

Specific and generic goals for project planning and the respective practices are set. According to CMM, reaching the various maturity levels is a task that requires good planning, and this should not be underestimated by organizations.

A detailed determination of the maturity level of project management is a comprehensive undertaking. The success of a project greatly depends on the selection and composition of the development team and, therefore, staff parameters are important to consider. The support of the top management and cooperation with the project manager are key success factors. If a project is not sufficiently supported by top management, the project may not be successfully carried out and its realization may be seriously threatened. The consequences are obvious: inefficacy, delays, budget overruns and, last, but not least, failure of the project.

The project manager is a key success factor. He is responsible for achieving the objectives stated in the project definition: deadline, costs and product quality. The project manager manages and steers the project, organizes tasks and work packages, and makes decisions. In his case, apart from professional qualifications, social skills are also needed. (Dammer et al., 2006).

Collaboration and cooperation are essential for the accomplishment of the projects. Teamwork and team spirit are indispensable for project's success. Clear role assignment is crucial for an orderly, structured and systematic project execution. The more efficiently a team works, the faster and more cost efficiently projects are carried out. A good team composition can create innovative ideas and solutions that could not have been achieved by a single person. The ability to work in a team requires employees to show that they are willing to cooperate, to be responsible, and that they will not let others do their work. (Handy, 1999)

The project management office (PMO) performs a broad range of tasks by order of the management, which can include top management and the project manager. Some of these tasks may refer to: coordinating resources, compiling documentation, project controlling, reporting and ensuring that contractual agreements are met. The PMO is also important to accurately apply and manage previously gained knowledge so that maximum benefit is obtained for the company. This makes sense to relieve the project team in the area of administrative and coordinating tasks. The PMO sets uniform procedures and supervises their application. Comparability of the projects can be achieved by the PMO. Thus, know-how does not have to be acquired repeatedly. The benefits of a PMO, as an independent organisational unit, lies in the uniform handling, evaluation, selection, and realisation of the projects, as well as, in the increased value contribution of the projects, achieved through efficient management. With the comprehensive coordination of the use of resources, the PMO ensures that they are ideally distributed, supporting sustainability. Thus, the PMO is an important criterion for successful project management, in a sustainable context (Dammer, 2006).

Project portfolio controlling is an important part of Project Portfolio Management (PPM), as it allows for linking the business strategy with the progress of the projects. PPM needs controlling methods and indices to comprehensively plan, steer, supervise, evaluate, and control the portfolio (Campana, et al, 2005). Indices for project (portfolio) controlling can be established from quantitative, as well as qualitative criteria. Quantitative criteria compare costs, time, earnings and yield returns, while qualitative criteria refer to the potential or the attractiveness of a project (Huber, et al., 2011).

A series of quantitative indices used in project portfolio controlling are outlined in table 5. These derive from the classical capital budgeting. For example, internal investment and organisation projects should be evaluated based on quantitative indices, such as the return on investment.

Table 5: Quantitative indices for project portfolio controlling

Indices based on quantitative/monetary criteria		
Index	**Calculation**	**Description**
Cash flow	inflow – outflow	Cash flow indicates the surplus of inflows over outflows. Contrary to costs, it only considers the factors affecting payment. It does not include amortisation, for instance, although this is considered to be a cost.
Rate of return	(profit*100) / invested capital	The average annual profit is put in relation with the capital, which is additionally tied to projects. Instead of profit, saved expenses can be applied. Many businesses stipulate a rate of return of at least 10 to 20%.
Return on investment (ROI)	(profit / turnover) * (turnover / invested capital)	ROI is a special form of rate of return. It is the key performance indicator of an index system and shows the dependency of different indices.
Cash flow	(Cash flow / turnover) *	Contrary to ROI, the numerator is repre-

ROI (CFROI)	(turnover / invested capital)	sented by the cash flow, instead of the profit.
Amortisation duration (Ad)	initial investment / cash flow per year	The amortisation duration indicates how long it takes to regain the capital invested in a project.
Expected commercial value (ECV)	[(PV*Pcs-C)*Pts]-D	This method considers flexibility and risk. PV - discounted cash flows of the market phase (only incoming payments) Pcs - probability of economic success (0 to 1) C - market start up costs Pts - probability of technical success of development (0 to 1) D - remaining development costs

Source: Huber, et al., 2011

The exact measurement of the financial benefits is still an issue. Therefore, the value of benefit analyses or scoring methods is frequently employed for collecting qualitative criteria (Kunz, 2007). Table 6 presents a series of qualitative indices used in project portfolio controlling.

Table 6: Qualitative indices for project portfolio controlling

Indices based on qualitative criteria	
Index	**Description**
Strategic contribution	The project's contribution to the business' strategic goals.
Interdependencies	Content-related and resource-specific dependencies and interdependencies of the projects in the portfolio.
Risk	Risk evaluation by means of text description of risks and point evaluation. Frequent, occurrence probability and impacts are also evaluated.
Target achievement	Frequently based on milestones.
On specification	Often used in software programming. Share of fulfilled requirements. (often percentages or indices)

Source: Huber, et al., 2011

The parameters for the evaluation and prioritisation of projects are given by the strategic planning (annual and project planning). These define the strategic business goals, thus determining the essential selection criteria. The process of projects selection and prioritisation passes through several levels:

a) *Rough pre-selection.* Within the course of rough pre-selection – also often referred to as pre-screening – the number of projects that are to be evaluated, is supposed to be narrowed down. In this phase, it is checked, whether project proposals clearly adhere to the strategic goals; feasibility is questioned, too.
b) *Evaluating the attractiveness of projects*. Those projects that have passed the rough pre-selection process are explicitly evaluated in terms of their attractiveness to the company. The attractiveness expresses which projects should be realised, from the company's viewpoint. For this purpose, various criteria such as strategic meaning (e.g. customer focus, advantages in competition, process know-how), urgency, risk, resource requirements, profitability, and costs, can be used.
c) *Evaluation with scoring methods*. Scoring models can be used in the field of project multi-dimensional evaluation. After the calculation of each score, it is possible to aggregate specific values of the scoring models, to visualise them in a portfolio diagram.
d) *Evaluation of all strategy contributions of different project portfolios: "House of projects"*. The next step implies the evaluation of projects in different project portfolios based on all company strategies and functional strategies. It is not distinguished whether the strategies are directly allocatable to a certain portfolio. The advantage of this methodology is that, for example, R&D projects can also be checked for possible contributions to marketing and production strategies. It should be especially pointed out that, with this method, it becomes immediately transparent when certain functional strategies are not supported by strategic projects. Furthermore, it is assumed that the contributions of the projects can be positive, as well as negative.

A model that supports the process of project selection, focusing of the last phase, especially through highlighting the evaluation developed in "house of projects", is presented in table 7.

Table 7:Project evaluation in "House of Projects"

Strategy		**Emphasis (Σ 100)**	**R&D-projects**			**Organisation projects**		
			Project 1	Project 2	Project ...	Project 1	Project 2	Project ...
R&D-portfolio	R&D strategy 1	**5**	**+**		**++**	**--**		**+**
	R&D strategy 2	**8**		**+**			**++**	
	R&D strategy N	**10**	**++**		**-**	**+**		**+**
IT-portfolio	IT-strategy 1	**5**		**+**			**--**	
	IT-strategy 2	**7**	**-**	**-**		**+**	**-**	
	IT-strategy N	**9**		**++**	**-**	**+**		
...	...	...	...	...	...	...	...	...
Strategy relevance absolute (ARB)			**50**	**40**	**35**	**21**	**40**	**17**
Strategy relevance relative (RRB)			**10**	**8**	**7**	**4**	**8**	**3**

Legend: Contribution of project to the strategy (in points)	***Positive***		***Negative***	
	++=3	+=1	-=-1	--=-3

Source: own elaboration

In the model, the individual projects of a project portfolio are evaluated with the functional strategies of another project portfolio. The range of values of the contributions lies between +3 and -3. The specific contributions of a project are multiplied by the emphasis of the respective functional strategy and added up to an absolute strategic relevance. In a further step, the relative strategic relevance is calculated to obtain a standardised view of all projects. For the calculation of the relative strategic relevance, the respective absolute strategic value of a project is divided by the highest absolute value that was reached by a project. Multiplying by the factor 10, makes possible a depiction of a project's relative strategic relevance as the dimension "strategic relevance" in a graphic project portfolio diagram.

The results from the evaluation of individual projects/plans or of a project portfolio can be depicted in a project portfolio diagram for visualisation and further analysis. (Figure 7)

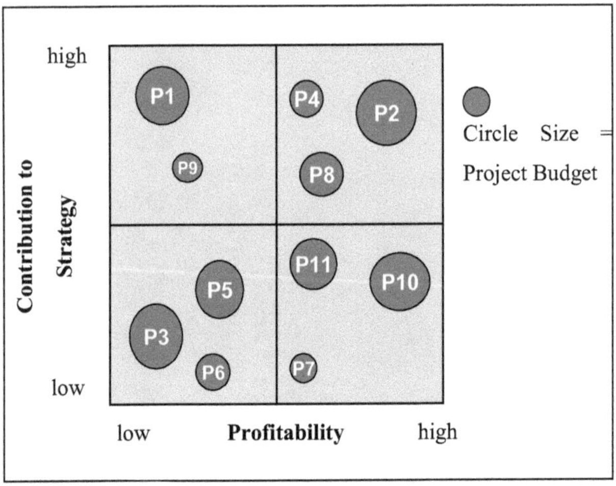

Figure 7:Project portfolio diagram according to strategy contribution and profitability

Source: own representation

The project portfolio diagram in figure 7 can be used in order to outline the connection between the strategic benefit and the viability of projects and plans, with additional consideration of the individual project budgets (equivalent to circle size). Compared to the other projects of the project portfolio, the projects in the left lower quadrant (P3, P5, P6) contribute to a small extent to strategy and profitability. This can be seen as a potential indicator for improvement and these projects should be looked at more closely, as they take up a considerable budget in the project portfolio. Depending on the strategic goal and considering the continual interdependencies, urgency, resource interdependencies, and "mandatory project" requirements, scenarios are simulated until the ideal project portfolio is compiled.

The following figure illustrates an ideal type of an evaluation and prioritisation process.

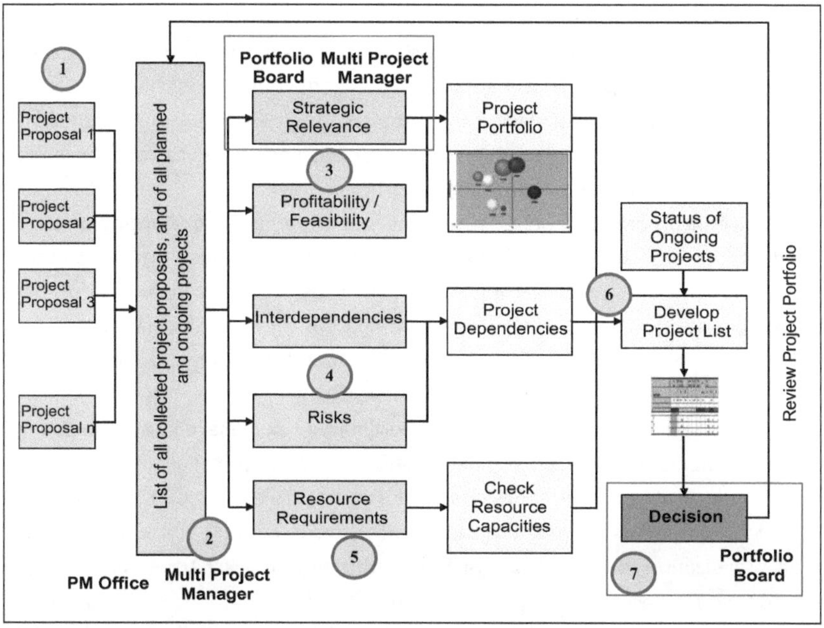

Figure 8: The ideal type of an evaluation and prioritisation process

Source: own representation

Besides project management, risk management is also vital for achieving business goals. Likewise, by supporting basic leadership and change of productivity and viability of procedures and association, risk management is extremely important for organizations. In the same framework, sustainable risk management should bolster towards accomplishing the ideal result of an organization and towards lessening the vulnerability of its results (Paul, 2014).

In respect of viability and achievement, sustainable risk management is satisfactory to the level of risk. However, this should be lined up with different exercises inside the association. Risk management should not be disengaged, but rather inserted inside an organized approach which likewise permits adaptability for iterative improvement.

The risk management approach for each organization is controlled by market, but also by the multifaceted nature of the association and the risk it faces. Risk management is a procedure that depends on a few basic advances, such as recognizing, breaking down, assessing, treating, checking, and investigating (Shin-Wie, 2012). The procedures and system are important for risk management inside an association, which is an indispensable piece of Enterprise risk management (ERM).

The coordination of exercises, which are identified with screen and control risks, are secured with the expression "risk management". A risk management system (e.g. the COSO-system, ISO 310000 and so forth) comprises of hierarchical segments to actualize and execute risk management. The risk management process itself guarantees the treatment of risks, as distinguishing, assessing, observing, and detailing. Risk management is a continuous process.

ERM incorporates various procedures and strategies, representing a coordinated way to deal with the risks in organizations. Due to expansion in ecological complexity, an institutionalized approach of managing risks and openings isn't just helpful, but also significant for business continuation. The way associations manage such risks is the key part for progress and can be found in the organization's general performance (Global Corporate and Specialty SE, 2016).

ERM should provide a structure to coordinated risk management to meet lawful commitments, guarantee risk mindfulness and practical management of recognized risks inside the organizations' association and processes (Zu, 2013).

ERM influences the vital basic leadership process, directly impacting the yield of an organization (e.g. tolerating or moderating risks will impact items, advertise enhancement, conveyance of administrations and so forth.).

As indicated by ISO 31000: 2009 risk is characterized as a deviation from the normal, which prompts vulnerability on achieving association's targets. "Enterprise risks" may be encountered in all elements of an organization, whatever the sources or nature are. ERM is "an ongoing process in an entity, developed by people at every level of an organization, applied in strategy setting and across the enterprise, at every level and unit. This includes approaching the risk from the persepctive of a porfolio, designed to identify potential events that may affect the entity in case they occur. This is able to provide reasonable assurance to an entity's management and board of directors, geared to achieve all the objectives, in one or more separate, but overlapping categories" (Takehiko et al., 2006). As indicated by the Committee of Sponsoring Organizations of the Treadway Commission's (COSO), risks can be separated into various classifications, e.g. vital, tasks, revealing and consistence.

In this thesis, risk is characterized as any occasion or condition that could unfavourably influence the accomplishment of business goals.

Risk taking and its appropriate management are significant for developing and building up an association. Proactive risk methodologies may prompt enhancements in strategic and agent regions, since choices and potential outcomes are examined in more depth (Paul, 2014).

Risks may be assesses using both quantitative (monetary) and qualitative (subjective) techniques. Quantitative techniques are, generally, centred around the calculation of certain monetary factors and their connection (e.g. affectability examination, situation investigation), while subjective techniques regularly accentuate the information of risk proprietors or risk takers (e.g. interviews, cross-useful workshops). Frequently, operational, market or business risks are assessed based on what can happen in the next year. Major key or liquidity risks can be assessed considering a period of up to 5 following or past years.

Risks ought to be assessed regarding their subjective and monetary outcome (positive or negative). Impacts ought to be surveyed in terms of the detailing gathering and allocated to risk classes. Also, the subjective impacts of risks must be surveyed. Due to their temperament, not all risks can be assessed in connection to money-related effects (Anderson, 2005).

The expanding effect of social and ecological issues on business success, plus the European control with respect to non-monetary data on sustainability and social obligation (EU order 2014/95/EU), lead organizations to focus on sustainability. In this way, sustainability needs to be incorporated in management, risk methodologies and practices (Zu, 2013). Sustainability covers political, monetary and social angles, whereby sustainability-related risks should be a key element in investigating the risks of an organization, especially when considering their potential budgetary effects (Leon, 2014). The compromise of these long time impacts and changes with effect on fund and general business achievement is a test which additionally impacts risk management (Smith, 2003).

The distinguishing proof and treatment of risks as a feature of risk management are pivotal for accomplishing business goals. ERM is a coordinated way to deal with, and to control the risks related with the business exercises by providing a steady structure of strategies and procedures to screen and react to occasions or conditions that could influence the accomplishment of business targets (Institute of Risk Management, 2006). Organizations' way to deal with ERM ought to be lined up with centre business procedures, such as business arranging, venture management and outside yearly announcing, yet in addition with other applicable corporate administration components, such as Compliance Management, Internal Control System and Internal Audit, to guarantee viability. Adapting high straightforwardness about accessible risk data is basic for compelling ERM.

The principle undertakings of ERM are to help vital and very much educated basic leadership and to give a versatile and viable approach for risk and openings all through the business. ERM intends to distinguish and react to circumstances and risks, influencing the accomplishment of business goals in a compelling and coordinated way (Anderson, 2005). Business achievement calls for ponder risk-taking. The way to deal with risk management serves to fittingly control the risks emerging from business movement with a sober minded and steady strategy. Different standards apply to empower successful ERM. Viable ERM is a necessary piece of organizations' business forms, everyday management and corporate culture sorted out by the leading group of management.

A compelling ERM depends on risks and their assessment, especially in terms of their subjective and budgetary effect. For a wide understanding of the risks, a definite depiction ought to guarantee a typical comprehension of the risk and distinguish obligations (Poser & Tobin 2012).

To demonstrate the intrinsic level of the risks regarding probability and size and to show the feasible risk control system which may be connected, scholars promote the use of a risk frame. Different risk management approaches are outlined in the scientific literature. Thus, it is imperative to underline the demarcation between the risk management standard, the risk management process and the risk management structure, focusing on their meanings used in the thesis. The risk management standard sets out the general way to deal with the effective risk management. This covers the risk management process itself, and the structure. The risk management structure covers the reason, vision and mission of the organization and its mix inside risk management. The risk management process and the risk management structure should consider the present condition of information, yet in addition give individual authoritative modifications and improvements.

Today, companies have a great responsibility to their customers, the global community and the earth's resources. This means satisfying the information needs of customers and stakeholders through a convincing sustainability concept. In addition, a healthy corporate philosophy is also subject to a behavioural ethic, namely a responsibility towards the Earth as a habitat. Consequently, it is the companies' responsibility to make the sustainability performance of their business processes tangible. While some aspects of sustainability, such as a declining energy consumption with constant efficiency, are relatively easy to identify, there are other sub-areas whose measurement is not explicitly possible. Problems arise, for example, when measuring effects that are attributable to higher employee motivation (IHK Nürnberg, 2015).

A few years ago, Professor Frank Figge developed the so-called "Sustainable Value Approach", which measures the social and ecological use of resources and the subsequent economic effects for the company. In this process, the company's use of resources is compared with that of a benchmark. The principle of the concept is, according to Professor Figge, the following: "Sustainable added value, sustainable value, is achieved by companies when they use their economic, environmental and social resources more efficiently than their competitors" (IHK Nürnberg, 2015). Another way to gain an overview of a company's sustainability performance is the Dow Jones Sustainability Index (DJSI). This serves as a criterion for the assessment of investment decisions, since it only includes those companies in each sector that are best placed to act in all three sustainability dimensions (Hansmann, 2003).

Companies usually measure their sustainability performance using special indicators, so-called key performance indicators (KPIs), since their use is seen as a promising method for measuring the sustainability of business processes. A large number of key figures can be accessed from different sources, which are more or less suitable, depending on the sector and company.

Further on, the chapter focuses on KPIs, outlining a detailed description of their basic functions. Afterwards, general requirements for indicators and, finally, their weaknesses are identified. A detailed examination of the KPI fundamentals is intended to facilitate the selection of suitable key figures for a given problem. To select the optimal key figures for measuring the economic sustainability of a company, it is important to first deal with its functions. The essential functions of key figures or key figure systems are outlined in figure 9. Acceptance of the key figures, which is achieved by correct data acquisition and processing, forms the basis for all functionalities of the KPIs (Posselt, 2014).

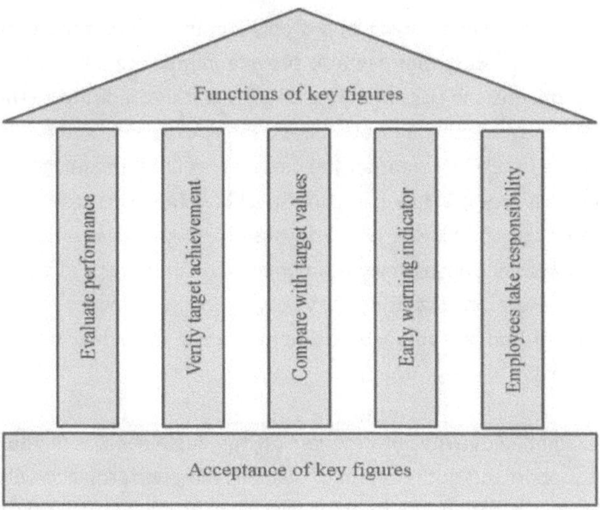

Figure 9: Central functions of key figures

Source: Posselt, 2014

The essential functions of key figures refer to (Posselt, 2014):

- *Evaluate performance*. The primary function of key figures is to assess and control the entrepreneurial performance. They enable companies to measure the results of their business processes and present selected, relevant information in a compact form. The measured results help to make the complexity of reality more manageable and serve as a reflection of the actual company performance for those in charge and shareholders.
- *Verify target achievement*. The most important function of key figures is to check the achievement of objectives. First of all, the selection of suitable key figures is essential for the precise formulation of objectives within a company. The actual values can be compared at any time with the previously defined target values (targets) and thus provide information on the degree of target achievement.
- *Compare with target values*. A valid evaluation of the company's performance is only possible if the used key figures are comparable with reference values that have similar initial parameters. In this way, intuitive judgments are to be replaced by verifiable information as far as possible, thus enabling the examination, evaluation and discussion of the collected data of a company.
- *Early warning indicators*. Key figures can not only identify future opportunities for a company or process, but can also provide immediate information on approaching problems and risks by acting as early warning indicators. The existence of these early warning indicators is essential, especially in times of crisis, as they enable timely intervention and can prevent greater damage.
- *Responsibility of employees*: While company-specific data – such as the liquidity situation of the company – was previously only known to selected executives, nowadays, its transparency is an important component of a successful corporate culture. By disclosing these key figures, employees can be informed, motivated and encouraged to improve their individual performance.

KPIs can provide companies with information on the sustainability of their business processes and support the optimization of sustainability performance with the help of defined targets. Grundfald (2006) emphasize that "working with indicators is principally without alternatives", but their use can lead to application problems, since not every indicator is suitable for every practical case (Posselt, 2014).

In order for key figures to serve as a reliable basis for information and decision-making, they must meet certain requirements. First of all, it is important that the selected key figures are empirically ascertainable and precisely measurable. Furthermore, the required effort for collecting the necessary data should be justifiable. In order to carry out a reliable and meaningful target/actual comparison, the determination of data on a regular basis, for example in an annual cycle, must be possible (Bardt, 2011).

Ultimately, the decisive factor for the selection of a specific key figure is the extent to which it can provide precise and reliable statements about the specific problem. Key figures and key figure systems also help companies to set and review their corporate objectives.

In sustainability management, on one hand, key figures serve to derive sustainability targets. On the other hand, they help to measure the company's sustainability performance and, if necessary, to introduce sustainability measures (Tachkov, 2011). Key figures mainly provide historical data. Therefore, it is important to always look at and evaluate the collected data over several, consecutive measuring points and always in comparison to the target value.

A major problem that arises when measuring sustainability performance with the help of key figures is the frequent manipulation or misinterpretation of the collected data. This can be primarily attributed to the incorrect or inadequate selection of indicators or to the isolated consideration of the individual ratios. Therefore, a company must always ensure that the key figure evaluations are based on correct data. The best way to minimize the weaknesses of key figures is to select suitable key figures for the problem. This is the root for effective sustainability measurement. It must be ensured that the used indicators are providing sufficient information about the respective problem. Often, looking at selected key figures in isolation, is not enough. Therefore, a combination of several key figures into key figure systems should be accomplished, to achieve a high-quality result, and thus to obtain sustainable statements on economic sustainability (Tachkov, 2011).

3.2 Assessing Risk Management In The Conext Of Business Performance

In the ERM assessment process, the singularity of each organization must be considered. Approaching ERM as a proper way to deal with the different risks an association might face (counting risks with regards to sustainability), it appears to be legitimate to assess the result in monetary figures as well as from other perspectives. Thus, along with quantitative methodologies, subjective ones are expected to comprehend the importance of ERM for each organization. In this way, the usage of KPIs, as well as vital objectives, the association and every connected procedure as to the sustainability point, is pertinent.

For the assessment of ERM viability, the scientific literature proposes the usage of an improved Balanced Scorecard, which examines ERM and its commitment to accomplishing budgetary and non-budgetary related objectives (Parvaneh, et al., 2014). ERM ought to be assessed with respect to "execution"; its estimation can be founded on the Balanced Scorecard technique and incorporate the utilization of Economic Value Added (EVA) (EVA, 2003; Hawawini, 2003). The adjusted scorecard technique is a management device which measures the association's advance toward accomplishing key objectives and evaluates the advance in different aspects (money related execution, consumer loyalty, inner procedures, learning and development for workers), focusing on systems, comparable with the classifications proposed by COSO (The Sponsoring Organizations of the Tread way Commission, 1992).

Taking into account the strategy for sustainable ERM, the scientific literature promotes a model for evaluating ERM and measuring the execution of organizations' risk management (Kopia, et al., 2016). The model (figure 10) depends on existing strategies and aims to distinguish approaches for practically assessing ERM.

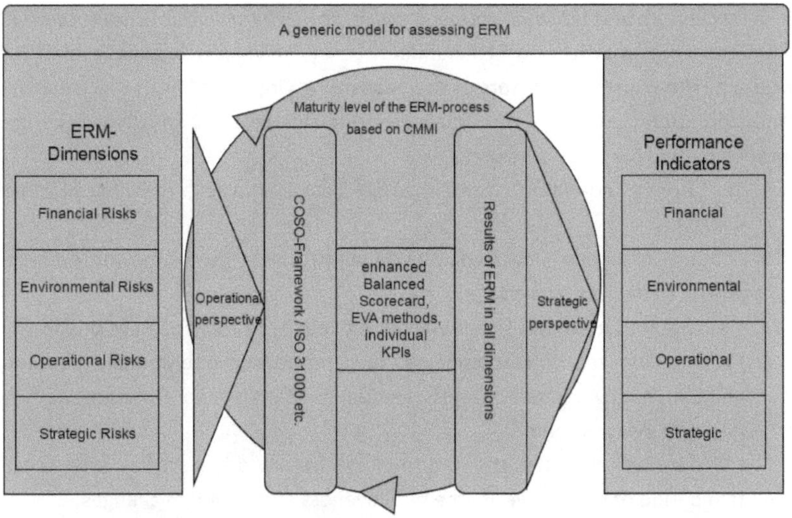

Figure 10: Generic model for ERM assessment

Source: Kopia, et al., 2016

It is necessary to create a clear understanding of identifying and assessing risks, as well as, of monitoring and measuring the process individually, for each company. Structures give fundamental procedures to ERM, whereby the change of the risk management forms is a basic part. Numerous current investigations attempt to assess the effect of ERM by exclusively utilizing monetary figures. Yet, for the most part, ERM can not face a top to bottom approach, especially due to its multifaceted nature.

In such a context, this sub-chapter explains a contextual analysis to pick up bits of knowledge into the unpredictability of ERM inside an association. This contextual analysis demonstrates the adaption and usage of hypothetical parts of risk management, however, may likewise serve to assess the convenience of the proposed estimation system for ERM. Furthermore, the chapter provides a typical view on structures, forms and KPI.

Risks are characteristic to a wide range of associations and capacities. For actualizing conventional risk management efficiently and successfully, different benchmarks and controls exist. KPI assess the accomplishment of an association's goals or of a specific action. Characterizing KPI for risk management is, by all accounts, an intelligent advance to assess ERM inside an organization. KPI are likewise utilized by various ERM-structures. Methodologies which built up an inner control – for example, COSO – demonstrate to organizations the need to assess their inward control framework and risk management. Inside the structure, the "inward control" is characterized as a process which is influenced by individuals at each level of the association. The Board of Directors of the Sponsoring Organizations of the Treadway Commission (1992) – COSO – recognizes five interrelated parts to break down authoritative inward control frameworks:

1. The "control condition" establishes the basic setup (e.g. meaning of moral values).
2. "Control exercises" covers directions, which might guarantee the essential strides to deal with risks.
3. The "evaluation of risks" is a basic piece of each risk management process.
4. "Information and correspondence" (e.g. reports on operational, monetary and consistence related data) is essential in an inward control framework to guarantee data stream.
5. "Monitoring" evaluates the nature of the framework execution after a certain period of time, to verify the effectiveness and to obtain changes.

The four classifications (key, tasks, detailing and consistence) stretch out the structure to guarantee the accomplishment of characterized authoritative destinations. ERM itself needs to consider the human factor, which may prompt lacking basic leadership in regards to risks – this is hard to consider inside a hypothetical structure, however it requires a singular management (Christian, 2009).

The ISO 31000 standard can be viewed as an accumulation of risk management rehearses. This isn't centred around ERM yet rather it is a non-specific, generally useful way to deal with risk management. It characterizes standards, outlines, executes and keeps up a risk management process inside an organization. As other ISO standards, too, it characterizes a cyclic best level-process with the accompanying risk parts: commitment of the risk theme, plan of a risk management, usage of the risk management, observation of the risk management, and enhancement of the risk management. Inside these procedures, certain important advances are characterized. These may refer to creating a risk setting, risk ID, risk appraisal, risk alleviation, risk checking.

There are different strategies and systems which are valuable with regards to ERM. The adjusted scorecard technique is a management device which measures the association's advance toward accomplishing key goals. While ERM directs through the different risks while guiding toward vital objectives, adjusted scorecard measures the advance toward it. The adjusted scorecard can be utilized together with ERM for several reasons. The adjusted scorecard evaluates the advance in different measurements (budgetary execution, consumer loyalty, inner procedures, learning and development for workers) and with an attention on techniques, comparable as the classes proposed by COSO. It assesses an organization that uses execution measures on an endeavour wide point of view; the same is valid for ERM. Both are top-down and comprehensively, ceaselessly, and continuous methodologies which seek after an adjusted and predictable approach over numerous measurements of an enterprise (Beasley, et al., 2006).

Further on, it is outlined how to incorporate an ERM approach into the adjusted scorecard technique for an inventory network procedure of a venture, given a decent case on the most proficient method to utilize the two strategies together. Comparable methodologies were developed by various scholars (Takehiko, et al, 2006; Parvaneh, et al., 2014). Saeidi proposed the usage of an improved Balanced Scorecard approach. "Risk-BSC" should expressly cover ERM highlights and their commitment to accomplishing budgetary and non-money related objectives of the substance (EVA, 2014). ERM is a controlled framework which can be evaluated utilizing multidimensional destinations of various types. EVA can be valuable while assessing the impacts of ERM (Hawawini, et al., 2003). This is an investigation apparatus which evaluates the financial benefit of an association from the investor point of view (Youthful, 1997). EVA and Balanced Scorecard make them cover points and can both be utilized to make execution markers (Woods, 2007).

In a business, the concentration key targets are unique. In this manner, an unmistakable arrangement of execution pointers can't be predefined. In any case, every association ought to adjust a system which controls the ERM procedure through a multi-dimensional estimation approach which is lined up with the key targets.

ERM ought to cover risks related to sustainability and to approach sustainability in risk management methodologies and practices (Zu, 2013). Thereby, sustainability should seriously be considered in political, monetary and social measurements terms. Accordingly, sustainability-related risks ought to be a key component in an organization's risk examination process in regard to its financial impact (Leon, 2014). As conceivable affecting elements on fund and general business achievement, risk measurements of sustainability might be lined up with the organization's approach to risk management (Smith, 2003).

All the information outlined in this chapter is synthetically explained and applied on the ERM assessment model specific to company X. Company X is a global company, among the leaders of the industry it activates in. This represents the unit of analysis specific to the case study research outlined in chapter 5 of the thesis. Further information about the company and its activity are highlighted in chapter 5. The model outlines the following:

- The company did not take after any broad existing best practice, yet rather picked its own particular approach of evaluating the ERM. Rather, the company uses a devoted revealing framework, in view of quantitative and subjective pointers.
- The company sets up management framework norms (as ISO 14001 Environmental management framework) to utilize best practice approaches in particular territories and characterized singular key execution pointers to survey the ERM framework.
- The company builds up an individual integrative quality management framework with an open correspondence.
- The company incorporated its management frameworks (as the quality management framework and the ISO 14001 EMS) into the ERM forms by connecting them, based on key execution pointers which introduce the risk status of the business zone.
- The consistent KPI report from various divisions is evaluated by the venture risk board of directors, producing a normal risk status for the association, in light of risk effect and risk probability using an institutionalized technique (ISO 31000). The roots of these risks are related to the fact that they were developed inside various divisions. They can be in the area of economic value, item quality, data security consistence and so forth. The outcomes from the ERM perspective is a summed-up risk status of the whole company – the execution of the organization, seen from a risk management viewpoint.

To model points out that Company X uses most of the non-specific approaches to ERM assessment. Sustainability, with its related risks should not be analysed detached but rather distinguished, and it has to be assessed and checked inside the risk management procedures of the organization. The ERM-appraisal model can be used for various purposes in all associations which confront the issue of incorporating a few unique risks originating from a wide range of regions, into extensive ERM system.

3.3 Key Performance Indicators For Assessing Business Sustainability

This chapter focuses on *economic sustainability* indicators. First, possibilities for measuring or evaluating the sustainability performance of companies are identified. Subsequently, Key Performance Indicators (KPIs) are approached, focusing on thoroughly describing their basic functions. In order to facilitate the selection of suitable key figures for the given problem, the general requirements for indicators are set up.

All economic indicators already used in practice or recommended in the scientific literature are collected in a table and then evaluated. This is followed by a detailed explanation and discussion of four selected *economic sustainability* indicators: *sales growth, operating income, equity ratio, and profitability.*

The study conducted by the Ludwigshafen am Rhein University of Applied Sciences provides information on how widespread indicators of the individual sustainability dimensions are in each company. The economic dimension is the most important factor and is therefore the most frequently used indicator in companies. For example, in the industrial sector, almost all companies counted on economic indicators, while in the services sector almost 92%, as illustrated in figure 11. While social indicators are also very often included in the sustainability measurement by the studied companies (92-93%), ecological KPIs are only used in just over half of the service providers (58%) (Tachkov, 2011).

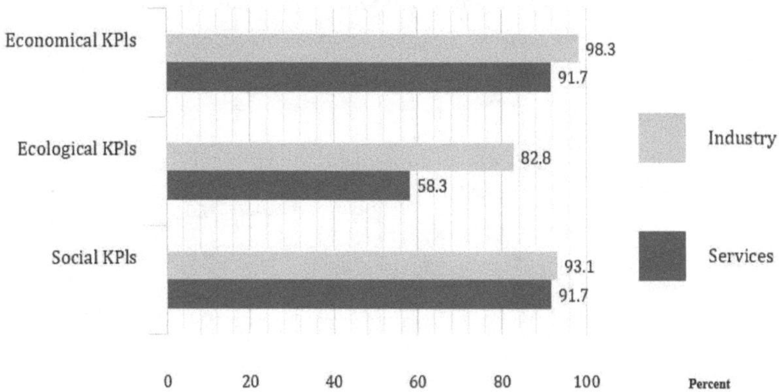

Figure 11: Dissemination of the three categories of sustainability indicators

Source: Tachkov, 2011

In industrial companies, key figures for measuring *ecological sustainability* are used more frequently, which can be primarily attributed to the increasing number of environmental guidelines, but also to public pressure. The study has also looked at the dissemination of the specific sustainability indicators of the three dimensions of the triple bottom line model. To this end, companies should mark the indicators that are used in their company on a list of predefined indicators. Figure 12 shows the degree of dissemination of specific *economic sustainability* indicators. In determining their *economic sustainability* performance, industrial companies primarily rely on lagging indicators such as profit and return (93% and 90%) and almost two-thirds of the surveyed companies in the industrial sector (64%-72%) also use early indicators (customer satisfaction, R&D expenditure and product quality and safety) to measure *economic sustainability*. Only large companies use taxes paid and contributions to local or regional economic development as indicators. Due to the way in which services are provided, customer satisfaction (79%) is the most common *economic sustainability* indicator within the service sector. In addition, more than 70% of the service companies surveyed use the late indicators, profit and return on investment to measure sustainability. The indicators R&D expenditure and product quality and safety are less relevant compared to the industrial sector. Overall, only few companies in both sectors (12%-29%) use contributions to local or regional economic development, as well as taxes and dividends paid, as indicators of *economic sustainability*. Sumarising, only the following five economic indicators are used in more than half of the surveyed companies: profit development, yield development, customer satisfaction, product quality and safety, and R&D expenditure. (Tachkov, 2011).

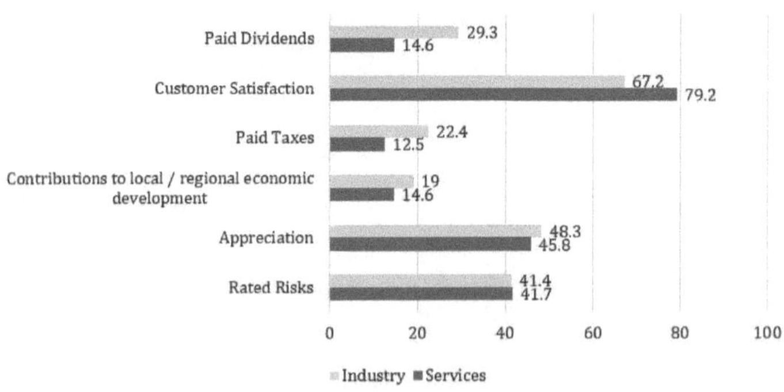

Figure 12: Degree of dissemination of economic sustainability indicators

Source: Tachkov, 2011

The selection of suitable indicators is essential for efficient sustainability measurement. When selecting *economic sustainability* indicators, a large number of indicators from corporate practice can be used. In addition, there are various guidelines that are intended to help companies to select their sustainability indicators. The two most important sustainability guidelines are presented below.

The Global Reporting Initiative (GRI) was founded in 1997 and since then this has been supporting governments and large corporations by developing and publishing guidelines for the preparation of sustainability reports that include, among other things, more than 120 key figures from the fields of business, ecology and society. They currently serve as a reference point for more than 5000 companies, associations and organisations worldwide to measure their own sustainability performance. The directive includes key performance indicators, which are considered to be significant for most companies, and supplementary indicators, which can be added to the directive, depending on the company (Hauff, 2014).

Within the economic dimension, the GRI lists the following core indicators:

- *economic performance*: added value (revenue, operating costs, salaries, donations, taxes), financial consequences of climate change, corporate social benefits, public financial inflows (subsidies);
- *market presence*: local personnel, suppliers on site;
- *indirect economic impact*: sum of infrastructure investments.

The Association of German Engineers (VDI) has developed a guideline for sustainable development for small and medium-sized enterprises (SMEs). The VDI Guideline 4070 Sheet 1 is planned to support the strategy of sustainable business processes and thus the implementation of the global guiding principle of "sustainability". The guideline is also based on the three magnitudes of the triple-bottom-line approach and has, therefore, divided the selected indicators into the areas of economy, ecology and social issues (Dürr, 2011). Similar to the GRI, it is recommended to select additional supplementary and complementary parameters, depending on the sector and company.

The guideline provides a total of 17 key figures for the economic sub-area, which can be grouped as follows (Dürr, 2011):

- *earnings indicators*: operating result, net value added, *sales growth*, value added;
- *asset and financial indicators*: *equity ratio*, *return on equity*, return on debt, development of fixed assets, return on investment (ROI), development of working capital (WC);

- *production-oriented indicators*: capacity utilisation rate, scrap rate, error costs, percentage of certified suppliers, market share, R&D share, productivity.

Further economic indicators can be found in various publications or in public sustainability reports of companies (Henkel, 2017; Siemens, 2015; Deutsche, 2013). The following table summarizes the *economic sustainability* indicators and their characteristics, which are commonly used in business practice and frequently discussed in the literature. Some economic performance indicators, such as Gross Domestic Product (GDP) per capita, employment or government debt, are often cited in the literature but not in the table, as these are only used to measure the sustainability of countries (Statistisches Bundesamt, 2017).

Table 8: Economic sustainability indicators as resulted from practice and the scientific literature

Indicator	**Description**
Asset intensity	Ratio of fixed assets to total assets of the company
Fixed assets	Changes in fixed assets: Non-current assets not held for sale.
Percentage of defective products	Percentage of defective products in total production that have been rejected due to poor quality (%)
Number of employees	Stability of the number of employees
Operating profit / EBIT	Comparison of operating income and operating expenses
Gross value added	Total value of all goods and services produced, less intermediate consumption.
Cashflow	Inflow of cash: Company surplus after deduction of expenses
Dividend per share	The portion of retained earnings that is distributed to shareholders (dividend yield %)
Economic Value Added (EVA)	Revenue less cost of capital
Equity ratio	Ratio of equity to total capital
Return on equity	Ratio of profit (net income for the year) to equity
Development of the number of customers	Net increase / decrease in customer numbers

Share of R&D	Share of R&D investment in total investments
Defect costs	Costs in the company caused by faulty production and its effects
Financial consequences and risks of climate change	Implications for the organisation's activities and other risks associated with climate change
R&D services	Total R&D services
Debt ratio	Ratio of debt to *Equity ratio*
Capacity utilisation rate	Ratio between actual production volume and maximum achievable production volume
Market share (sales market)	Ratio of own sales (revenues) to total sales (sales) of all suppliers (%)
Net value added	Gross value added less depreciation and amortization
Productivity	Ratio between produced goods and the required production factors
Regional share of procurement	Proportion of procurement goods originating from the region of the company
Return on Capital Employed (ROCE)	Ratio of NOPAT to (total capital - current FK - cash and cash equivalents)
Subsidies	Unilateral transfers from public funds
Sales growth	Economic development
Working Capital	Development of working capital: Difference between current assets and current liabilities
Certified suppliers	Number of certified suppliers
Interest	Interest paid to debt capital providers

Source: GRI, 2006

Further on, the following selected *economic sustainability* indicators are presented and evaluated on the basis of their usefulness for companies:

- *Sales growth*
- *Operating result (EBIT)*
- *Equity ratio*
- *Return on equity*

Usually, each of the key figures only provides a reliable statement on the sustainability performance of companies in conjunction with other indicators. In addition, the use of key figure systems reduces the risk that a key figure may provide an incorrect statement due to currency collapses or other one-off events.

Sales growth is one of the classic earnings ratios within the company's key figures and represents the positive or negative changes in a company's sales compared to the base period. The *sales growth* of a company is therefore calculated as follows (Vahs & Schäfer-Kunz, 2012):

$$Sales\ growth = \frac{Revenues\ for\ the\ period\ under\ review}{Revenues\ in\ the\ base\ period}\ [\%] \qquad (1)$$

A company's sales include all revenues from provided goods and services. Sales therefore describe all income resulting from the sale of company's products and services. The key figure "sales revenue" is regularly reported in a company's income statement. The earnings ratio enables customers, competitors or investors to follow the developments of a company in recent years and identify trends. A continuously positive sales development over several periods secures the constant existence of the company. It suggests a stable position and thus a future-oriented management of the company (Dürr, 2011).

Operating result (EBIT - Earning before interest and taxes): This outlines the company's operating result before interest and taxes (Dürr, 2011). EBIT is calculated in accordance with the International Financial Reporting Standards (IFRS), as presented in table 9.

Table 9: Calculation of EBIT

Net income for the year
+ Tax
+ Financial result
= **EBIT** = earnings before interest and taxes

Source: Scheffler, 2011

The advantage of operating earnings is that they are internationally comparable, in contrast to other key earnings figures, such as the annual result; EBIT is a common indicator in an international comparison of companies' success (Behringer, 2014). EBIT allows "statements about the future viability of a company" and thus also about its *economic sustainability*. In this way, an increase in EBIT can be interpreted as a successful development of the company, guaranteeing its existence continuity. On the contrary, a negative operating result often indicates losses that "tend to jeopardize the future viability of the company" (Dürr, 2011).

However, EBIT ratio has no uniform use or definition worldwide despite existing standards and regulations (IFRS or HGB). For example, in the case of corporate use, it may be adjusted for additional effects, such as income from participations.

Equity ratio: An enterprise can be financed by equity and debt. The ratio of equity to total capital is known as the *equity ratio*. This key figure provides information about the capital structure of a company. The formula for its calculation is the following (Vahs & Schäfer-Kunz, 2012):

$$Equity\ ratio = \frac{Equity\ capital}{total\ capital}\ [\%] \qquad (2)$$

The more equity capital a company contributes, the better the *equity ratio*. A higher *equity ratio* entails a higher risk for the owners of the company, who are dependent on the development of the company. According to the so-called "vertical capital structure rule, as much equity as debt capital [is to be used in the company]", so that the equity investors have less risks. Contrary to the vertical capital structure rule, however, companies are increasingly using a higher proportion of debt capital. The reason for this is usually the so-called leverage effect, which affects the *return on equity* (Vahs & Schäfer-Kunz, 2012).

The *equity ratio* not only offers information on the capital structure, but also shows how creditworthy a company is. However, in order to assess the economic situation and thus the sustainability of a company, the *return on equity* of the company should also be considered.

Return on equity: The *return on equity* is a ratio of the net income for the year to the equity brought in. This is one of the most significant key earnings figures and offers information on the level of *return on equity* in the company (Behringer, 2014).

$$Return\ on\ equity = \frac{Net\ profit\ of\ the\ year}{Equity\ capital}\ [\%] \qquad (3)$$

The *return on equity* can be used to measure the company's profitability. It is therefore possible to see to what extent the company can make profits from the capital provided by shareholders (Laier, 2011). It has already been mentioned that the leverage effect is important when considering the *return on equity*. "The *return on equity* invested in an enterprise can be increased by a higher level of indebtedness if the overall profitability achieved in the enterprise is greater than the interest rate at which debt can be borrowed" (Vahs & Schäfer-Kunz, 2012). However, it is critical to note that a higher *return on equity* entails a greater risk for the stability of the company. This can be described by the fact that the arrangement of a high proportion of debt and a declining overall *return on equity* is having an equally rapid adverse effect on the *return on equity*. In the long term, companies can end up in over-indebtedness and insolvency due to the consequences (Vahs & Schäfer-Kunz, 2012).

The analysis of the *equity ratio* and *return on equity* provide a clear image on the current capital structure and the economic situation of the company. This can be used to draw conclusions about the degree of *economic sustainability* of corporate processes, since long-term economic stability is one of the main objectives of *economic sustainability*.

3.4 The Implementation of EFQM In Project Management

The importance of quality in a company continuously increases (Schmelzer & Sesselmann, 2013). Consequently, it is not surprising that different standards, regarding the issue of quality and quality management, exist. Exemplary, the EFQM system is used as a benchmark for quality management as well as project portfolio management for project management.

Project management influences the success of an enterprise as well as its growth (Mathias, 2013). Project Excellence Model affects the achievement of business goals. Accordingly, an organization, which tries to be effective ought to apply the Project Excellence Model or EFQM inside the task administration process. Consequently, it is indisputable, that EFQM and the Project Excellence Model cohere concerning sustainable business success. All these insights into scientific evidence concerning project management and EFQM are based on a valid thorough literature survey.

The competition between the three biggest economic areas – the North American Free Trade Area, the European Union and the industrialized countries of East Asia – led to the establishment of the European Foundation for Quality Management (EFQM). The EFQM awards the European Quality Award. This aims at emphasising a holistic quality management, creating incentives for individuals and companies to develop activities in quality improvement, and presenting the achieved results of all departments. The goal of the EFQM is to increase the competitiveness of its members and to create role models for other companies by honouring them (Just, 2016). The EFQM Excellence Model evaluates all the processes of a company.

Figure 13 provides a clear overview of the basic concept and fundamental principles related to EFQM. Fulfilling the following basic concepts is important for an efficient management system.

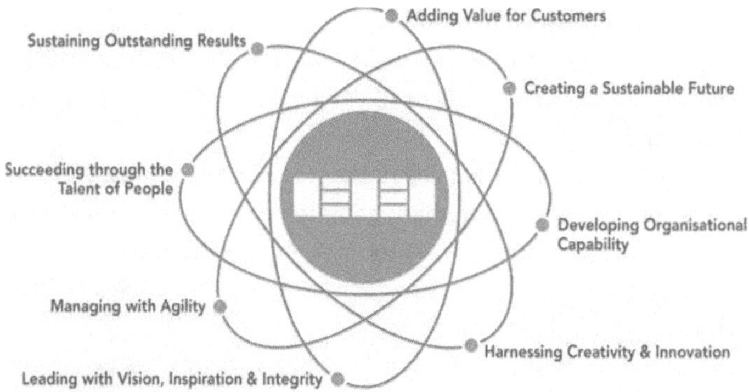

Figure 13: EFQM basic concepts

Source: Swiss Association for Quality, 2011

These are detailed in the following paragraphs.

Achieving balanced results: A requirement for this is that current and future needs and beliefs of the stakeholders are recognized. The gained knowledge must be reflected in the vision, mission and policy of the company.

Creating benefits for the customer: Another important requirement for an excellent organization is the alignment towards the customer. The customer decides upon the success or failure; therefore, it is very important to properly assess them. The superiority of the products and services must be aligned to the needs of current and potential customers. In this context, a very good customer relationship management is especially important (Just, 2016).

Leading with vision, inspiration and integrity: Excellence requires motivated and visionary executives. Only if executives show clarity and constancy of purpose in their behaviour, employees will feel encouraged.

Managing with processes: Excellent organisations are managed by structured and strategically aligned processes. These were designed upon fact-based decisions to achieve long-term improvements and to take potential risks into account.

Being successful through employees: Staff potential is strengthened and developed through employee development and integration. Common values and a culture of trust allow employees to participate in the design process and to enrich their professional development.

Fostering innovation and creativity: Continuous learning which leads to innovation and improvements is the underlying idea of excellence. The reason behind this is that the performance of a company systematically builds and leverages knowledge through consequent knowledge management and knowledge sharing. This is reflected in innovative products and services.

Building partnerships: Excellent organizations work more effectively when they build and maintain lasting relationships to all of their partners; this is a win-win situation for all parties involved.

Assuming responsibility for a sustainable future: To meet the company's long-term interests, the employees act in an ethical and ecological manner. Excellence reflects an outstanding and superior corporate social responsibility. Social responsibility and sustained ecological behaviour can be found in the organization's mission statement (Just, 2016).

A model was developed to be applied to all industries, companies of all sizes and all cultural frameworks. Figure 14 provides an overview of the basic structure of the EFQM valuation model.

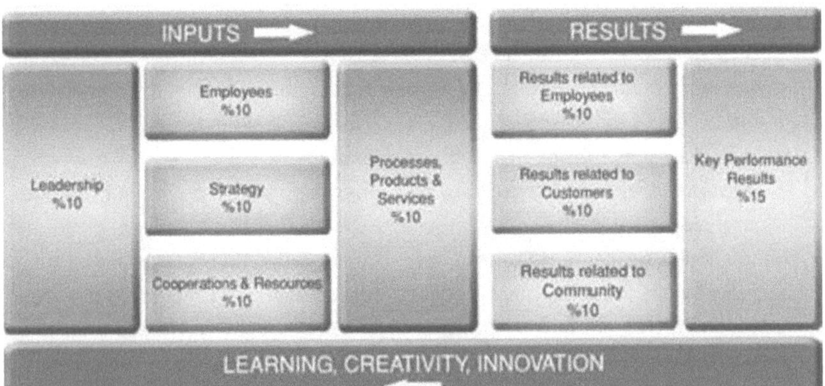

Figure 14: The basic structure of the EFQM model

Source: Swiss Association for Quality, 2011

The EFQM Model serves as a tool to recognize potential for improvement on the way to excellence. It gives a company the possibility to recognize its strengths and weaknesses during an assessment and to introduce improvement measures, if necessary (Michael, 2016).

The EFQM valuation model consists of nine assessment areas that are differently weighted, as illustrated in figure 14. Each of these nine criteria is divided into several sub-categories based on which the evaluation is carried out:

- The first criterion of the EFQM Excellence Model is leadership as it plays an essential role in every company. The leadership of a company determines the direction and assumes the responsibility for the company. Without the dedication of the top management, far-reaching measures for business excellence cannot be taken. (Just, 2016)
- The second criterion addresses policies and strategy. This criterion deals with how policies and strategies are developed and translated into practice. Its essence lays in the aspects concerning the raison d'être, the company's values, mission statement and strategic alignment so that the basic principle of constant improvement is anchored in this area as well. In this context, it is important to note that the policy and strategy contribute to the achievement of the company's goals; this must be embedded in employees' mind. Otherwise, the best strategy is of no use. Policies and strategies become highly visible, especially in constructing the company's image and in the communication with customers. (Just, 2016)
- The criterion "Employees" deals with the involvement of the employees in the continuous improvement processes. Essentially, it deals with how the organization uses its human capital and promotes employees. The EFQM not only focuses on promoting the individual but also on promoting and developing team potential (Michael, 2016).
- Increasing customer satisfaction and quality is the most important objective of all total quality management approaches. This fourth criterion focuses on achieving outstanding market performance, through efficient and effective use of resources. Avoiding waste of resources is required to achieve this criterion. The success of the organization significantly depends on handling resources in an efficient manner. Important resources for a company are, for instance, finances, information, material, technology, buildings and floors, and knowledge. (Just, 2016)
- The fifth criterion focuses on the processes that are aligned with the customer. TQM concepts, which have already been described, include these in the implementation activity. These TQM concepts deal with the achievement of goals such as improvements of process flows, reducing throughput time and strong customer retention. It is important to recognize all processes and intercepts of an organization and gear them towards customer satisfaction.

Management, core and supporting processes must be perfectly coordinated. (Just, 2016)

- In contrast to the previous criteria, the sixth criterion – customer-oriented results – belongs to the result criteria and has the highest weighting factor. Customer satisfaction is a company's primary goal. Thus, it is important to exactly know customer groups and market segments. Customer expectations must always be satisfied. This is why all aspects that provide information about the customer's satisfaction and expectations must be considered. (Just, 2016)
- Just like "customer-oriented results", the seventh criterion, referring to "employee-oriented results", must be defined by indexes, too. This is primarily done through surveys, but also through analyses.
- The second to last criterion of the EFQM Excellence Model refer to society-oriented results. "Society-oriented results arise from the perception of tasks and implementations that must be derived from ethical, moral, political or economic interests with respect to the community" (Klug, 2012). For example, all efforts related to environmental protection – such as sustainable management and corporate social responsibility – are included in these criteria.
- The last criterion of the EFQM Excellence Model refers to the key results. Key results refer to all measures aiming to secure the organization's results for the long-term. For this, financial and result indexes for innovation and improvements are necessary (Nielsen, 2012).

Following these criteria, organizations can measure their performance. The criteria must be reviewed and assessed on a regular basis, so that strategies for improvement can be derived. This leads to a continuous improvement of the organisation (Deutsche, 2016).

The key part of the evaluation according to the EFQM is the RADAR logic, which is based on five elements:

- Results;
- Approach;
- Deployment;
- Assessment;
- Review.

The systematics of the continuous improvement process is applied. As shown in figure 15, the Plan-Do-Check-Act Cycle illustrates the importance of the alignment of the action to achieving the aimed results.

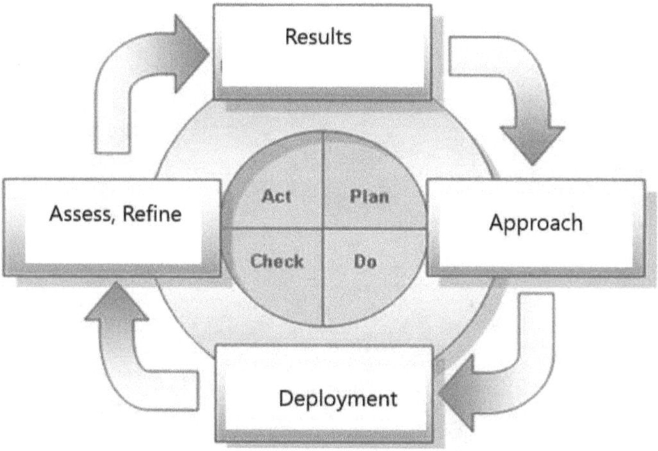

Figure 15: The RADAR logic in accordance with the PDCA cycle

Source: Deutsche Gesellschaft für Qualität e.V., 1999: 14

The reasoning behind this logic is the following: First, an organization should specify the desired/expected results from the strategy and planning process. For this, a well-founded approach must be planned, and its implementation has to be worked out. It is vital that the described processes are executed. In the end, the applied approaches and their implementation must be assessed and reviewed and, if applicable, improvements must be made.

In 1996, the GPM derived the Project Excellence Model from the EFQM Excellence Model. The basic structures were maintained, and the congruences were applied to project management (Lemmer, 2012). Since the EFQM Excellence Model has been thoroughly described, only essential differences of the Project Excellence Model are outlined.

The Project Excellence Model consists of nine criteria that are divided into two main groups – project management and project results (Figure 16).

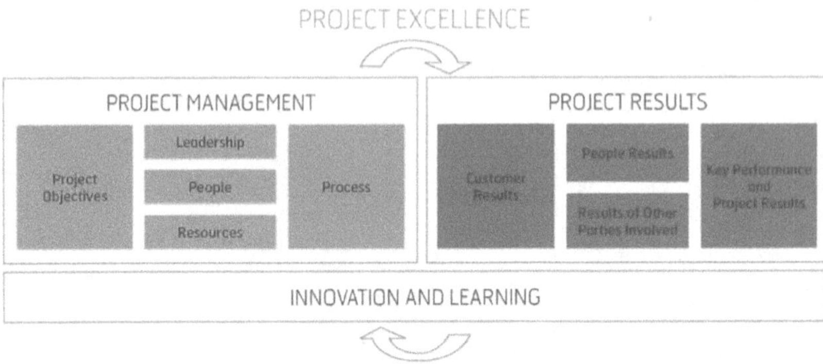

Figure 16: Project Excellence Model

Source: GPM, 2011

Project management answers the question of how the project runs and is being managed and assesses the course of action during the entire life cycle of the project. The project results answer the question of what the project accomplishes and what results will be achieved with the project. "The Project Excellence Model serves as self-reflection for a project team, to recognise and leverage strengths and potential for improvement, and as assessment in the context of an application for the German Project Management Award" (Perrini, 2006). Just as with the EFQM Excellence Mode, the elements of the Project Excellence Model are based on the TQM.

The basic strategies are:

- *Customer orientation*: All decisions are made depending on the customer. He determines the quality of the product or service. A project-oriented company must fully satisfy these needs and requirements.
- *Employee development and involvement*: Project employees are involved in the decision-making process and their potential is recognised and leveraged.
- *Partnerships and suppliers*: A trusting relationship with partners and suppliers is maintained. All parties benefit from good cooperation.
- *Leadership and constancy of purpose*: Executives must efficiently allocate resources. They steer the project and employees in a goal-oriented manner. Leadership qualities and skills are mandatory.
- *Social responsibility*: Projects and results cannot happen independently from the company. Social responsibility and ethics play an essential role.
- *Processes*: Work packages are systematically described as processes and are perfected by a continuous improvement process. Indexes are used as a basis for decisions.

- *Result orientation*: The interest groups of an organization expect long-term results and have high expectations, so all requirements and expectations must be reasonably balanced.

With the Project Excellence Model, project management success can be increased for the long-term (Smith & White, 1987). The continuous improvement and optimization of the processes lead to success. The first recommended step is to carry out a self-assessment that offers the possibility to uncover initial weaknesses. Furthermore, projects can be compared internally, and it can be identified which projects were especially successful. This leads to an internal exchange of particularly good methods and approaches for project management, whereby the project excellence model combines the quantity as well as quality enabler and results of all success factors of project management (Grant, 1996).

4 Trends In Performant Business Models In A Sustainable Context. A Case Study In The Transport Industry

Since the start of the twentieth century industries have changed from concentrating on raw materials and on activities specific to the primary sector, to assembling, administrations, optional division and other activities specific to the tertiary sector. All organizations are influenced by this advancement and they are presently orienting towards benefit-based models.

The interest in mobility is described and affected by demography, legislative and governmental issues, economy, innovation, and social patterns (Institut für Mobilitätsforschung, 2015). With a specific end goal to meet future prerequisites concerning the outline of feasible urban portability, future situations and their effects are of high significance. Due to urbanization, the lessening in utilization of assets, constrained monetary assets, higher interest for adaptability concerning portability represent necessities for practical future urban versatility to react to these adjustments in the best way.

4.1 Assessing Present And Future Transport Modes And Their Influence On The-Businesses Active In The Industry

Different social, economic, demographic, political etc. changes societies face nowadays, are highly impacting the current characteristics of mobility. Investigating the case of Germany, such particular challenges may be translated in:

- Urbanization.
- Aging population.
- Reduction of people number per household.
- Reduction in consumption of resources (including crude oil).
- Limited financial resources for infrastructure.
- Increase in demand for multimodality.
- Higher demand for flexibility in regard to mobility.

Considering these changes, in order to face them in the most effective and efficient manner, a series of requirements can be identified for developing a sustainable future urban mobility. To determine these requirements, the modal split in Germany (figure 17) represents the starting point in the analysis outlined in this chapter. This aims to set the requirements towards the future design of an innovative and sustainable mobility system in Germany.

V. Just, *Sustainable Business Processes in Global Companies*,
Sustainable Management, Wertschöpfung und Effizienz,
https://doi.org/10.1007/978-3-658-28196-0_5

Figure 17 reveals that individual traffic is the preferable option to satisfy the need for mobility. Based on this modal split, reasons for the choice of each transport mode (private individual transport: car/motorbike; bike; public transport: rail/tram/bus, carsharing, footpath) shall be interpreted considering also quantitative secondary sources.

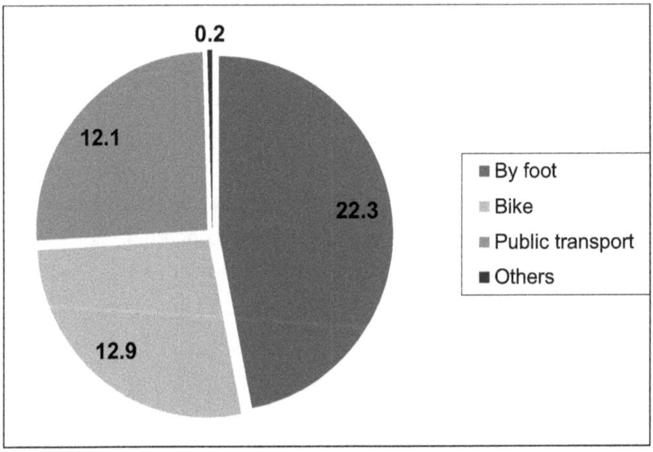

Figure 17: Modal split in Germany

Source: KIT 2015: 108

Versatility itself does not portray a thought process, but rather is utilized to physically achieve another objective: development. The decision of transport modes depends on various criteria, especially on individual conditions. These criteria can be derived from the marketing mix. The weaknesses of each transport mode become obvious, making necessary its improvement using innovative approaches, especially to meet the public needs regarding:

- *product;*
- *price;*
- *place;*
- *promotion.*

The marketing mix connects the strategic general conditions with the operative implementation of a possible product. The marketing mix is usually characterized by the four "4 Ps", but it can be reduced to three (product and price are combined under one "P") or extended to up to seven "Ps" in the area of services (Pepels, 2015). The following interpretation of the classical marketing mix (with 4 "Ps"), focuses on identifying and outlining main reasons for choosing different transport modes:

- The *product* describes the characteristics of each transport mode. The characteristics include comfort, time saving, ecological awareness, availability, accessibility and reliability.
- The *price* of the transport mode depends on the owner. Speaking about public transport mode, prices are either paid by single trips or by season tickets. The same pricing scheme applies to carsharing. Individual transport modes, such as the car, motorbike and bicycle require asset and maintenance costs.
- The *place* shall be defined as the place of the provision of the mode of transport. As for individual mobility (car/motorbike, bicycle, by foot), the transport mode is directly provided at the location of the individual. As for public transport, the individual is required to cover a certain expense to the place of pick-up and after drop-off to the final destination.
- The *promotion* can be considered the least important dimension of the marketing mix, when aiming to compare different transport modes. As both public and private mobility is advertised, the reasons for choosing one or the other are rather dependent on the above- mentioned factors. Therefore, this dimension will not be considered further on.

According to population preferences in terms of transport modes, the car is placed on top of their preferences for everyday use, followed by public transport, bicycle and by foot. (Figure 18)

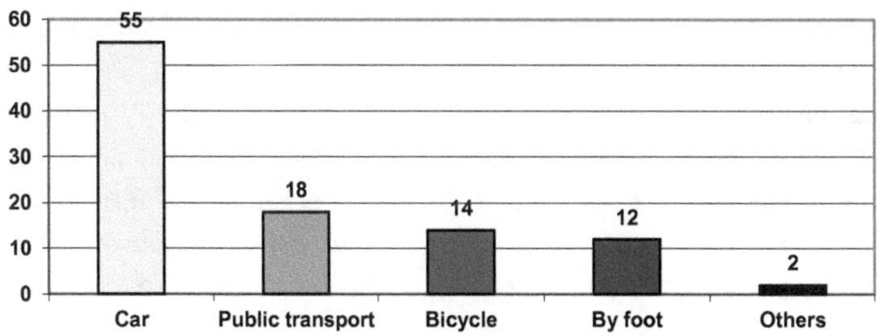

Figure 18: Population preferences for transport modes

Source: Statista, 2016

Facts outlined in figure 17 and figure 18 uncover a distinction in the desired transport modes and actual transport modes. The inclination of using a car is higher than it is in use. The greater distinction can be found in the inclination for public transport and the actual use: 18% prefer this transport means, while just 12% really use it.

After highlighting the transport modes wanted and used by individuals, the main reasons for these choices are discussed further on. Because of their usual usage on short distances of up to 3,4 km, bicycles and foot are excluded from the analysis of the transport means, when compared to travelling by private motorized vehicles or public transport (Statistisches Bundesamt, 2016).

Cars' quality, security and cost are of broad significance to the general population, trailed by fuel utilization and environmental-friendly features (Ernst and Young, 2012). A normal auto is utilized for just 1 hour per day, making this transport mode a generally costly one, contrasted with open transport or carsharing (Verkehrsclub Deutschland, 2016). Albeit private autos are considered as extremely adaptable and agreeable, as far as accessibility and dependability are concerned, they require customary examinations, protection, filling and space for stopping. Carsharing, as part of individual motorized travel, deals with the problem for a certain distance, from door to carsharing station or car location (Puls, 2013). However, this is not a very used transport mode. Berylls Strategy Advisors (2016) distinguished further reasons against carsharing in one of their examinations and discovered that the main motivations are vulnerability about accessibility (28%), the distress of driving another person's auto (26%), the exertion and intricacy of leasing (25%) and the absence of carsharing offers close-by. Contrasting the carsharing offer with a private auto, this requires less effort in terms of maintenance as this is typically done through the carsharing supplier.

Another investigation developed by Verkehrsclub Duetschland (VDV) uncovered the reasons for public transport. The primary reason is adaptability (75%), trailed by gaining time (52%) and promptness (51%). Other reasons refer to comfort, accessibility, low costs (42%) (VCD, 2014a). Furthermore, public transport is accessible to anyone living in a region with accessibility, while the private auto requires the existence of a driver's permit.

However, decisions upon the used transport means, are finally made on an individual base; individual's preferences play a key role in this process. Derived from these, it is probably going to distribute the likelihood of self-driving autos in a carsharing model through the instrument of situating. This marketing strategy that joins to the previously mentioned marketing mix is utilized to position this thought in the prospects' brain (Trout, 2001)

Positioning is characterized by the product (self-driving autos in a carsharing model), its distinctive features and the attributes of the clients. All these attributes are schematically illustrated and synthesised in figure 19.

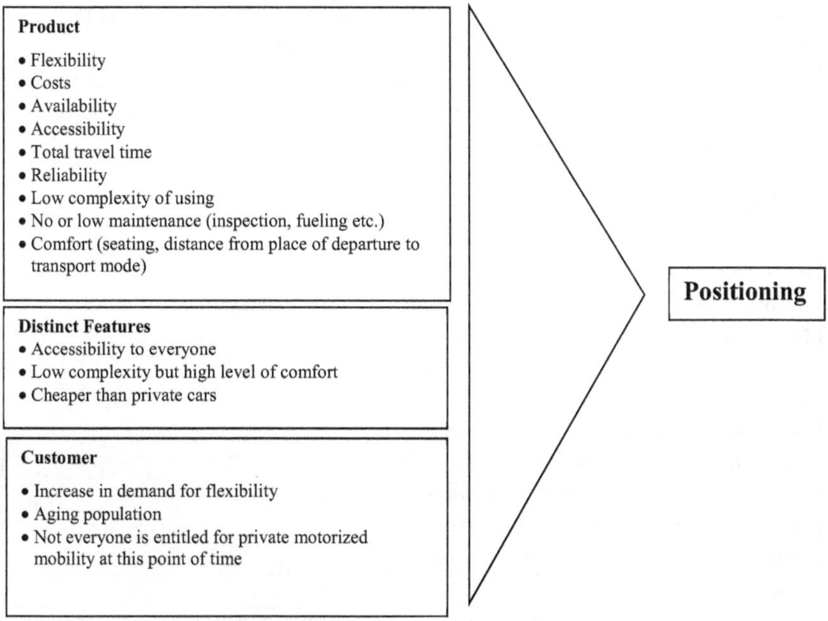

Figure 19: The positioning of self-driving cars in a carsharing model

Source: own representation based on Geldmacher, 2016

Further on, these requirements are additionally coordinated with the chance of self-driving autos in a carsharing model.

Such a self-driving carsharing model could be given by the state (open transport) or by private mobility suppliers, such as automotive manufacturers or software provides as Google, for example. If such a model could be widely implemented in a country, this could respond to socio-demographic changes, as well as to a considerable number of other important present issues in the portability area. Considering the marketing mix, the product of self-driving cars in a carsharing model could be set up as outlined in table 10.

Table 10: Potential marketing mix specific to self-driving cars in a car-sharing model

Product	**Place**
Cars are provided by a third part → no need for registration, maintenance etc. Reduction in accidents in comparison to normal cars Environment-friendly Full availability when called via e.g. app Full accessibility (broader group can be reached than for private car or public transport: e.g. elderly people who don't want to drive anymore, children, blind people, etc.) Full reliability: car arrives when called at any time of day (no long waiting time as for e.g. public transport) Time saving: e.g. no waiting for public transport, no search for parking space Comfort: high level of comfort as seating is guaranteed and no need of interference allows time for other activities e.g. reading	Self-driving cars can be provided from place of departure to final destination (door-to-door mobility) An app can support the booking of a car to provide the car at the desired place
Price	**Promotion**
Making full usage of a car (no parking) Highly efficient in fuel consumption Sharing the ride, shares the fuel expenses Different price schemes (flat rate, minute packages, price/minute) can address different customer groups: high-use customers (e.g. commuters), medium use customers (e.g. housewifes), low-use customers (e.g. students)	The provision of self-driving carsharing model would require a certain amount of promotion to attract new customers, especially in the starting phase. Self-driving cars attract new customers

Source: own representation

Socio-demographic changes and increase in the demand for mobility require a paradigm shift in the establishment of mobility services. After analysing the most well-known methods of transport, it can be outlined that many of the present transport modes can't satisfy the wants and needs of the Germans. In such a context, innovative solutions should be developed by both existing companies and start-ups acting in the transport industry. Implementing a self-driving car-sharing model in

Germany would shift the existing mobility towards a more sustainable, future-oriented one.

"The automotive industry is changing as new technologies are arising. This forces manufacturers to rethink their core product – the car. One of the most discussed trends in this branch is digitalization and connected car technologies. They target various sides from vehicle management, entertainment and security, up to self-driving capabilities. This chapter is particularly approaching the last topic as this is the latest addition to the connected car environment and its market potential is prospected to rise to 39,6 bln. € in 2021 (from a value of 9,5 bln. € registered in 2016). Such development would result in the second most important digital technological advancement in the automotive industry next to security aspects (with estimated 49,3 bln. € in 2021)". (Viereckl, et al., 2015 cited in Kompalla, et a., 2017) This is reflected in figure 20.

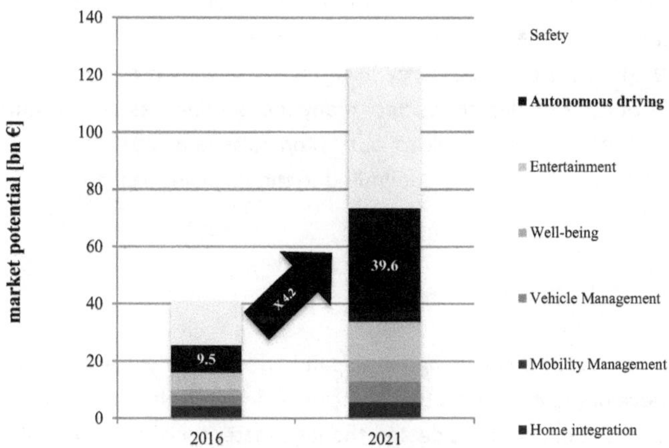

Figure 20: Market potential in connected car technologies

Source: Own representation based on Viereckl, et al. 2015

"Assisted driving systems have been continually including functionalities up to the level of semi-automated driving. This advancement depends on some worldwide megatrends specific to the most recent decades. Prerequisites towards future portability and suppositions for an adjustment in the mobility system depend on demographic changes, legislative issues, economy, innovative patterns and social changes in a globalized world. The improvement of autonomously driving cars is a continuous process, which started out with driver assistance systems that supported the driver in certain circumstances, e.g. parking. In order to describe the process from classic cars to self-driving cars, a 5-level classification system is used" (BMVI, 2015 cited in Kompalla, et a., 2017):

- Level 0: Driver only.
- Level 1: Assisted driving.
- Level 2: Partly automated.
- Level 3: Highly automated.
- Level 4: Fully automated.
- Level 5: Autonomous.

"While assistance systems are already in place, the process for the development of fully automated cars is still ongoing. Future self-driving cars are required to be equipped with sensors, cameras (including Light detection and ranging systems) and GPS to allocate their own position, map the surrounding, identify next steps and its own need for action. This sensor-based solution is extended to a vehicle-to-vehicle communication to benefit from the convergence (International Transport Forum & OECD, 2015). While the technology itself for self-driving cars is under development and test rides are being conducted, many more influences are currently under investigation until large-scale public rollout." (Kompalla, et a., 2017)

Current obstacles include, but are not limited to the following aspects:

- social acceptance;
- legal situation;
- costs (adaption of infrastructure etc.).

Despite the fact that the launching time span stays unclearly specified, considering previous developments three situations can be inferred. In an "aggressive scenario", where both the innovative side and the legitimate, social and political issues are tackled, self-driving autos would face an extreme increase in their demand and would rapidly get to the mass market. The "traditionalist scenario" depicts a moderate way towards the mass-advertise rollout, as mechanical and all other issues are solved along the course of events and after that prompt a fast increment in item selection at last. The "base case situation" promotes a mix of the two previously mentioned scenarios. It outlines a consecutive development, while early adopters already exist (Silberg, et al., 2012). Car manufacturers have different time horizons in their mind for the intense promotion of self-driving automobiles. Current studies developed by organizations provide rankings and relationships of car original equipment manufacturers (OEMs) with respect to their status of commitment and wisdom in cutting-edge designs, especially centred around prosperity. Nevertheless, the usage of self-driving automobiles isn't simply associated with the required development and programming models, yet notwithstanding their mobility advantages.

Mobility services consider an extensive variety of items, from financing arrangements, to client and item encounter offices, or after deals alternatives. These can be portrayed in different ways. The principal set of "embedded services" targets alternatives, which are connected to the item itself (e.g. support benefit). The second category of "comprehensive services" refers to services able to generate added value besides the product itself (e.g. financing models). The third category is focusing on "integrated solutions", which are utilized to mix the product with a service (Wise & Baumgartner, 1999)

As the auto (as a product) gets an impressive extent of a client's normal wage and since the usage rate is, or may be low, customers become especially interested in sharing solutions. Auto sharing may exist in two particular models – free-coasting and perpetual station car-sharing models – that are depicted by their (versatile) get and drop-off zone. The majority of registered customers are located in Europe, followed by North-America and Asia. In spite of the fact that the market is generally new, there are about 150 diverse specialist organizations found exclusively in Germany (Kompalla, et a., 2017). The potential market in Germany has been estimated at 8 million clients (Statista, 2015b); currently, there are 1,26 million active users (Bundesverband, 2015). This is contrasted with a 55 million people who are owning a driver's permit (Statista, 2015a). However, the worldwide market for this "novel" car-sharing services is expected to increase by 50 times, reaching a value of 1.500 billion US-dollars in 2030 (compared to the actual value of 30 billion US-dollars) which demonstrates the attractiveness of this industry (McKinsey & StanfordUniversity, 2016).

Key drivers for the increase in car-sharing solutions and customers may refer to cost savings, environmental friendliness, administrational effort reduction, and fun, among other aspects. However, the most representative, especially in attracting clients, are low costs and car availability (Puls, 2013 cited in Kompalla, et a., 2017).

4.2 Car-Sharing With Self-Driving Cars As A Sustainable Business Model In The Transport Industry

From a key perspective, automotive manufacturers act in different ways to alleviate, or even to eradicate, the challenges outlined in the previous sub-chapter. However, they generally orient towards two main dimensions: source and intensity.

Manufacturers can choose if they want to apply all their activity plans while they are developing new capacities, expanding resources and changing structures or while they aim at expanding through mergers and acquisitions. These conventional "make-or-purchase" choices are pivotal parts of key administration and influence the financial situation of the enterprise, as well as its further development (Huth, et al., 2015). The scientific literature provides different approaches aiming to break-down this decision via a simulation model considering risk analysis (Mock & Miller, 1970; Raunick & Fisher, 1972), financial results (Paisittanand & Olson, 2006) or the uncertainty of input variables (Sari, 2010).

Automotive OEMs can choose how much hazard and quality they will face in such a context. Considering their personal perception on success as well as on their future contribution to the yearly income, they can be either conservative or progressive. In the event that they decide to rather be traditionalist, this may be translated into low investments in start-ups in the car-sharing area or in digitalization, or low investments in developing the internal structure of the company. Furthermore, they could alleviate different risks through developing different key partnerships with OEMs or through eliminating competitors. Since 2009, this pattern became highly applied, facing increased notoriety, in accordance with the consolidation in the automotive industry (Diehlmann & Häcker, 2013). If they take bigger risks, they need to strongly invest in mergers and acquisitions, and solid changes in the hierarchical culture, authoritative structure, and the business procedure might occur, while inner ventures achieve new auxiliaries and board regions.

Figure 21 outlines strategic ways that car manufacturers may follow to face digitalization and service-oriented business models.

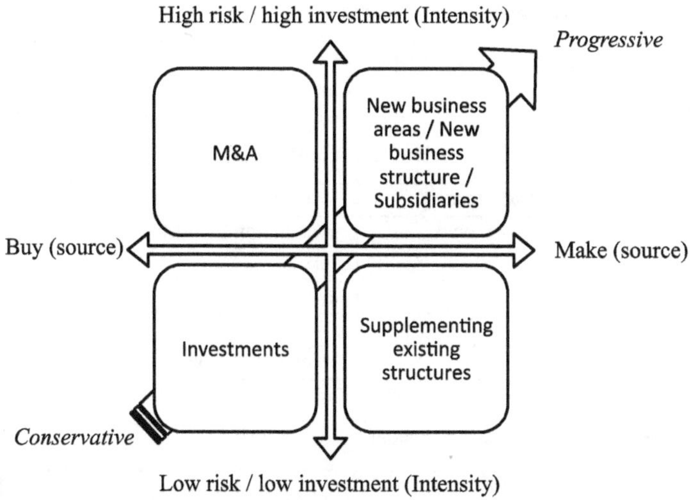

Figure 21: Strategic options for facing digitalization and service-oriented models

Source: Own representation based on Diehlmann & Häcker, 2013

In such a framework, the present chapter aims to:

- investigate if current car manufacturers are simultaneously competing on different sectors of the matrix or if they are specializing on several aspects while acquiring or partially investing in others.
- analyse the current positioning of automotive OEMs regarding the two megatrends of digitalization and (mobility) services orientation.

Tables 11 and 12 and figure 22 outline current investments specific to four important global car manufacturers and one emerging manufacturer, focusing on electric-driven vehicles (Tesla). Furthermore, due to comparison reasons, a possible substitute company (Apple) is also investigated.

Table 11: Overview of activities regarding mobility services

Positioning regarding mobility services (car-sharing)		
Brand	**Source**	**Intensity**
Volkswagen	Gett / Mobility Division	Investment (300 Mil. Dollar) / Inhouse
Daimler	MyTaxi, Hailo	Investment via subsidiary Moovel
GM	Lyft / Maven	Investment (500 Mil. Dollar) / Own service
Toyota	Uber	Investment (500 Mil. Dollar)
Tesla	-	-
Apple	Didi	Investment (1 Bln. Dollar)

Source: Vogt, 2016; Davies, 2016 cited in Kompalla, et a., 2017

Table 12: Overview of activities regarding digitalization

Positioning regarding digitalization		
Brand	**Source**	**Intensity**
Volkswagen (& Porsche)	Autonomous driving subsidiary (inhouse)	Porsche: Small team (50 persons) with satellites in major regions General: Intense hiring of specialists (1600 IT-Specialists at Porsche)
Daimler	Digital strategy (no subsidiary due to strong connections with existing departments)	General: Strategic investments with suppliers and supplementing existing structures
GM	Research centre (inhouse)	1 Billion Dollar
Toyota	Research centre (inhouse)	1 Billion Dollar
Tesla	Inhouse	-
Apple	Inhouse / Separate structure	-
In general:	Strategic planning with suppliers	

Source: Volkswagen Press, 2016; Buhr, 2016; Pretzlaff et. al., 2016; Joann, 2015; Manager Magazin, 2016 cited in Kompalla, et a., 2017

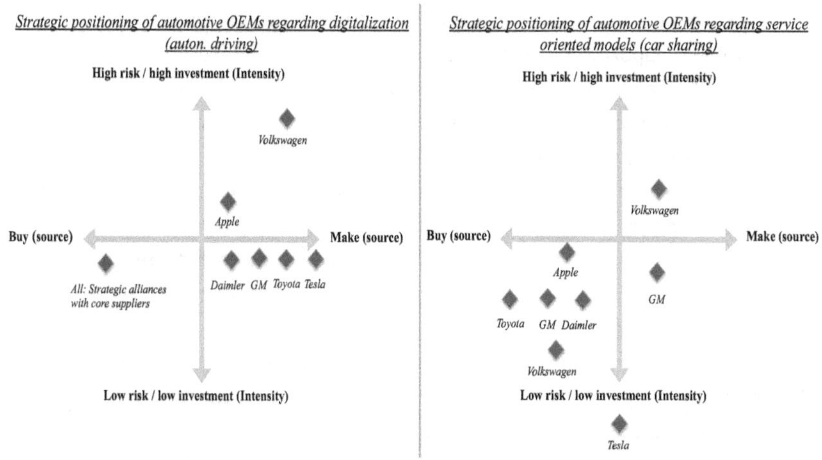

Figure 22: The positioning of car manufacturers in the context of digitalization and service-oriented models

Source: Own representation based on information outlined in tables 11 and 12

Relating the positioning of OEMs about the make-or-purchase measurement, a tendency arises: digitalization is somewhat changing the business inside through developing know-how and close relationships with the suppliers than concentrating on acquisitions for greater providers.

According to official press releases, companies acting in the automotive industry are concentrating their efforts towards understanding how customers use and benefit of their services. Some manufacturers are offering value-adding services to the car-sharing experience itself. "A relevant example may be represented by the development of applications specific to a car-sharing customer or offering leasing contracts for them. The most advanced collaboration model could be represented by providing fully autonomous vehicles to car-sharing service providers (Vogt, 2016). Tesla is also promoting a strategy of autonomous driving and car-sharing services, supporting the car-sharing business model. However, this did not invest yet into existing providers (DeBord, 2016)" (Kompalla, et a., 2017).

There are different potential ways through which auto makers can change their business from one based just on the pure production of vehicles to one that also provides substantial additional services. However, the focus of this chapter is on three potential models: Car-sharing offerings, autonomous-driving taxis and transport on-request (Reidel, 2016). As specialized and legitimate settings are not yet prepared for self-driving vehicles, the car manufacturers are mainly focusing on the car-sharing possibilites on the short run. In this way, they consider both risk based (protective) and opportunity-related perspectives.

From the risk perspective, auto producers should realize that, small and reasonable car-sharing providers will not become key players on the market. Moreover, they have to consider that their present auto opponents, in the future may become important players on the car-sharing services market, generating important obstacles for smaller player in terms of customer attraction.

On the other hand, car manufacturers likewise need to consider the chances of the auto sharing alternative, giving another arrangement of clients while producing less communication and sales costs. Generally, service orientation depends on a lower resource and venture base, leading to lower incomes (contrasted with the core function of vehicles production). However, services provision is the one that strongly connects the customer with the company, building relationships for the long run. Moreover, new selling models could be produced, leaving the one-time purchasing process and changing into yearly service contracts.

With a specific end goal to diminish the danger of high ventures, which might possibly pay out, automotive OEMs develop new start-ups. Particularly for new innovations and business models, an entire increase of inner assets and the required joining into the authoritative and administrational association is expensive and, somehow, irreversible. Another hypotheses into new organizations is that the auto manufacturing industry secures a specific and customary viewpoint with a consideration on creation, quality and arrangements, which can't be easily changed. New settled and uncommonly versatile small ventures from different branches possess the necessary features to compete with important key players on the market such as, for instance, Google and Tesla, as demonstrated by Porter's five forces (Dietz, 2016). Start-ups approaches are usually related to investment reserves or business incubators. For example, BMW is focusing on both ways.

There are diverse ways to deal with new megatrends. For example, Porsche Inc. is concentrating on digitalization, implicitly self-driving vehicle innovation, through developing new sub-association. "Digitalization" determines entrepreneurs to either invest in their own business or to develop new ventures. This technique ensures that the parent association can revolve around current focus activities and future advances can be separated and directed (Dietz, 2016). Sub-associations and even separate brands are moreover notable for shared organizations inside the auto business. Daimler, for example, achieved independence through developing a separated brand for small cars, called SMART as they might not want to mix the customer demands among Mercedes and the new vehicle. Their auto car-sharing administrations did not totally integrate into the association structure. In such a context, Daimler used the characteristics of Moovel and Car2GO for offering exceptional car-sharing services.

Investments into recognized, but rather smaller car-sharing services providers, are based on various incentives. Maybe the main reason lays in the fact that the key player on the market, Uber, should not become a monopoly. If so, it would be almost impossible to face it, and, by the time the car-sharing services increment benefits, classic automotive OEMs will not be able to take advantage of it.

The automotive business is managing a pattern which is concentrating on expanding the innovation rate inside their conventional mechanical items. In this way, an improvement can be accomplished, as well as in other industries, in case the creation of vehicles is accompanied by services provision in the future. The change from a mechanical designing organization to a service provider for exceptionally advanced items is testing particularly in a conventional industry, as the automotive branch, and should be guided by means of a complementary business strategy. While previous endeavour objectives and plans of action have been concentrating on conveying a top-notch item and expanding deals inside exceptionally proficient interior structures, new business models and structure need to catch the new difficulties of digitalization and portability services. The mixture of the two viewpoints could tentatively outcome in the replacing of private autos with self-driving auto sharing or auto renting models bringing about a total different approach in the business models specific to the automotive industry (Cusumano, et al., 2006).

Keeping in mind the end goal to adjust their assets, organizations make an arrangement, which plots subjective and quantitative targets. In view of the megatrend of digitalization, increasing demand for mobility services rather than for simple products and expanding the number of competitors leads automotive manufacturers to adapt their current business strategies to their customers' needs and demands. The automotive businesses adjust to these patterns and need to confront new rivals in the market, which have their centre skills and aptitude inside this field.

Digitalization likewise prompts interconnected clients, sharing data quickly and with significantly more different clients than in the past. Instead of a one-time pitching purchasing association with the client, there will be various associations and items for the client. Consequently, the energy of the client is, and turns out to be, more imperative than ever before. The traditional end-customer becomes less product-driven and requires mobility solutions. Thus, the pull trigger comes from the customer. Companies that will be able to respond to their customers needs in the most effective and efficient manner will gain supremacy on the market.

A car-sharing model with self-driving cars could hypothetically be considered in the future for not only replacing individual motorized traffic, but also in the public transport (Greenblatt & Shaheen, 2015). The idea of self-driving cars in a car-sharing model is based on the classical model of taxi companies, which is characterized by flexible places of return. With many of these providers, customers have the opportunity of ordering a vehicle via a smartphone to their site or to locate a vehicle in the vicinity while the payment of the service can be carried out directly via an app. Unlike the current system with drivers, the idea of a model with self-driving vehicles could incorporate a much higher flexibility: vehicles are distributed automatically according to the transport flow analysis throughout the city centre to reduce the waiting time for customers as best as possible. At the same time, the function of a smart carpooling solution may be integrated, due to customers' demands. This would mean that customers will take a small detour to reduce their own travel costs while automatically being shared through the system with other customers in the vehicle.

Car-sharing, as part of individual motorized transportation, currently deals various issues. One of the most representative is related to the distance from door to car-sharing station or car location. If this distance could be minimized, more people would use this transport mode. Comparing the car-sharing offer with the use of private car, this requires less effort in terms of maintenance as this is usually done through the car-sharing provider. Factors against car-sharing may refer to uncertainty about availability, the discomfort of driving someone else's car, the effort and complexity of renting and the lack of car-sharing offers close-by.

However, some of these issues may be solved through focusing on the "positioning" component of the marketing mix when considering the possibility of self-driving cars in the development of a car-sharing model. Positioning is characterized by the product (self-driving cars in a car-sharing model), its distinct features in contrast to present transport modes, and the characteristics of the customer. Positioning relates to flexibility, costs, availability, accessibility, total travel time, reliability, low complexity of using, no or low maintenance, comfort. It terms of the distinctive features of positioning, products become accessibility to everyone, there is low complexity but high level of comfort. In terms of customers' satisfaction, positioning leads to increase in demand for flexibility. Self-driving cars can be provided from place of departure to final destination (door-to-door mobility). An app can support the booking of a car to provide the car at the desired place. Cars are provided by a third party, and there is no need for registration, maintenance etc. It also saves time as there will be no waiting time for public transport, and no time related to searching for parking space. It allows for ecological friendliness as the car arrives when called at any time of day, and a broader group can be reached than for private car or public transport: e.g. elderly people who don't want to drive anymore or children, blind people etc. Usually, self-driving cars attract new customers (Ries, 2001).

Self-driving vehicles in a car-sharing model simultaneously bear several challenges and obstacles, which could lead to problems or even failure of such a business model. These challenges include technical, operational, political and social aspects. While the social challenge is minimized to the factor of acceptance, the technical challenge refers to the vehicles themselves and less to the car-sharing model. Technology acceptance is understood as a psychological process that starts with pure interest in an innovation and leads toward the regular use of this innovation. Consequently, acceptance can be defined as a collection of evaluation and effects. Acceptance represents a critical success factor when dealing with innovations. Self-driving cars in a car-sharing model represent a sustainable mobility concept that takes the changing environment into account and implements most motives from a customer perspective in regard to transport choice.

The political challenge is currently strongly determined by the legislation, which must be adjusted according to the technology and the possibilities of autonomous cars in order to allow a large-scale deployment and expansion. Ultimately, the challenge lies in the operation and maintenance of self-driving vehicles in a car-sharing model and the associated services, for example app development, generally for smartphones.

Based on technological and innovation advances, corelated with society's requests that depend on changing social and economic patterns, autonomous cars face an ascending trend. Even though this imaginative transport mode is described by a few focal points, there are also various shortcomings and dangers that incorporate social acknowledgment. Acknowledgment among the general public is therefor a key achievement factor for self-driving cars and can be characterized as both a positive assessment and coming about effect.

During recent decades, models and theories on innovation acknowledgment have been developed. An examination of the most crucial acknowledgment models and theories has uncovered three key factors (Geldmacher & Plesea, 2016): individual influencing factors, external influencing factors, and stages or phases of use.

Acceptance is a fundamental criterion, indicating the success of such a model. Since this cannot be easily measured due to the lack of implementation, a modified acceptance model has been developed, based on the existing ones. The three-dimensional model displays a structure of external and internal influencing factors (Springer, 2017), their specific features being outlined further on.

Classic acceptance model

This encompasses numerous models for the analysis of acceptance and the consideration of various influencing factors. These models describe the basis for the measurement of acceptance, but, due to the general and non-specific themes approach, usually, they cannot be regarded as an exhaustive list of influence factors. One of the first fundamental models is the "theory of reasoned action" which displays the influence and trigger factors of a particular behaviour. The theory has been transformed over the years in the "theory of planned behaviour". This theory describes an extension and includes the definition of influencing factors. The rational model is based upon a combination of these factors with maximum expression of a subsequent behavioural intention and the behaviour itself.

Technology acceptance model

This model is centred on the theory of planned behaviour. This acceptance model analyzes the perceived usefulness and the perceived ease of use of an innovation. Based on this model, the updated technology acceptance model represents one of the most popular models for explaining the personal shaping of acceptance. Yet, exactly like other models, this model needs to be critically considered, as it describes a simplified process of shaping acceptance and can hardly be reduced to the definition of external and influencing factors. This model can be applied to a vast variety of innovations. This influences acceptance by three key factors: system configuration (form, function and utility of the innovation), task characteristics (importance and frequency in use) and user characteristics (skills or motivation).

In addition, the model foresees influences by: gender, age, experience and voluntariness of use. External factors, individual factors and phases of use or process can determine a person's acceptance towards an innovation. The individual model's building blocks are composed of external as well as individual influencing factors, which can lead to different behaviour and ultimately to acceptance, in the course of various phases of use.

It is worth stressing out that the models outlined above are two-dimensional and cannot represent the direct relationship between influencing factors, the time, and the respective acceptance phase (VCD, 2014a).

Modified acceptance model

The modified acceptance model is mainly for responding to the supposed individuality of the acceptance of self-driving cars in a car-sharing model. To this end, the individual, as well as the external influences, are combined and lead to a different behaviour in different stages of use and, ultimately, to user acceptance (VCD, 2014b).

To determine the influencing factors of self-driving cars in a car-sharing model, reasons for selecting particular modes of transport are considered. Some of the main ones refer to the total driving time, flexibility and convenience, while the environmental performance, privacy and security represent less relevant motives. Examining these reasons, the advantages and disadvantages are clear, highlighting the differences between the individual transport modes, from a customer perspective. Public transport (bus, train, tram, etc.) and motorized individual transport (usually car) are compared based on a simplified network diagram with the purposes for selecting the respective transport mode (Koschnick, 1983).

It is obvious that different customer groups, with different travel purposes, influence the decision of transport mode. Derived from these reasons, a model that also considers all influencing external and internal factors for customers, is developed. The modified model shall incorporate different user phases and it could lead to the use of an innovative means of transport (acceptance): self-driving cars in a car-sharing model. These stages shall be incorporated in the adapted acceptance model. In the so-called recruitment stage, the potential customer has not yet tested the product itself, but he is familiar with the self-driving cars through media and society. Along with the above described individual phases, the modified acceptance model also considers the timeframe. Hence, time is a critical success factor for the creation of acceptance. Furthermore, the modified acceptance model provides a three-dimensional structure, where the (potential) user passes through the different phases to reach the level of acceptance, while he is simultaneously affected by individual and external influencing factors. Accordingly, the modified acceptance model provides a three-dimensional structure, which incorporates the time factor (first dimension), represents the level of acceptance (second dimension) and considers the impact of individual and external factors (third dimension). In doing so, influencing factors are considered in the setting and action phase, before achieving the final status, respectively the acceptance. In this model, a possible retrogression of acceptance is depicted.

The determination of the level of acceptance is influenced by certain factors, the most important being:

- **Information and knowledge**. Information is characterized as the (new) knowledge acquired about a question, a man or conditions (Springer, 2017). Learning depends on broad information. Information is described as an essential for learning that develops through time. Knowledge on comparative items or administrations and their particular meanings is shown on innovation. Information can be picked up effectively or inactively and can be cathegorised as follows with respect to items and administrations (Brucks, 1986):
    - Abstract-declarative: general knowledge about products and their characteristics (e.g. driver assistance technologies in cars).
    - Specific-declarative: knowledge about a specific product and its characteristics (e.g. Tesla's software for self-driving cars).
    - Abstract-procedural: knowledge about product handling (e.g. turning driver assistance systems on or off).
    - Specific-procedural: knowledge that is gained through individual habits and experiences (e.g. experience with self-driving cars).
    - Evaluative: Knowledge that is directly identified with an individual constructive or adverse evaluation of a product or service (individual inclination to drive autos with driver help frameworks).

  The relationship between information, knowledge and acceptance can be explained as follows: information helps to acquire knowledge. The customer who has acquired knowledge may now accept the proposed information. When there is acceptance, evaluation can be made. And will further affects the customer's state of living. (figure 23)

Figure 23: The process from information to knowledge and acceptance

Source: Geldmacher, et al., 2017

Keeping in mind the end goal to confirm that acceptance is an outcome of information or learning, a definition for "acceptance" is required: Acceptance portrays a mental procedure that is described as a mixture of evaluation and influence (Geldmacher, 2017). Consolidating the above illustrated definitions, the accompanying observational equations can be determined, demonstrating the relationship between information, learning and acceptance:

$I * x = K$ (4)

$A = EV + EF$ (5)

Hypothesis: $K + x = EV + AF$ (6)

Where:

A = Acceptance

K = Knowledge

I = Information

EV = Evaluation

Af = Affect

- **Evaluation**. Understood innovation acknowledgment models have avoided the part of data and information in the acknowledgment shaping procedure to the best conceivable degree. Particularly as to developments, existing comprehension can impact human's conduct with respect to evaluation in influencing acknowledgment. Information is a standout amongst the most vital hotspots for evaluation, as learning can comprehend the item's qualities. Evaluation, regardless the distinguished occasion, is portrayed by a constructive or antagonistic individual implication. Evaluation of the occasions is to be reconfirmed by a specific influence when considering that acknowledgment is a mixture of optimistic evaluation and influence. Evaluation, as an outcome of learning, is portrayed by impediments. Notwithstanding these impediments, an approach that can halfway demonstrate the relationship of evaluation and influence with information, was developed. This approach is sectioned by three stages and identifies with the time span mid-2012 until mid-2017 (Schnobrich and Barz, 2013):
    - analyse the level of data/information on self-driving vehicles (in view of Google Trends);
    - estimate the subjective evaluation of the recognized pinnacles (occasions) that prompt an expansion of wanted data (thus an increment of the hunt list);
    - compare the normal evaluation with consequences for the share trading system.

The following analysis is based on actively sought information measured by Google Trends. In any case, this kind of investigation has its confinements as it does exclude latently picked up data or produced information. This confinement can be avoided by surveying the level of data and learning, paying little respect to the shape (effectively or latently) through a poll and associate their effect on the acknowledgment level.

The news about self-driving vehicles have subjectively expanded in the most recent year. To check this subjective inclination and the significance of information and learning as to acceptance, the Google look list was utilized as an indication. Google looks are considered as a wellspring of information, that would then be able to be changed into learning and, perhaps into acceptance per inferred observational equation. As the research particularly envisaged the case of Germany, this was developed based on the usage of German terms; however, their equivalent in English is provided. The accompanying German comparable terms that are utilized as a part of the writing and in daily paper articles are sought to characterize the most widely recognized term that identifies with self-driving cars: "selbstfahrende Kraftfahrzeuge" (equivalent to "self-driving vehicles"), "selbstfahrende Autos" (equivalent to "self-driving cars"), "autonome Autos" (equivalent to "autonomous cars"), "autonome Kraftfahrzeuge" (equivalent to "self-driving vehicles").

Google Trends demonstrates an unmistakable online inquiry inclination of the expression "selbstfahrende Kraftfahrzeuge" (equivalent to "self-driving vehicles"), trailed by "selbstfahrende Autos" (equal to "self-driving cars"). The pattern analysis that ranges back similar to 2012, likewise plainly demonstrates an expanding look file until July 2017 with a few perceptible pinnacles and lows. Notwithstanding an unmistakable pursuit inclination of a specific term, the pattern analysis uncovers a general rising quest file for this subject (and every single examined term), showing a consistently expanding interest, in this manner an abnormal state of information and thus a broad learning on this topic. Google Trends list for the chosen terms identified with self-driving vehicles and self-driving cars are outlined in figure 24.

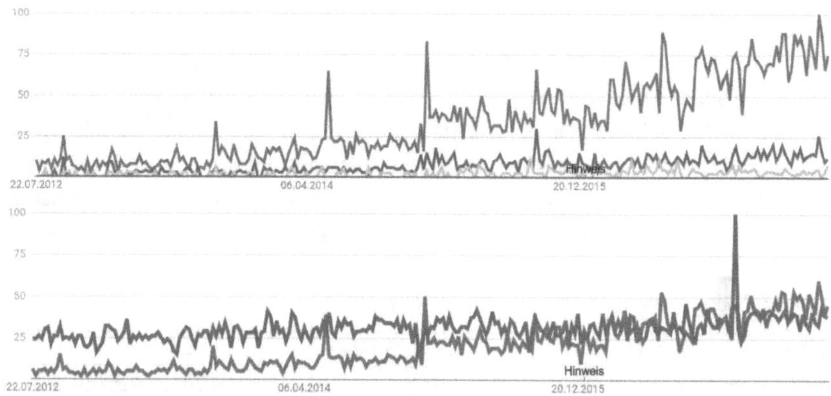

Figure 24: Google Trends list (2012 - 2017) for self-driving vehicles (up) and self-driving cars (down)

Source: Google Trends, 2018

Placing the most researched term of the above selected similar terms "selbstfahrende Kraftfahrzeuge" (equivalent to "self-driving vehicles") in correlation with "Fahrerassistenzsystem" (equivalent to driver assistance systems), an interesting improvement can be observed: While the measure of scans for the two terms is generally low in 2012, the two terms ascend in significance all through the most recent four years. Nonetheless, while driver help frameworks were of higher research significance from 2012 until 2015, the last quarter of 2015 uncovers a pattern change. From 2015 until mid 2017 the Google list of self-driving vehicles has overtaken driver-help frameworks with one remarkable top in December 2016.

Furthermore, five noteworthy peaks for looking through the term "selbstfahrende Kraftfahrzeuge" (equal to "self-driving vehicles") from the most recent 5 years are highlighted in figure 25, for expanding the analysis.

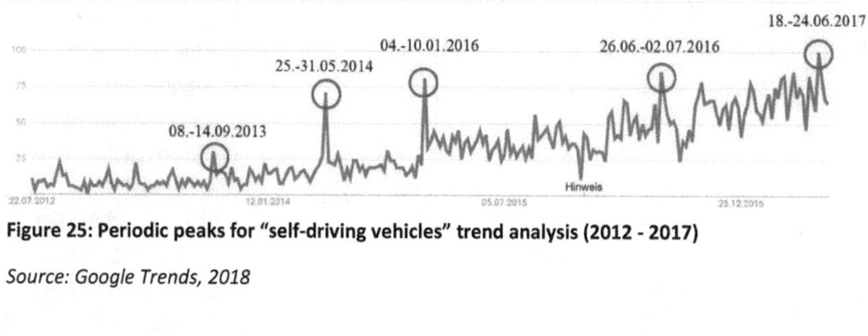

Figure 25: Periodic peaks for "self-driving vehicles" trend analysis (2012 - 2017)

Source: Google Trends, 2018

The above distinguished pinnacles are further on examined concerning the discharged news on the separate dates. The look for news is done through Google and restricted to the particular time span of the pinnacle. The inquiry is finished with the above alluded most utilized terms: "selbstfahrende Kraftfahrzeuge" (comparable to "self-driving vehicles") and "selbstfahrende Autos" (equivalent to "self-driving cars"). The recognizable proof of explanations behind pinnacles uncover real occasions that range from the introduction of models with self-driving capacities to declarations and administrative adaption. Table 13 outlines these occasions.

Table 13: Major events and news around self-driving vehicles

Date	Event/ news	Company	Source
08-14 September 2013	International Motor Show (IAA) as the world's biggest exhibition for the automotive industry Release of new technologies that are presented at the IAA	-	http://www.spiegel.de/auto/aktuell/autonomes-fahren-unterwegs-mit-einer-s-klasse-auf-autopilot-a-920803.html
25-31 May 2014	Presentation of the Google self-driving car project	Google	https://www.youtube.com/watch?v=CqSDWoAhvLU
04-10 January 2016	Advertisment on the launching of self-driving cars by Renault and Nissan in 2016	Renault & Nissan	http://www.handelsblatt.com/auto/nachrichten/renault-und-nissan-selbstfahrende-autos-noch-2016/12805626.html
26 June - 02 July 2016	Accident with a Tesla car	Tesla	http://www.spiegel.de/auto/aktuell/tesla-die-wichtigsten-fakten-zum-toedlichen-unfall-in-den-usa-a-1100803.html
	Announcement of BMW to release a self-driving vehicle until 2021	BMW	http://www.handelsblatt.com/unternehmen/industrie/kooperation-mit-intel-und-mobileye-bmw-

			will-bis-2021-selbstfahrende-autos-bau-en/13819180.html
18-24 June 2017	Definition of ethical requirements for self-driving cars	-	https://www.welt.de/wirtschaft/article165745124/Ein-kluges-Auto-darf-niemals-ein-Opfer-auswaehlen.html
	Full implementation of self-driving cars is expected by 2040	-	http://www.dw.com/de/selbstfahrende-autos-erst-in-jahrzehnten/a-39306821

Source: Google Trends, 2018

As a second step in the analysis, a subjective approach to all the events and news outlined in table 13 is presented table 14.

Table 14: Subjective evaluation of selected news and events

Event/ news	Subjective evaluation
Presentation of the Google self-driving car project	Positive connotation
Advertisment on the launching of self-driving cars by Renault and Nissan in 2016	Positive connotation
Accident with a Tesla car	Negative connotation
Announcement of BMW to release a self-driving vehicle until 2021	Positive connotation

Source: Google Trends, 2018

In the third and last advance, the evaluation of the occasions is going to be reconfirmed by a specific influence when considering that acceptance is a combination of positive evaluation and influence. The influence is evened out by a response on financial markets for the concerned organization. As a general guideline, positive occasions prompt a positive advancement on the stock exchange, while negative occasions prompt a negative stock value (Schnobrich & Barz, 2013).

To break down the subjective evaluation and its impact on the share trading system, the stock cost of the individual organizations is analysed one month ahead and one month after the news release. A synopsis of this examination is outlined in table 15.

Table 15: Implications of events and news on the development of the investigated companies' shares on the stock market

Event/ news	Company	Development stock market
Presentation of the Google self-driving car project	Google	523,10 USD (25.04.2016) **571,65 USD (30.05.2016)** 685,20 USD (24.06.2016) Trend: positive 14.07.2017: 976,91 USD 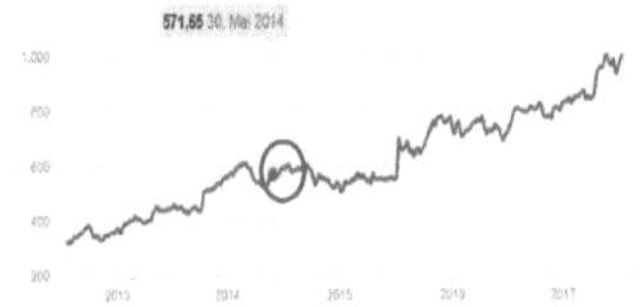
Advertisment on the launching of self-driving cars by Renault and Nissan in 2016	Renault & Nissan	**Renault** 92,85 EUR (04.12.2015) **83,77 EUR (08.01.2016)** 73,42 EUR (05.02.2016) Trend: negative 14.07.2017: 83,41 EUR 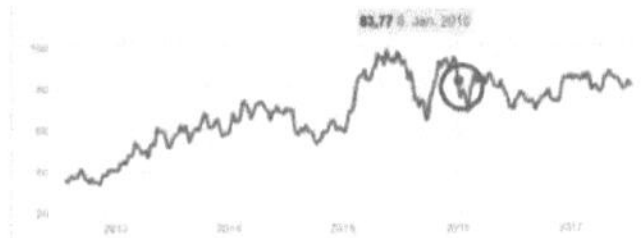 **Nissan** 1262,00 JPY (04.12.2015) **1073,50 JPY (05.02.2016)** 1141,50 JPY (08.01.2016) Trend: positive 14.07.2017: 1150,00 JPY 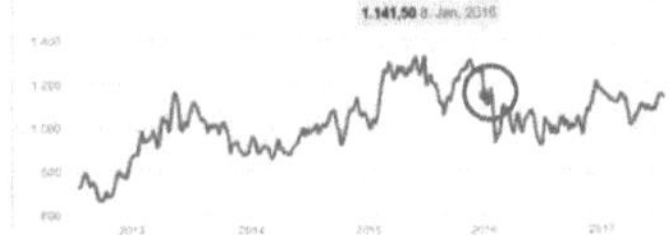

Accident with a Tesla car	Tesla	218,99 USD (03.06.2016) **216,50 USD (01.07.2016)** 230,03 USD (05.08.2016) Trend: negative (if compared to June 2016) 14.07.2017:327,78 USD 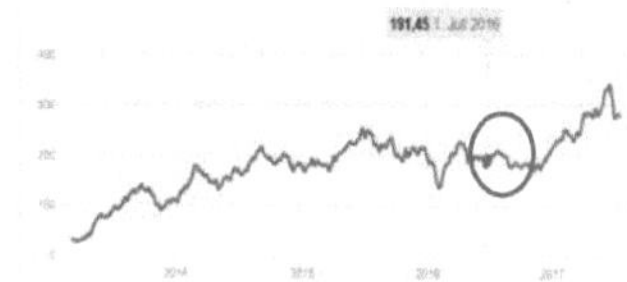
Announcement of BMW to release a self-driving vehicle until 2021	BMW	72,27 EUR (03.06.2016) **67,79 EUR (01.07.2016)** 77,92 EUR (05.08.2016) Trend: positive 14.07.2017: 83,74 EUR 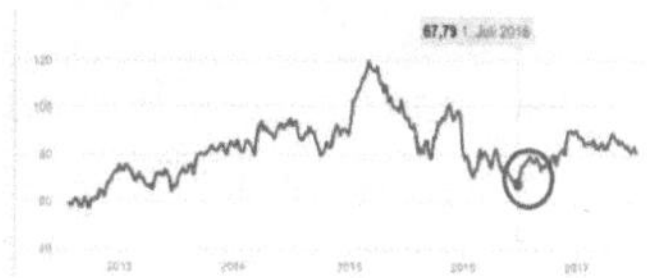

Source: Schnobrich & Barz, 2013

The pattern analysis of financial markets demonstrates a reasonable connection of subjective evaluation and stock cost for deepest explored cases (3 out of 4). However, the declaration of the arrival of self-driving cars by Renault portrayed with a parallel diminishing stock price. (Table 16)

Table 16: The correlation of evaluation and stock market trend (= affect)

Event/ news	**Subjective evaluation**	**Stock market trend**	**Match of evaluation and stock market trend**
Presentation of the Google self-driving car project	Positive connotation	⇗	✓
Advertisment on the launching of self-driving cars by Renault	Positive connotation	⇗⇘	(✓)

and Nissan in 2016			
Accident with a Tesla car	Negative connotation	⇘ (if compared to previous month)	✓
Announcement of BMW to release a self-driving vehicle until 2021	Positive connotation	⇗	✓

Source: Geldmacher, et al., 2016

In light of these outcomes, the above proposed hypothesis (K + x = EV + AF) is, to a substantial degree, confirmed. As previously mentioned, the picked approach has its points of confinement, as the share trading system cost is likewise affected by assist occasions. The hypothesis related to the recommendation to incorporate information and learning in acceptance models (Geldmacher et al., 2016) was also confirmed in the above accomplished analysis. The chosen approach that assessed acceptance exclusively in view of the share trading system advancement is prescribed to be reconfirmed by advanced analysis of the relationship of information/learning and acceptance.

Innovation acceptance models have barred the part of information and learning in the acceptance shaping procedure to the best conceivable extent. Existing insights can impact human's conduct concerning evaluation and influence (acceptance), as learning can comprehend the item's attributes. While learning on comparable products or services and their individual implications is shown on the advancement (self-driving cars), information is a standout amongst the most critical hotspots for evaluation (Herbig & Kramer, 1994).

4.3 Future Directions And Challenges

In the near future, vehicles and transportation modes will significantly change. In the coming decade, there will be numerous changes in a car - motor, fuel, materials, yet particularly brilliant internals. Sensors and PCs will make it conceivable to co-ordinate car development and have PCs drive cars. Individuals who need to take a Sunday drive can get a Sunday ride. Expansive scale co-ordinated systems of vehicles will rise, like ventures such as ULTra. Cars may move from streets to control ways or string rails. Flying cars will be presented. Inventive substitutions, for example, Segway will end up well known (Miller, 2014).

All through the previous decade, one of the best walks in car innovation, with the attention on independent cars, could be observed. Head ways have quickened with the support of the main car designers including BMW, Ford, Audi; Google and Tesla later joined them. Even if potential customers have been recently familiarized with self-driving vehicles, specialists have been focusing on developing self-driving vehicles for more than 45 years (Adhikari, 2016).

For example, an article published in the July 1969 issue of the IEEE Spectrum revealed various specialized research and experimentations carried out to deliver the main vehicle that will work independently (Jordan, 2016). It is estimated that the eventual fate of mechanized vehicles would depend on "keen framework" that would control cars on roadways. One approach to address the requirements for cutting-edge foundation is through coordinating reference points and different sensors into existing movement hardware like street cones. This will enable self-driving cars to explore securely, while additionally alarming people about hazardous environment.

While the expectations are not very far away, the eventual fate of self-driving cars advancing toward the heading of cars can be observed. This can decipher and act in view of their prompt condition. The fate of savvy cars depends upon the onboard innovation of every car. As progress will be registered, the utilization of innovation will change towards the truth of self-driving vehicles. Different strategies will be utilized to enable vehicles to comprehend their encompassing condition in a dynamic driving condition. Vehicles must have the capacity to act due to particular changes in their condition. These vehicles require a wide scope of advancements and foundations to work appropriately (Horwitz & Heathe, 2018). Every vehicle is required to constantly gather and decipher tremendous measures of data. Each arrangement of the car must work with the encompassing conditions, and innovative progressions must be made to guarantee self-sufficient vehicles work inside a few settings, including long-extend radar, LIDAR (laser filter), Cameras, Short/medium-run radar, Ultrasound (Brian, 2018).

These advances will be utilized as a part of various limits in light of a specific need of the vehicle. Additionally, this innovation needs to work with signals made for people like security cones, so automakers need to think about robots and people in the meantime. For instance, cameras will get visual data to enable the car to decide movement flags and cross activity cautioning. Ultrasound will be utilized to educate about the quick condition for stopping help. Each of these innovations will gather diverse data for the vehicle. In view of the general gathered data, cars will be able to make elucidations and to react in the most adequate manner in particular circumstances.

Disregarding the different advantages to expanded vehicle robotization, some predictable difficulties delay the time expected to turn the current supply of vehicles from nonautonomous to autonomous (Richard, 2016). Some of these are related to various debates concerning the associated risks, mainly consisting in protection by people to relinquish control of their cars, client worry about the wellbeing of driverless cars, the execution of lawful system and foundation of government directions for self-driving cars, different impediments that could be missing driver involvement in conceivably risky circumstances, moral issues in circumstances where an autonomous car is constrained amid an unavoidable collide, and perhaps inadequate adaptation to gestures and non-verbal signs by police and pedestrians (Worstall, 2014). Conceivable innovative difficulties for autonomous cars reside in the man-made brainpower and these may refer to the fact that a car can't work legitimately in confused inward city situations, a car's PC could possibly be traded of, as could also be a correspondence framework between cars. Weakness of the car's detecting and route frameworks to various kinds of climate (for example, snow) ar also debatable. Autonomous cars may require professional specific maps to work appropriately. However, where these maps might be obsolete, they should have the capacity to fall back to sensible practices. Field programmability for the frameworks will require careful assessment of item improvement and the segment store network. Current street foundation may require changes for autonomous cars to work ideally. Inconsistency between individuals' convictions of the fundamental government intercession may cause a deferral in tolerating autonomous cars. Regardless of whether the general population wants no change in existing laws, government direction, or another arrangement, the system of control will probably bring about contrasts of assessment.

5 Research On The Improvement Of Business Processes In Global Companies Within A Sustainable Framework

Organizations are concentrating on corporate supportability in different ways. In any case, effective maintainability programs systematically address vital, operational, synergistic, and administration prerequisites. The United Nations Environment Program (UNEP) Finance Initiative, addresses the connection between business organizations and four general gatherings of partners: suppliers, inner (representatives), customers and investors, society and the environment. Also, four essential ways by which actualizing Sustainability Management and Reporting (SMR) can provide advantages to business foundations, particularly in rising and creating economies, are distinguished as: Revenue development, Risk administration, Access to capital, Cost reserve funds and effectiveness.

Since every organization contains a large number of processes with relevant impact on enterprise success, there is an urge to implement accurate processes and a proper management for developing sustainable organizations.

5.1 Research Methodology

This research aims to reveal insight into the structure and difficulties related with sustainable business processes development, keeping in mind the end goal of generating a system for supporting directors in enhancing their business models. Due to the absence of exact experiences into these angles, a subjective contextual analysis approach is utilized (Eisenhardt, 1989; Yin, 2009). In accordance with the expectation of building up a generalizable system, a contextual investigation configuration was developed for the expansiveness of perceptions and for acquiring wealthier bits of knowledge into the basic subjects.

Focusing on a contemporary phenomenon outlined in its real-life context, the main research method implied was the exploratory and descriptive case study research, grounded on Yin's (2003) premises. Aiming to answer to the main research question referring to *how business processes can be improved in global companies in a sustainable context*, a single-case study was developed, based on a holistic approach. However, some other small pieces of research were carried out mainly for strengthening the case study results. The supplementary pieces of research consisted in analysing various articles, news etc. about other global companies, important players in their field of activity.

V. Just, *Sustainable Business Processes in Global Companies*,
Sustainable Management, Wertschöpfung und Effizienz,
https://doi.org/10.1007/978-3-658-28196-0_6

The case study's unit of analysis is represented by a leading company in its area. Due to confidential reasons its name is not revealed, being referred to as Company X. Strong arguments in favour of its choice are highlighted in the following paragraphs.

The organization of examination is a worldwide undertaking with numerous production lines and backups more than 50.000 representatives. The company offers a worldwide system of excellent individuals and solid brands. As a main maker of home machines and arrangements, it propels things to make individuals' lives less demanding. Everybody's attention is on innovation, which is the reason it offers entrancing openings for work for individuals interested in developing promising careers. The company seeks after business magnificence by constantly enhancing effectiveness and quality, as well as by giving associated items and arrangements. Its likewise centre is around buyers' needs. The mix of remarkable skills and innovative advances empowers the company to develop products that blend enthusiasm and it guarantees that its brands keep on being among the most grounded in the industry.

Devoted workers live for the company, they motivate each other and they all get advantages due to their joint effort. In an environment described by receptiveness, trust and profitable trade, everybody is urged to contribute with their thoughts and arrangements.

The organization is seen by its clients, providers and the general public as a capable and solid business partner. The shopper is at the focal point of the greater part of the organizations' advancements. Enhancing the buyer's personal satisfaction is the key generator of organization's processes.

The company's organization rests on two pillars: organizational structure and process organization. These must satisfy the following requirements:

- *Effectiveness*: The organization should be in line with its strategy and must support the achievement of company objectives. It must be able to react to the changing circumstances in the market, especially when competition is referred. It should therefore support company's vision of becoming the benchmark for its sector.
- *Efficiency*: The organization should ensure the smooth and productive running of business processes and choices. Clearness with respect to duties and portrayals of undertakings are required, to stay away from duplication of work. The organizational structure governs which tasks are assigned to which organizational unit. The management structure of the company serves to coordinate the various operational areas of the company and the tasks performed in them. The management activity is particularly characterized by

decision-making, directing, using initiative, taking responsibility, and representation.

Unlike the organizational structure, process organization is not based on functions but on cross-functional workflows, so called processes. Processes generally cross departmental and well-designed boundaries. The major challenge is to link and harmonize processes in such a way that the workflow is optimized, and the result meets the requirements and expectations of the customer.

The company documentation on organizational structure and processes is accessible to all employees on the intranet and updated on a regular basis; documents are available in a central location, in a standardized form that is accessible to all. The usage of the intranet creates transparency and serves as a knowledge platform to provide information on workflows and process responsibility within the context of process management.

The aim of the company's process management is to strengthen process orientation group-wide and to increase competitiveness through transparency, synergy, quality, and speed. Process management structures the company according to activities – so-called processes – to continually improve the general company performance. Thereby, process orientation means optimal implementation of the corporate vision and the derived strategies and understanding the company as an entire system of interdependent processes.

The process management of the Company X consists of various elements, as illustrated in the figure below.

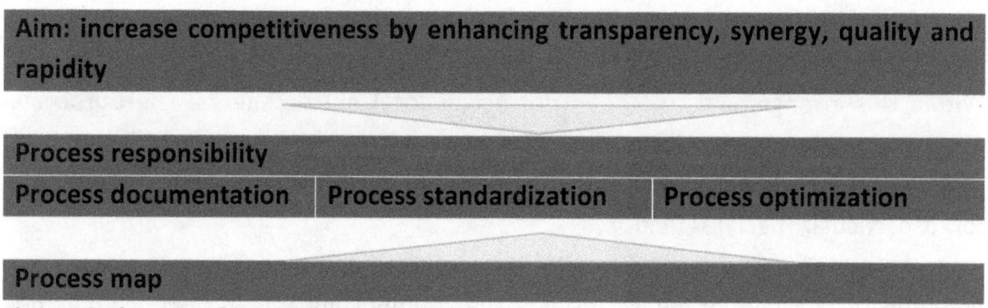

Figure 26: Elements of Process Management

Source: Own representation

The Company's X process map is seen as basis for its process management. It provides a graphical overview of the enterprise processes at group level and represents the starting point for defining process responsibility, as well as for documentation, standardization and optimization of various processes, which are divided into:

- management processes (strategic activities);
- core processes (value-creating activities);
- support processes (supplying activities).

The operative processes are structured according to responsibilities. Therefore, process responsibility is particularly important as process management can only work successfully and sustainably if responsibilities for processes are clearly set up.

Process documentation is crucial when dealing with processes. To enable an effective and efficient workflow, it is very important to document processes. The visualization and the documentation of a process build the foundation for its following optimization. Documentation serves as a basis for certification according to quality management standards.

The aim of process documentation is to create transparency regarding the processes, this way fulfilling an important requirement for process analysis, process steering and process optimization.

To make the best use of the potential synergies that exist, Company X is working to standardize frequent and similar processes. In detail, process standardization means to standardize the key elements of a process. Local differences are allowed if they are needed (e.g.: for the reason of different legal situations).

Once processes are documented and standardized, they can be improved, and process management becomes evident – therefore process optimization is a logical step in the implementation of process management in Company X.

The Company X is primarily structured according to Regions. The Regions with their subsidiaries assure optimum market exploitation in their regions. They define the sales channel strategy and the competitive sales structures that are coordinated with it and are also responsible for the necessary associated business processes. Within this arrangement, the countries act as local entrepreneurs. The Corporate Areas are responsible for the fulfilment of group-wide functions. They fulfil coordination tasks on a company-wide basis and each has overriding controlling obligations for its particular specialist field.

Within the case study, five pilot countries are analysed. These represent the basis for the meaning of measures and have an important role in the upcoming development of business requirements and general findings. These countries represent a mixture of smaller and bigger subsidiaries, from Western and Eastern Europe and include a sub-region. However, the developed case study may be approached as valid and representative for Europe. (Figure 27)

Figure 27: Selected countries within the case study

Source: own representation

The thesis is centred on a case study to increase process efficiency, quality and agility in business processes, by taking the example of sales support processes in various countries. In the case study, the methodology approach within the phase 'process evaluation' consists of four phases to determine and implement the best-practice reference processes. Phases 1 and 2 aim at setting-up the project and gaining a detailed understanding of the processes being considered. With this information, decisions regarding the focus of phases 3 and 4, and their detailed planning, will be determined:

- Activity-based review of differences between countries.
- Activity-based assessment of potentials for process optimization.
- Description of aggregated measures for process improvement.
- Description of costs, benefits and risks for selected measures.

The overall aim of the case study is to ensure quick adaptability of processes through standardization and further automation that shall support the sustainability of processes.

In order to implement Company X/NextLevel and to improve operational excellence with respect to Sales and Sales Support processes, the target of this case study is to develop a Company X Sales and Sales Support reference process landscape and to describe selected best-practice reference processes in detail. These reference processes will then be utilized as basis for the implementation within Company X for Europe Region (REU).

A common process framework shall (Chesbrough, 2007):

- ensure a high level of process quality;
- develop transparency and comparability of processes and activities;
- lessening the complexity of processes and activities;
- consider future developments within the process design.

With these aims in mind, the following objectives were defined:

- Develop a common process framework for all Company X subsidiaries.
- Ensure high levels of process quality.
- Consider future developments within the process design.
- Improve transparency and comparability of Company X processes and activities.
- Reduce the complexity of Company X processes and activities.
- Reduce IT costs by minimizing the differences between systems and settings.
- Increase the speed of adjustment when introducing new systems.
- Harmonize customer master data.

The case study will be designed and developed based on the principles outlined in the following figures.

Figure below sets up the premises of the case study, highlighting how customer needs influence customer processes, implicitly Company's X business processes.

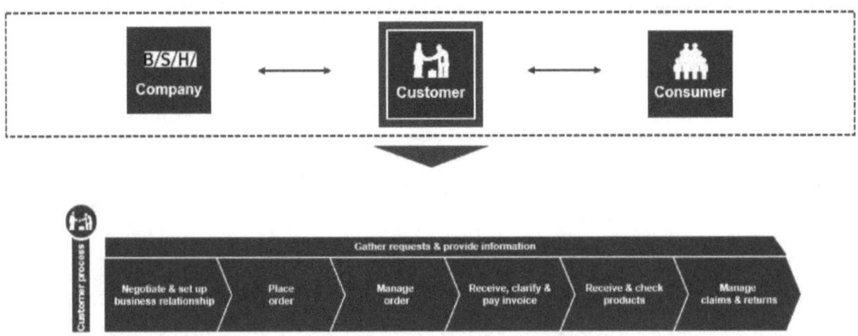

Figure 28: Customer process as relevant input for business processes

Source: own representation

The initiation, process assessment, process evaluation and implementation of the case study are synthetically presented in the next figure.

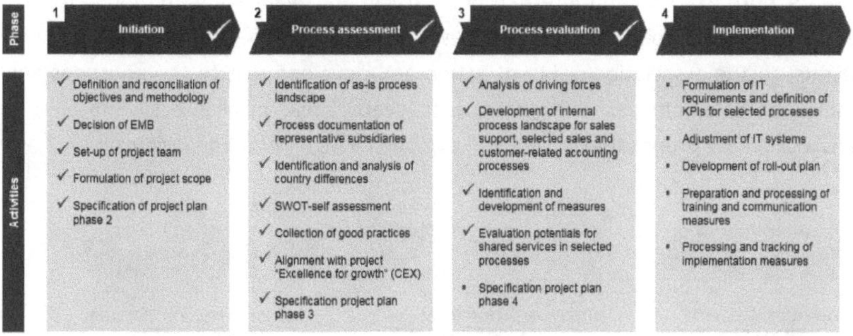

Figure 29: Case study: Initiation, process assessment, process evaluation and implementation

Source: own representation

The overall approach to process assessment is described in figure 30.

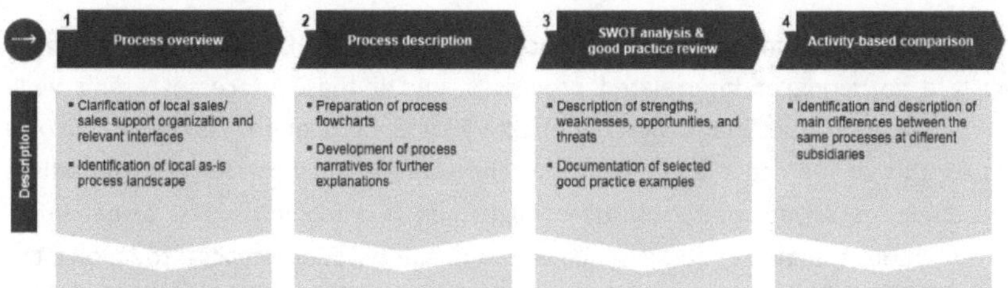

Figure 30: Process assessment

Source: own representation

The engineers of Company X are expected to be aware of the complex changes faced by the organization and of the need to assess the association's capacity and structure, to comprehend organizational drivers that will affect the change, and to be able to adjust the association to effectively embrace the change. Company X utilizes organizational assessments to provide executives and directors with adequate support and business knowledge, to effectively lead the change. Organizational assessments are accomplished based on a standardised framework. The approach implies data collection and analysis, focusing on the factors that effect organizational activity; this way, regions with high quality processes are revealed. There are various excellent models for comprehending and investigating information amid an organizational change assessment. As illustrated in figure 31, there are various reliant components, both external and internal, that exist in an organization and influence the development of its specific activities. These reliant factors go from external spending weights, to the association's way of action and development, to the aptitudes and conduct of its employees from the lowest levels. These provide a system able to translate, create proposals, convey, and oversee change inside the organization.

INTRODUCTION INTO SALES AND SALES SUPPORT
- Introduction into local organization/ clarification on responsibilities and contact persons
- Past projects and topics
- Actual projects and topics
- Current challenges

IDENTIFICATION OF AS-IS-PROCESS LANDSCAPE
- Name of the processes
- Short description of the process
- Process variants
- Identification of process owner
- Process customer
- Affected parties
- Interfaces to other processes
- IT-systems

IDENTIFICATION OF FURTHER SALES SUPPORT TASKS
- Name of the task
- Short description of the task
- Responsible person
- Customer of the task
- Interfaces to other processes/ tasks
- IT-systems

Figure 31: Process assessment: Organization Assessment

Source: own representation

Process documentation is a key activity for any organization. A business is basically a gathering of interrelated processes, and if these processes aren't well-connected, difficulties may occur. For effective tasks, Company X has repeatable processes; this way, process documentation represents a vital guide for representatives and directors. An adequate approach might aim two major targets: to get information about the quality and essence of the documentation process; to involve the proper team of employees in the process. Usually, the approach is selected, implemented and coordinated by the creator of the specialized report. Any mix of qualified or unqualified workforce (from inside or outside the organization) might be incorporated, as appears to be suitable. Strolling through a process can enable the discovery of potentials for improvement, and every one of the divisions will work autonomously, exactly like they will do also in the new process. The organization's director is responsible for the portfolio specific to a closed task. This represents the starting point in developing future processes. It might incorporate maps, illustrations, necessities, client data, and endorsement records. The SWOT analysis in social work rehearse system is valuable since it enables organizations to assess whether a goal is realistic or not. This empowers organizations to set achievable targets and to advance the social change or group improvement exertion. It enables organizations to assemble important data to maximize their potential. Accomplishing a SWOT analysis is a valuable process, especially when key organizational needs are considered. All this information is graphically summarised in figure 32.

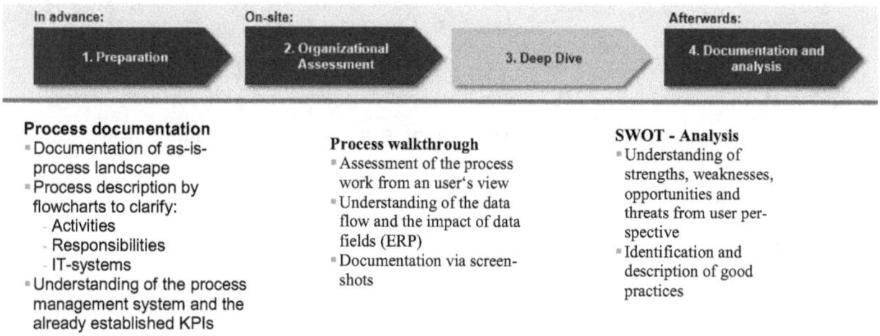

Figure 32: Process assessment: Deep Dive

Source: own representation

Documentary analysis is a sort of subjective research. Analysing documents includes coding content into subjects like how central gathering or meeting transcripts are explored. Figure 33 describes the process assessment in the documentation and analysis phase.

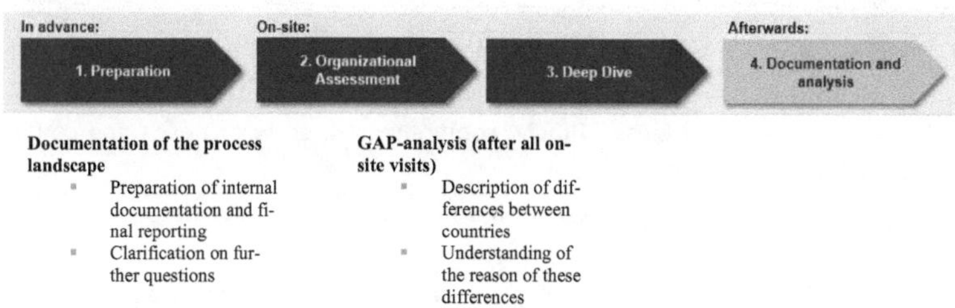

Figure 33: Process Assessment – Documentation and Analysis

Source: own representation

The following table shows the measures which have been elaborated to improve process efficiency and sustainability. The measures and their numbers match to the process landscape developed for business processes.

Table 17: Process evaluation: Result – Overview of proposed measures

S/N	Process	Measure Title
1	A. Gather requests & provide information	Provision of documents and process-related information to the customers via online portal
2	A. Gather requests & provide information	Provision of information via online portal to Company internal departments (self-service)
3	A. Gather requests & provide information	Creation of a possibility to request non-standard information via the online portal
4	A. Gather requests & provide information	Analysing which sales-related information is relevant for customer self-service functionalities in the online portal
5	A. Gather requests & provide information	Increased quota of electronic information exchange (e.g. EDI)
6	A. Gather requests & provide information	Analysis of potentials regarding fax utilization
7	A. Gather requests & provide information	Establish a system for the routing of incoming customer requests
8	A. Gather requests & provide information	Development of the possibility to document manual customer requests
9	A. Gather requests & provide information	Utilization of possibilities for electronic archiving of documents
10	1. Negotiate & set up business relationships	Development of a REU-wide IT solution for contract management
11	1. Negotiate & set up business relationships	Timely, comprehensive entry of prices and conditions
12	1. Negotiate & set up business relationships	Establish a REU customer master data governance organization
13	1. Negotiate & set up business relationships	Implement a REU-wide standardized customer master data process
14	2. Receive & enter orders	Creation of the possibility to enter orders via online portal for customer and sales
15	2. Receive & enter orders	Transparency regarding availability of products / expected date of delivery
16	2. Receive & enter orders	Transparency regarding maintained prices and conditions
17	2. Receive & enter orders	Entering of discounts on position level only
18	2. Receive & enter orders	Development of workflow for the entry of mass-orders
19	2. Receive & enter orders	Development of a workflow for the entry of home delivery orders

20	2. Receive & enter orders	Development of a workflow for the entry of free-of-charge orders
21	2. Receive & enter orders	Development of a workflow for the entry of exhibition orders
22	2. Receive & enter orders	Creation of the possibility for the management of consignment orders via online portal
23	2. Receive & enter orders	Development of the possibility for ordering of spare parts
24	3. Process & adjust orders	Conduct a benchmarking regarding rules of checking incomplete orders
25	3. Process & adjust orders	Development of a standardized approach for order entry check
26	3. Process & adjust orders	Utilization of manual order blocks on position level
27	3. Process & adjust orders	Utilization of electronic order confirmations (where possible)
28	3. Process & adjust orders	Development of a functionality within the online portal that allows both the customer and sales representative to enter order changes and to trigger the related approval workflows
29	3. Process & adjust orders	Development of a workflow for the identification and management of backorder situations
30	3. Process & adjust orders	Development of a process for proactive management of upcoming backorder situations
31	4. Generate & send invoices / credit notes	Establish a workflow for the entry, approval and posting of credit notes via online portal
32	4. Generate & send invoices / credit notes	Establish a KPI-based governance and management system to monitor the issued credit notes
33	4. Generate & send invoices / credit notes	Establish a customer accounting and credit management user group
34	4. Generate & send invoices / credit notes	REU wide roll-out of existing best practices regarding customer account management solutions
35	4. Generate & send invoices / credit notes	Enable announcement of invoice or credit note related incidents via online portal and ensure connection to DMS / KLP solution
36	4. Generate & send invoices / credit notes	Implementation of a REU-wide standardized already available DMS / KLP solution
37	4. Generate & send invoices / credit notes	Establish a portal that facilitates the administration of the DMS / KLP solution
38	4. Generate & send invoices / credit notes	Establish a KPI-based directing system for clarification incidents

39	4. Generate & send invoices / credit notes	REU-wide implementation of a standardized solution supporting credit management activities
40	6. Handle claims & returns	Development of a workflow (via online portal) to support and streamline communication in case of delivery incidents
41	6. Handle claims & returns	Development of a workflow (via online portal) to support and streamline communication in case the customer refuses acceptance of a delivery
42	6. Handle claims & returns	Development of a workflow (via online portal) streamline communication and clarification in case of a wrong quantity delivered to the customer
43	6. Handle claims & returns	Development of an IT-based workflow (via online portal) for the processing of returns
44	6. Handle claims & returns	Development of a workflow (via online portal) to avoid returns by usage of stock transfer from one customer to another
45	6. Handle claims & returns	Prevention of not announced returns
46	6. Handle claims & returns	Development of a functionality to trigger customer service request directly via the online portal

Source: own representation

The case study research is based on a comprehensive literature review process and on a complex analysis of company's internal records and documents. Furthermore, qualitative pieces of research were also carried out to expand the methods for data collection and to bring new insights about the investigated issues. Onsite visits were accomplished, unstructured interviews were carried out and video conferences were held. All the research outcomes are interpreted and complemented with the authors' extensive knowledge and expertise in global companies.

Preparation of onsite visits considering organizational matters as well as knowledge of local organization and processes consisted in announcement to local CFO, scheduling of visit, provision of scope (relevant processes), identification of contact persons, preparation of meeting schedule, clarification of travel and administrative issues, preparation of country specific information, identification and interview of persons with local process knowledge, located in Germany.

At the end of 2016 and the beginning of 2017 fourteen unstructured interviews were carried out with CFOs. The interviews were unformal, mostly of them being face to face. However, video conferences were also held, especially to get in touch with the local CFOs. Due to the organization of the company, the centralized experts are located in Germany and are responsible for the standardization and benchmarking, but the local experts have the regional expertise. Therefore, the interviews were important to gain local insights before visiting. In average, the interviews lasted for two hours and subjects related to business process, IT infrastructure, problems and expectations of the visit, were extensively approached.

The strategy for information gathering in this exploration incorporates the writing audit on the comprehension of the sustainability in business forms by integrating how scholars utilize the idea and how they outline it from related fields. In view of the proposals of vom Brocke et al. (2009) and Webster and Watson (2002), an efficient writing look approach is used. It incorporates its outcomes from a wide arrangement of insightful databases. All accessible inventories were studied, including the extensive Business Source Complete database. Articles were diminished physically by dealing with clear copies, non-English articles, non-academic articles, and book surveys. The writing base was examined for specified related ideas, the chosen units of investigation, the consideration given to the plan of action development, and further regular subjects.

The case assessment incorporated the exhaustive survey and examination of the gathered information. In this way, the case was comprehended as a solitary unit and accordingly examined. The assessment was trailed by an iterative procedure of enveloping writing, contrasting the discoveries against hypothesis, and creating extra experiences from training. The last part was accomplished by displaying draft discoveries. This contributed impressively to the deliberation and speculation of the discoveries.

All the information explained in the results section of the chapter is based on the pieces of research accomplished within the case study research framework. Following an inductive approach, all the information is structured and outlined as the outcome of the case study research, being thoroughly detailed in the following chapter.

5.2 Case Study Results – Focus On Business Processes

Our environment is changing. Company X has a need for action to increase operational excellence. (Figure 34)

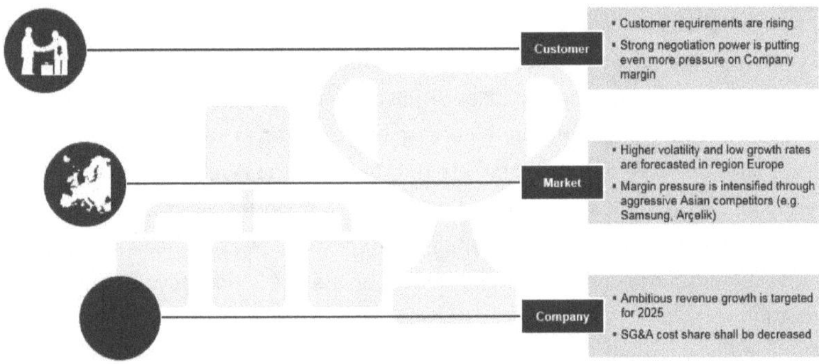

Figure 34: The changing environment

Source: Own representation

Supervision is a standout amongst the most vital tasks in all organizations, regardless of their structure, size, market or industry. A corporate task force is a cross-practical group selected to address a specific target. Regardless of whether big or little, a task force comprises of people from different levels and divisions. The intricacy of a group's aptitudes and experience gives an extensive variety of perspectives that provides the group with the necessary features for achieving progress.

Organization representatives should be replaced using a four-to-five stage approach:

1. Discovery/Assessment.
2. Solution Design/Planning.
3. Testing and Pilot.
4. Service Assumption.
5. Steady State Turnover/Implementation.

Each stage comprises of at least one tasks creating no less than one deliverable and finish criteria. This must be met to ensure the advancement to the following stage. The breakthroughs and expectations delivered by these tasks give a progressing quality survey process that supervises if the last item ensures the desired outcomes.

Commerce is as old as mankind itself. People have always traded and exchanged goods, gained advantages by selling goods and satisfied their own needs (Buhr, 2011). Hundreds of years ago, sales strategies were developed, a large number of people were organised, and the most diverse distribution channels were used and established. In addition to the actual exchange or sales product, the human factor has not been negligible so far.

However, in present times, the selling system faces important challenges and changes. The rapid development of technologies and the constant exchange of knowledge and information among people can be traced back to some important, ground-breaking innovations such as the Internet (Buhr, 2011). Nowadays there is hardly any company, no matter how small, that doesn't have its own website, no virtual mailbox or is not accessible from all over the world.

Admittedly, not every company can afford to "kidnap" its customers into a virtual showroom or perform big data analyses to better market its products (Binckebanck & Elste, 2016). Nevertheless, the increasing digitisation of the world comes with many advantages, but also responsibilities for companies. In such a context, many tasks have to be mastered in a modern sales organisation. Some examples may refer to adapting modern and efficient sales strategies, developing new sales and marketing channels and customer ordering behaviour, being always one step ahead of the customer and addressing customer problems individually instead of offering standard solutions.

This underlines the importance of pure (sales) competencies, processes and strategic partnerships. All business processes are becoming more transparent for the customer. The very common and often lived slogan "One Face to the Customer" is also having a "virtual mask" with the digitization, reaching new dimensions. In order to ensure success in such a process-oriented, competitive industry, trends must be identified and exploited at an early stage, especially in sales organizations. Sales have already undergone an enormous change - but the real revolution is still to come. Before a company's sales organization can be planned, the actual strategic orientation must be thoroughly worked out and thought through. The sales strategy is regarded as a long-term orientation of all sales activities of a company, which are adapted to customer and market requirements. For the sales management, this means recognizing market changes and changes in customer needs at an early stage, considering in the same time all possible dangers. If this advanced planning fails, no reasonable sales strategy can be derived; this way, the continued existence of the entire company is in danger in the long term. At the same time, a well-designed sales strategy enables the anticipation of the market potential that might be exploited to achieve long-term and sustainable corporate success through competitive advantages and to minimize risks. Accordingly, in addition to sales management, appropriate company resources must be made available for this task (Pufahl, 2015).

In addition to the specific markets and products, the core content of a sales strategy is the selection of the company's target customer groups and the proper sales channels. Other elements of a sales strategy include sales volumes, prices, resources, profit contributions, risks, and revenue streams. The different sales agents necessary for developing this process and the distribution channel structures that can be considered are described later in the chapter. In order to define these strategy contents and parameters in a meaningful way, the sales management has to have an accurate, realistic image of the current status. However, future developments should also be taken into account. A practically proven method for developing the target business model is the so-called 7C model (Hedman & Kalling, 2003) outlined in figure 35.

Figure 35: The 7C model for business model development

Source: Pufahl, 2015

The starting point in this model is the strategic core of the company, which consists of the range of services, the customer segments and the markets relevant to the company. The following six factors are derived from this core, considering both the current and the future/target status (Pufahl, 2015):

- ***Customer Perception***: In what form will the company and its activities, such as the acquisition of new products and services, be managed? How are products, services or offers perceived by the customer and how can their perception be influenced?

- ***Customer Interface***: How does the process of interchanging information between the corporation and the client run? What are the current interfaces with the customer and how will the customer do business with the company in the future (CRM, sales channels or service)?
- ***Internal Value Chain***: How are the internal structures around the company's sales process defined? Are there clearly defined processes from the initial contact with the customer to order management and after-sales services?
- ***Cooperation partner (cooperation)***: Are there any current sales cooperation for selling the company services and how are they measured? Are several sales agents and distribution channels used?
- ***Concepts for the Future***: Are market and industry changes and demand adjustments considered in the business model when developing the sales strategy?
- ***Employee qualification (Human Capital)***: Which requirements for employee qualification and knowledge management in the company are implicated by the business model?

The aim of this business model is to define the strengths and weaknesses of the company, its employees and customers. The strengths and weaknesses of the sales organization must always be viewed in relation with the environment. A strong sales force is reflected when the company is regarded by the customer as being better than the market leaders. Based on the sales strategy, the sales organization determines the team formation in sales. This has a decisive influence on the success of the company. An organizational structure is used to ensure the smooth running of sales and distribution (personnel and organizational) in order to increase sales efficiency (Pufahl, 2015).

In particular, personnel processes and organisational structures need to be planned and worked out thoroughly. Employees are considered to be the most valuable and most important capital in sales and should therefore have a clearly defined area of responsibility. If this is not the case, especially at the middle management level, the previously well-thought-out sales strategies can quickly fizzle out or even fail to reach the employees concerned. This is one of the main challenges in designing the sales organization, especially for internationally active organizations (IBM Global Business Services, 2012).

In order to have the company's customers efficiently served, especially in accordance with their individual needs, the sales management must define and design a sales organization structure. In general, this determines which customers are served by which employees, in which markets. This organisation can be classically regulated according to function, territory/region, products or product lines, customers or a mixture of these alternatives (Lichtenthaler, 2011):

- ***Organization by function***: In this organizational form, the assignment of customers or sales partners takes place according to the employee's function. The customer or sales partner is approached depending on his requests. Thus, the processed information requests and order placements are assigned to the relevant sales employees.
- ***Organization by Territory/Region***: In this form, customers and partners of the company are assigned to the appropriate sales representatives according to territorial characteristics such as country, city or postal code. This organizational assignment is often used by service providers such as insurance companies or sanitary companies. Often, territorial protection is even agreed upon, which, in turn, reduces the competition for customers in a region.
- ***Organization by product or product line***: In the case of technically demanding or complex products, the allocation of sales staff is often chosen based on the products concerned. The big advantage lays in the expert groups, which can inform and advise, in high detail, the customer or sales partner about the product.
- ***Organization by customer/customer class***: In this organizational form, the sales management classifies the customers which are afterwards assigned to the sales employees. Various criteria for classification may be represented by turnover, sales, company size or cooperation time. In addition, a distinction can be made between private and business customers, as well as individual and mass customers.

These traditional forms of organization are the most common, but they also have many disadvantages. The relatively rigid structures restrict the number of employees in their sales activities, negatively influencing the existing and potential sales. In addition, the strong economic fluctuations, hybrid customers with low customer loyalty, the intense competition caused by globalization and the increasing complexity of customer needs can hardly be mastered by these traditional sales organizations. Table 18 outlines a summary of the advantages and disadvantages of the classic sales organizations (McGrath, 2010):

Table 18: Advantages and disadvantages of traditional sales organizations

Organization according to...	Advantages	Disadvantages
...products	Very high product-specific know-how of the sales staff. Facilitated communication with product-oriented business units (e.g. development).	Lack of customer orientation leads to a lack of cross-selling potential and a diffuse or complicated appearance towards the company's customers and partners.
...customers	Comprehensive customer service and closer cooperation. Cross-selling potentials are exploited, and customer needs are faster recognised.	Less specific product know-how. Increased internal information expenditure. Several open questions to the customer indicate possible incompetence.
...regions	Regional market or customer characteristics are taken into account. Physical proximity to the customer.	Difficult coordination between the individual regions. It is difficult or, even, impossible to introduce quality standards for the selling activity. Problematic handling of international customers.
...sales channels	Very good knowledge of the individual distribution channels and sales agents.	Low customer and product-specific knowledge. Missing overall view.

Source: McGrath, 2010

Newer, more modern and, above all, dynamic forms of organisation are process organisation, project organisation, modular and virtual organisation, which, however, are only used to a limited extent in practice. In addition to the strategic orientation and organization of sales, sales controlling is the third dimension in the management of sales organizations. As part of the management and measurement of sales activities, various concepts are developed to measure the overall corporate success factors, such as turnover, sales or customer satisfaction. These, in turn, are based on the defined sales strategy and organization. The term "key performance indicators" (KPIs) refers to these key figures or control variables that relate to the success, performance or utilisation of the operation with its individual organizational units. The importance of control parameters is particularly relevant in sales and distribution. On one hand, they measure performance in sales, while on the other hand, they are able to determine measures at an early stage in the event of deviations between actual values and target values (Pufahl, 2015).

Some of the most relevant performance indicators and key performance indicators are outlined in table 19.

Table 19: Key Performance Indicators (KPI) and Performance Indicators (PI)

Key Performance Indicators (KPIs)	Performance Indicators (PIs)
- sales - turnover - revenue - gross profit - contribution margin - costs - incoming orders - customer satisfaction - ...	- market and customer potential - open & realized potential - number of leads / transformation quota - number of visits / visiting days - volume of contract conclusions/closing rate - volume of receivables - number of complaints - ...

Source: Pufahl, 2015

The key performance indicators play the most important role in a serious planning process. They are clearly related to the performance of the company and serve as a guide for management and as comparative or control values. The KPIs are delimited by the performance indicators (PIs) which serve for detailed and targeted control and the thorough controlling of smaller factors. The company's employees are primarily responsible for the key figures. In sales and distribution, personnel are a decisive success factor. Successful sales staff regularly identify potential customers, transforming them into existing customers and thus securing the company's long-term success (Pufahl, 2015).

The management of innovation processes in organization is the field of innovation management which is insufficiently investigated. Usually, in organizations, managers don't think about current methods and configuration devices for developing innovation processes, neither to the likelihood of their utilization for achieving a successful management in basic leadership conditions.

Innovations shape human's behaviour and decisions in all areas of their life. Most innovations are based on long years of research and development. Trends that determine the future directions in human's lives are already increasingly noticeable in present times (Industriemeister Flugzeugbau, 2015). The so-called basic innovations form the foundation of present and future lifestyles. To maintain this development, tendencies must be actively used today to create innovations and prepare for future changes. The entire development of technologies of the present age, implicitly human development is due to a few innovations. The term innovation management refers to all planning, decision making, controlling and other organisational tasks related to the research, development, production and market launch of new products and processes. Especially in the market launch, i.e. in sales, fatal mistakes can be made which have a significant influence on the development of new products. The right time, the right price and the right market are decisive for this. The requirements and areas of responsibility for sales organizations have also undergone fundamental changes as a result of basic innovations (Vahs & Schäfer-Kunz, 2012).

Something is considered to be an innovation when the first commercial use of an invention – i. e. the technical product resulted from research and development – is made in production and launched on the market, in the form of a novel product or process. A distinction is made between product innovations that have not yet been introduced on the market and company innovations that are only new to the company. Innovation management is part of a company's service provision and serves as an interface between different areas and stakeholders, such as the company's employees, customers, suppliers, production and marketing/sales. As early as 1926, the Russian economist Nikolai D. Kondratieff recognized the importance and influence of innovation on national economies and illustrated it in his model "long wave cycles" (Vahs & Schäfer-Kunz, 2012). In this model, the so-called Kondratieff cycles are achieved through certain basic innovations. These cycles last for 50 to 60 years and ensure an economic upswing and thus an increase in national income. The most important basic innovations to date and their cycles are shown in the following figure.

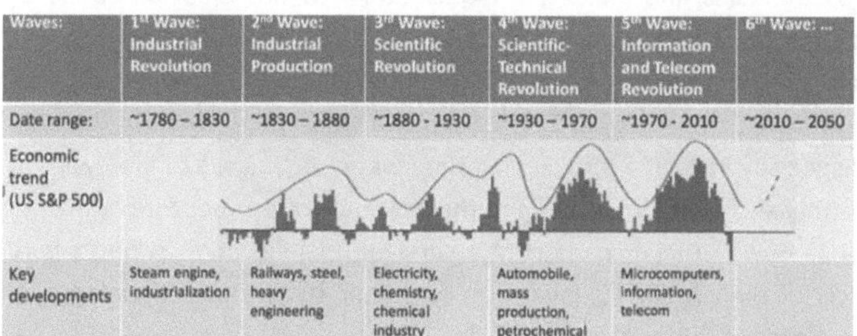

Figure 36: The five Kondratieff waves

Source: SRC, 2014

To date, a total of five Kondratieff cycles have been identified and arranged in chronological order. The sixth and next Kondratieff cycle is a basic innovation in the life sciences, including nutritional science, molecular biology, medicine, and neuroscience. Nowadays, the fifth cycle especially influences human's daily actions like ever before. Online platforms share points and other information technologies are now more mature and widespread than ever before. Automation, digitization and transparency are keywords that every company lives by, every customer demands and describe every process down to the last detail – without the 'human error factor'.

In addition to the many opportunities and advantages, there are also a number of risks and obstacles to innovation that accompany innovation management. These include, in particular, the following three main risks (Rappa, 2001):

- *Technical risks*: Not all demonstration, development or research projects carried out automatically lead to functional products or systems that can actually be used on the markets.
- *Market risks*: Due to a lack of customer interest, there is no market entry for the innovation.
- *Economical risks*: Not all innovations will generate profits.

Other obstacles to innovation can include internal resistance within the company, high innovation costs, long or incalculable amortisation periods, a lack of technical equipment, and a lack of know-how. Last but not least, this also applies to sales organizations, as the sales and marketing departments cannot meet all customer order options due to a lack of system infrastructure.

Ultimately, the competitiveness of internationally active companies depends on their ability to develop and exploit innovations and to establish them in the relevant markets. Especially in such a fast-moving time when the individual life cycles of products are getting shorter and shorter and the presence of competitor companies is increasing. That is why the management's handling of innovation support is of great importance for the company's long-term economic success and for safeguarding its existence (Vahs & Schäfer-Kunz, 2012).

The company analysis deals with internal factors of the company and compares possible specific strengths and weaknesses of the organisation with other market players in a sector. The analysis focuses on the company's strategic scope, its trained competencies and their impact on future business development. In addition to the analysis of internal strengths, weaknesses, risks and opportunities, the company's environment is also examined and analysed in more detail during the strategic planning process. As the term 'corporate environmental analysis' shows, corporate environmental analysis is always in the context of the corporate environment. Porter has developed a suitable method for determining the business environment, which defines and analyses the five competitive forces ("five forces") of an industry. These competitive forces include suppliers, customers, replacement products, the company's potential market supporters and existing industry competition. Porter's model is based on the company's relative position to the industry as a whole and how competitive forces are handled. The analysis focuses on direct competitors, customers and the company itself. The aim of this method and the measures derived from it is to achieve the best possible position in the industry and, implicitly generating higher incomes. On this basis, other instruments of company analysis can also be built up, such as competition analysis, opportunity and threat/risk analysis (SWOT) or the analysis of internal and external factors of a company (Jäger, 2008).

A classical tool for determining the external factors is the PESTEL analysis, which examines the political, economic, social, technological, environmental/ecological and legal dimensions of a company. As in case of most company or environment analyses, it is of great importance to regularly and conscientiously carry out the PESTEL analysis, as the above-mentioned dimensions of the analysis can constantly evolve and change.

It is important to determine the relevance of the factors for the company in order to evaluate the analyses. Not every factor is actually important for the company or the industry. It is therefore advisable to determine which dimensions are particularly essential and should be thoroughly examined before the analysis is carried out. The analysis of the internal and external factors can be accomplished for the entire industry, the company or just one organizational unit. The influencing factors of a sales organization are illustrated in the following figure.

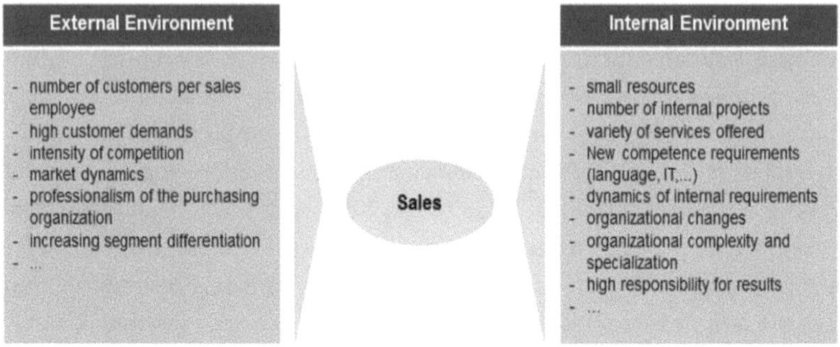

Figure 37: External and internal environment in sales

Source: Buob, 2010

When analysing a sales organization, the large number of internal and external factors and the resulting sales complexity becomes particularly clear. Requirements from both sides affect the sale of certain stakeholder groups. The resulting problems are intensified by the fact that many marketing initiatives, such as the marketing promotion of new products and services, are increasingly being launched. Development of new customer groups, product launches or CRM, can only be realized with adequate selling processes and strategies. In addition, there is a very strong internal network with the departments of logistics, development, technology and controlling, which, in turn, leads to a scarcity of resources for the employees. This, together with the high number of customers and their increasing demands, the growing and increasingly complex product range and the internal administrative demands placed on them generate an additional burden on the employees (Buob, 2010).

Lewin's Force Field Analysis is used to determine the factors and forces of a situation or organization that push a person to a certain state (driving forces) and those that prevent the person from doing so (restraining forces) (Change-Management-Coach, 2008).

Lewin's model can be used to document certain management decisions and thus make changes more acceptable, in the organization or workforce. The following figure presents and demonstrates this model.

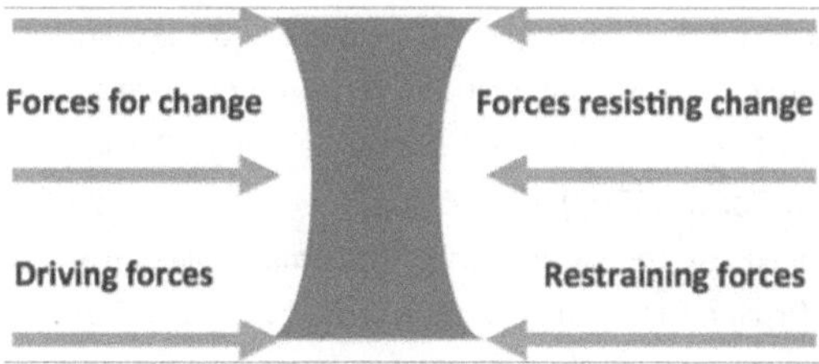

Figure 38: Lewin's Force Field Model

Source: Change-Management-Coach, 2008

Within the case study research frame, driving forces will be used to understand future environmental changes in sales and sales support processes, following the scheme: Current sales and sales support processes ➔ driving forces ➔ Current sales and sales support processes ➔ Transformation process – Implementation of measures ➔ Future sales and sales support processes.

Kurt Lewin was careful to ensure that the effective forces are more than just change properties. Rather, numerous emotions also underline the willingness to change certain situations. To understand which influencing factors lead the affected persons to vote against the changes, the values and experiences of the groups of persons have to be determined. To achieve this goal, the following seven steps are recommended in the form of an internal workshop (Change-Management-Coach, 2008):

- *Defining the change to be achieved*: Goals or visions of a future situation must be recorded in writing. Conversely, the preferred status quo must be precisely defined and recorded, unless the change that occurs is not intended.
- *Brainstorming or mind-map about the driving forces*: Determination of the forces for the situation change.
- *Brainstorming or mind map about the restraining forces*: Determination of the forces that work against a corresponding change of state.
- *Evaluation of the specific forces*: Determination of the influence of the respective forces from 1 (weak influence) to 5 (strong influence).
- *Revision of the forces*: It must be decided which of the forces worked out can be changed or neglected due to their insignificance.
- *Development of a strategy*: Development of a strategy concept that strengthens the driving forces and/or weakens the rest training forces.
- *Define and prioritize the next action steps*: Which are the greatest forces that need to be processed and how much time is required for this?

Sometimes, it is easier to attenuate a cautious force than to strengthen the actual driving force. Criticism of this model mainly includes the subjective selection and evaluation of the forces, which are usually carried out by persons who are already biased (Change-Management-Coach, 2008). This concept ensures that all future driving forces will be considered for the definition of upcoming measures on sales and sales support processes. Driving forces are parameters, which will influence a defined object in the future.

Similar to Kurt Lewin's force field analysis, the driving force analysis specifically deals with the driving forces. The method is used to define all current and future driving forces. The starting point is the current state of a situation or organization, and the already acting driving forces are defined. Driving forces are parameters that will influence a defined object in the future. They are divided into key internal forces – such as the level of knowledge of employees, the competence of management or the workforce – and external forces – such as the economic situation, market leader or technology standard (BusinessDictionary, 2017).

To derive the impact of the relevant driving forces, a five steps analysis was implemented. The current knowledge regarding the future process environment was also investigated.

Driving forces in an industry are the major hidden reasons for its change. Industry conditions change because essential forces are driving industry members (contenders, clients, or providers). The most widely recognized driving forces are: the changes in the industry development rate on the long term, expanding globalization, rising new web abilities and applications, changes in who purchases the product and how they utilize it (changes in purchaser socioeconomics), mechanical changes and assembling process advancement, marketing advancement, passage or exit of significant firms, dispersion of specialized expertise crosswise over more organizations and nations, changes in cost and productivity, decreases in vulnerability and business hazard, administrative impacts and government arrangement changes, changing societal concerns, states of mind and ways of life. When assessing the effect of the driving forces, three accompanying questions should be raised: (1) Are the driving forces acting to cause an expansion or an abatement in the interest for industry products?; (2) Are the driving forces acting to increase competition?; (3) Will the consolidated impact of the driving forces prompt higher or lower industry gainfulness? The last advance in driving forces analysis is for directors to reach a few inferences about what procedure modifications will be expected to manage the effects of the driving forces. At the point when all industry individuals seek after basically indistinguishable methodologies and have similar market positions, that industry will contain one vital gathering.

The approach to the driving forces specific to Company X in the case study is represented in the figure below.

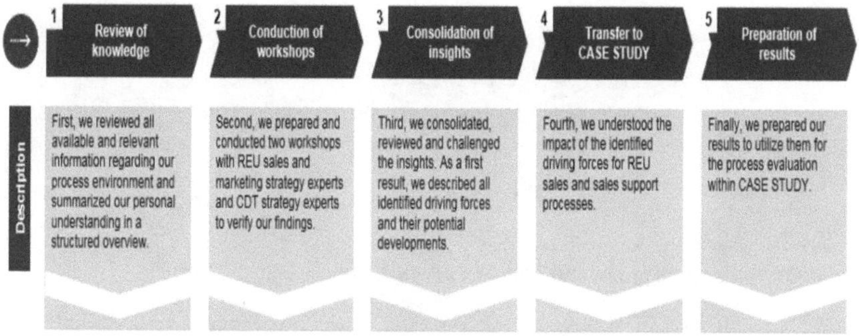

Figure 39: Specific approach to driving forces in the case study

Source: own representation

In order to get a picture of the future situation of the organisation, the internal factors must also be taken into account. Especially in sales organizations, these are characterized by a high degree of dynamics and complexity, which makes these influencing factors particularly important. Once all the driving forces are known and defined, they are also classified and evaluated according to their significance. The tasks of the internal sales department result from the company's sales strategy and the sales organization based on it. The office staff establishes the first contacts with potential customers, advises them on commercial and technical topics and researches important information for the sales field service in the background. In addition, the internal service department performs many tasks specific to the sales controlling (Buob, M., 2010).

Customer addresses are essential for a successful sale because every customer's contact is based on a contact address. No matter whether address, bank account, telephone number of the contact person or email address, these data must be correct. Before potential or new customers are approached or visited by the field service, the correctness of the address must be checked, and the right contact person must be found. The most important tasks of the internal sales department are shown in figure 40. This presentation can be supplemented by customer or company-specific tasks and serves as a rough overview of the range of tasks in the office.

Figure 40: (Previous) job profile of the internal sales department

Source: Schuler & Haller, 2008

As an interface between the company and its customers, the office staff ensures the flow of information and clarifies important questions. Coordination with the sales force is essential in order to provide customers with uniform and up-to-date information. Some examples may refer to (Fleig, 2017):

- Availability in stock and delivery time of the product sold. The internal departments affected are Production and Logistics.
- What prices are valid and can be expected with discounts or preferential conditions? Affected internal departments: Calculations of the corporate areas and sales.
- Do certain technical specifications have to be observed or technical adaptations made? Affected internal departments: development, design and product management.

Particularly in the instance of technically complex products, such as machines, tools or systems, other colleagues from various internal departments must be involved in the quotation process. For this purpose, some sales organizations are divided into a technical distribution and a commercial distribution, which deals with the terms of payment and delivery (Fleig, 2017).

From the variety of tasks and requirements of the internal sales department it quickly becomes evident that the supporting processes often run in the background and are usually not directly perceived. This fact is described by Schuler and Haller (2008) as a "schizophrenic situation", which places the internal service between praise and reprimand. The tasks of the internal sales department are interpreted and assessed in different manners by other departments, the field service or the customers. In this respect, the praise and reproach for the office staff are closely related, and certain extreme formulations precede the office workers. Some of these formulations are summarized in the following table.

Table 20: Praise and blame of Sales Support

Praise	Blame
The office workers are still the only ones in the company who keep track of things.	Nowadays, there is no essential for an office service. With modern technologies, the field service should be able to carry out all tasks independently.
The office staff handles the chaos created by the field service.	Indoor service is like a big black hole: no matter how many employees are made available, there are too few.
The office staff has the best network in the company and has connections in every department.	The office workers are never reachable and if they are, they are not the right contact person.
Field and office staff complement each other and are a well-coordinated team.	The office staff is neither result-oriented, nor sales-oriented. A superfluous department.

Source: Schuler & Haller, 2008

There are quite a lot of reasons for this two-way positioning to internal service, but they are established on the fact that the jobs and tasks of internal sales are not planned but defined where the work arises. However, this has various consequences (Schuler & Haller, 2008):

- *The range of tasks and the organizational structure of the office staff have grown historically and are not clearly defined*: Internal services in the company are of very different sizes and often located where the work is required. As the size of the business increases, this system also develops, but it is no longer useful. Tasks, work instructions and processes have not been defined.
- *There are no priorities nor special work instructions for internal sales staff*: Bills of materials, machine hours and work schedules – the normal daily routine in production. Every employee has a clearly defined task, his or her day-to-day routine and a timeline for each of his or her work steps, which is inconceivable for internal sales work. Tasks of superiors have to be processed spontaneously, any uncertainties have to be resolved and incoming emails have to be answered. Productivity or a specific work performance can be difficult to prove, which leads to certain prejudices.
- *Only few approaches are made to a standard between the individual employees in the office staff*: Guidelines for the execution of tasks are not docu-

mented. Each employee does his or her work in a different way and, therefore, naturally differently. The non-existent standards are the core purpose for the lack of transparency in the job profile of the office staff and the capacities required for this. Customers or partners of the company are not aware of how things are going, and what processing quality they should expect in the long term.

- *The tasks to be completed are hardly technically supported*: This is a situation which, unfortunately, is still too often encountered in many sales organizations. Paper clips, staples, stapling needles, semi-finished offers, punches and customer files cover the desk of the office workers. There is no trace of digitization and document management systems. Admittedly, many things have changed and improved in recent years, but the potential of customer portals, digitization and more is still being explored only to some extent.

The demands placed on an employee in the internal sales department are therefore high and varied. The office staff should know a lot, be able to answer questions from the sales force and customers, work efficiently, speak and understand several languages and be flexible and always available at best.

With the increasing digitisation, the simple administrators become generalists and specialists in a wide variety of fields, at the same time. Through internal and external networking, they know about the individual processes, connections and processes in the company and can even provide information to the business units on IT or departmental questions. (Alexy & George, 2011)

Despite common entrepreneurial goals, such as increasing sales and profit or winning new customers, the two types of sales force (inside and outside) are very different from each other. While the outside sales forece (field sales force) is engaged in customer acquisition and receives new orders for the company, the inside sales force (office staff) has to take care of the existing customers and try to live up to the promises of the field service towards the customers. (Arend, 2013).

With its areas of responsibility, the field service is the most important access to existing customers for a company. The field service is assigned to direct sales, whereby face-to-face sales take place here. Although there are some exponents who do not give this traditional, very personal form of sales force a long chance of survival, the majority of researchers and experts are certain that the sales force will continue to play an essential part in sales organizations and will have many advantages over other forms of sales (Buob, 2010).

One of the most important functions in the sales relationship is the field service employee (ADM), who personalizes the company vis-à-vis the customer. In addition to customer acquisition, ADM's scope of duties also includes concluding contracts, increasing customer satisfaction, obtaining information for the company and providing customer service tasks (Fleig, 2017). Some of the main tasks specific to the sales force are illustrated in figure 41.

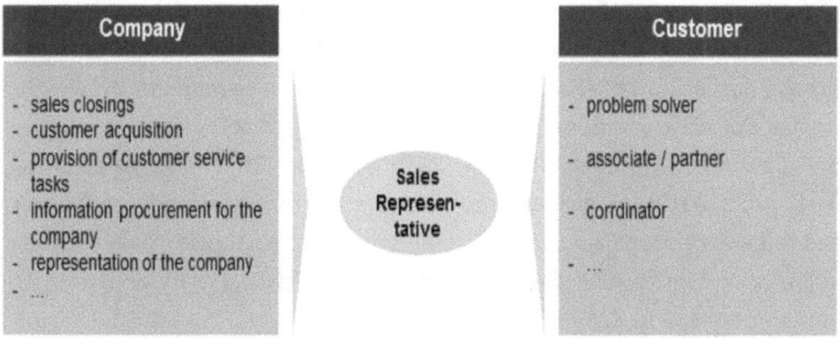

Figure 41: Tasks of sales force

Source: Buob, 2010

The sales representative must be able to identify the customer's individual problems and offer a tailored solution considering the company's product range. In addition to good social competences, he/she should also deliver a high level of technical understanding in order to be able to link the company's products with a solution to the customer's problem (Fleig, 2017).

A business model describes *"how a firm organizes itself to create and distribute value in a profitable manner"* (Baden-Fuller & Morgan, 2010). Consciously or not, every firm has (at least) one business model (Chesbrough, 2007a; Casadesus-Masanell & Ricart, 2010). This business model was taken as a pattern for a long time, as it represented the 'dominant logic' of doing business in the firm's industry (Prahalad & Bettis, 1986; Gassmann, Frankenberger & Csik, 2013; Lehoux, et al., 2014). Stable business models based on integrated manufacturing, in-house research and development, direct sales, and per-unit prices were the norm for the largest part of the 20th century (Slywotzky, 1996; Massa & Tucci, 2014). Lately, troublesome market contestants have shown the energy of creative business models and changed the predominant rationale of ventures. Apple's attack into the music business or Ikea's victory of furniture retail are representative examples (Giesen, et al., 2007). Accordingly, the business model has changed its place in officials' approach: progressively, settled firms understand that product and process innovation alone are not adequate to remain focused in the present quick moving economy

(Massa & Tucci, 2014). Rather, innovation endeavours should likewise be connected to a company's centre rationale of working together, its business model.

Scholars started to concede to some basic focal attributes of a business model (Zott & Amit, 2013). These are a business model's emphasis on the value creation model for all partners; the thought of significant value making exercises performed by parties outside the organization, similar to providers and clients; a complete way to deal with the value creation model of an organization; and the way that business models rise as another unit of examination in the academic environment. However, there still does not exist one generally accepted approached to business model by all scholars (Casadesus-Masanell & Ricart, 2010; Johnson, 2010; George & Bock, 2011; Zott & Amit, 2013), as one all around legitimate business model definition would need to be exceptionally expansive to be proper for each case. Such a standard definition isn't even conceivable, since it would need specificity and prompt mistaken assumptions (Zott & Amit, 2013).

Inside the huge number of business model definitions developed to date, Weill and Vitale (2001) view a business model as the portrayal of the parts and connections among a firm's customers, clients, partners, and providers that recognize the major flows of products, data, and cash, and the significant advantages to participants. Their business model system is centred around e-business and is constituted by the tended to target clients, product and administration offers, revenue sources, basic achievement factors, centre capabilities, channels, and IT foundation. Linder and Cantrell (2000) adopt an unique approach, considering that a business model is the "association's centre rationale for generating value". Referring to the business model configuration, pricing, income, channels and offer, represent the components portrayed by Weill and Vitale (2001). Differently, Linder and Cantrell (2000) outline a trade procedure model, connections, and the authoritative frame as further fundamental business model components. Afuah and Tucci (2003) promote the business model as a strategy to assemble and utilize a firm's assets to offer its clients' advantages over its rivals and to gain profit.

On the other hand, the business model of Osterwalder et al. (2005) – BMO – is considered a diagnostic system. In their work, they deliberately recognize the nine most normal business model segments outlined in the scientific literature by orchestrating the models and conceptualizations frequently referred to, specified, and inspected (Osterwalder et al., 2005). Moreover, the BMO has been produced with regards to data frameworks, which refers to an innovative centre of the IoT, is extensive, and includes an equivalently high range of business model parts fundamental for breaking down business models as totally as could reasonably be expected (Wirtz, et al., 2016). As indicated by Osterwalder, et al. (2005), a business model is a calculated apparatus that contains an arrangement of components and their connections facilitate the communication of the business model of a specific firm. It is a portrayal of the value an organization offers to one or more clients and of the design of the firm and its system of partners for making, marketing, and conveying this value and relationship capital, to produce profitable and practical revenue streams. To put in a nutshell, the "business model depicts the method of reasoning of how an association makes, conveys, and captures value" (Osterwalder & Pigneur, 2010). The middle is framed by the value proposition that portrays products and services that are particularly addressing to specific target customers – the company's offer. These target customers speak to the different groups of clients the organization expects to address. The distribution channels describe how the organization achieves its clients and speaks with them. The channels in this way convey the incentive to the clients. Relationships with the organization's clients are depicted in the component relationships and advance the offer. The value configuration portrays the exercises an organization needs to perform, to make the offer and run the whole business model. The centre capabilities are those assets that are mandatory to play out the urgent exercises and, thus, represent the premise of the business model's offer. Moreover, these two business model components permit the incentive. The firm's system of significant providers and other essential partners is depicted in the partners section. This affects key activities, which are encouraged or supplanted by partners. Hence, key partners bolster the offering of the incentive. The revenue model and the cost structure give some sign of the financial aspects, where the previous is based on the incentive and the last contains costs identified with value creation, marketing, and distribution/logistics (Osterwalder, et al., 2005). (Figure 42)

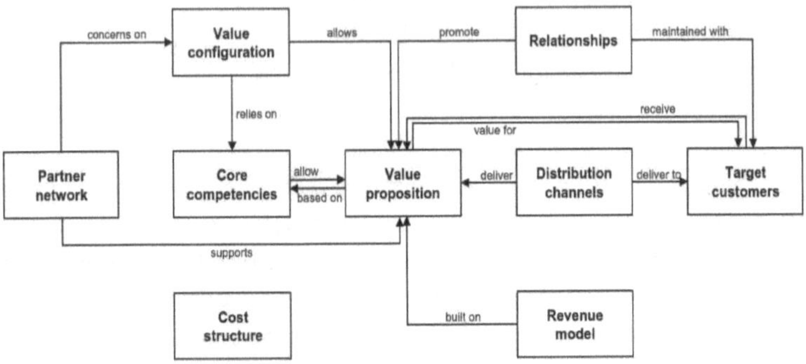

Figure 42: Relationships between the components of the business model

Source: Osterwalder, 2004

In present times, business model innovation is recognized as an important lever to achieve competitive advantage (Economist Intelligence Unit, 2005; Amit & Zott, 2012).

There are various nonexclusive procedures and headings which firms can take after to advance their business model (Mitchell and Coles, 2004a; Giesen, et al., 2007; Markides & Oyon, 2010; Amit & Zott, 2001, 2012). None of these bearings is a panacea which works in all specific situations or enterprises. One specific bearing emerges as a trademark found in numerous fruitful business model innovations crosswise over ventures: organizations have received 'open' business models, in which novel methods for working together with partners assume an essential part. For example, it is difficult to envision the achievement of Apple's iPhone without the numerous free programming designers who guarantee a consistent stream of new 'applications' to Apple's requesting clients (Amit & Zott, 2012). Similarly, enterprise software vendor SAP could hardly have become Europe's largest software company without its partners who account for one third of product sales and deliver the vast majority of SAP-related services (Antero, Hedman & Henningsson, 2013; Frankenberger, Weiblen & Gassmann, 2013). Lastly, consumer goods giant Procter & Gamble would hardly be as innovative as it is without its Connect Develop program which is the source of about half of its new products (Huston & Sakkab, 2006).

Observational confirmation proposes that opening up their business model for coordinated effort with partners is a promising course for firms to remain effective. IBM's CEO Survey 2012 uncovers that accomplishing innovation is the most grounded intention in top officials to look for joint effort with partners (IBM Global Business Services, 2012). Furthermore, Giesen, et al. (2007) demonstrate that 'system plays' (i.e., new organizations and joint effort) are the most widely recognized type of business model innovation in set up firms and that they are especially compelling for more established organizations, as they permit to use existing resources in another setting.

Business model research has, to a great extent, distinguished two main obstacles while in transit to an open business model. First, set up firms confront significant rigidities and different difficulties while advancing their business model (Chesbrough, 2010; Frankenberger, et al., 2013). Innovation management has just begun to analyse the procedure behind business model innovation and to give devices and direction to help this task (Björkdahl & Holmén, 2013; Schneider & Spieth, 2013; Eurich, Weiblen & Breitenmoser, 2014). Second, numerous open inquiries stay around the plan of effective open business model, their optimal setup and usage. Despite the fact that Venkatraman and Henderson (2008) propose that "business model innovation is to be confined in arrange driven (instead of firm-centric) terms with more noteworthy acknowledgment of co-formation of significant value", approaches to this correct co-production of significant value in open business models are still in their earliest stages (Coombes & Nicholson, 2013).

An open business model is viewed as a method for value creation, based on the understanding of the external environment. According to the studies promoted by the scientific literature, three influencing issues on the reasonable lucidity of the open business model can be distinguished: its misty definition that splits up into two streams; its likeness to open innovation; its similitude to the business model idea itself.

An essential for giving precise direction on business model innovation is to examine the procedure that organizations follow in developing and implementing their business model. First, the periods of the innovation procedure should be unmistakably characterized, alongside their particular difficulties. Hartley (2006) emphasizes this point, since the explanation of processes recognizes specific obstructions and facilitators at specific stages, and this might be of viable help to strategy developers and directors. Teece (2010) gives an abnormal state rundown of steps that organizations should take after to accomplish economical business model. Mitchell and Bruckner Coles (2004) depict business model innovation as a consistent procedure.

The models found in the scientific literature in the area of innovation management portray the innovation procedure on various levels/phases which are frequently custom-made to particular innovation items (Hartley, 2006). The main phase, regularly named start, outlines concerns about the revelation of the requirement for innovation. These are related to the catching of the underlying occasion, thought, or choice that starts the whole innovation process. This is trailed by a period of producing imaginative thoughts in the matter of how to respond to the motivation. This ideation stage goes for opening up the arrangement space and for creating an arrangement of conceivable choices. The third stage takes up one of the promising potential outcomes and spotlights on its elaboration and advancement; or, as Eveleens (2010) highlights, in this stage, the (chosen) thought is translated into a substantial product, process or service. The fourth and last period of the innovation procedure normally is the one in which the innovation is executed and conveyed to the market. These four non-specific stages – specifically start, ideation, reconciliation, and usage – should manage further examination and system development. Even though researchers in the area of business model, so far, have not intensively approached business model innovations from procedure's point of view, some of their commitments fit well into this bland four-arrange model, thus supporting its application. For instance, the approach proposed by McGrath (2010) concerns about growing new business models through experimentation in reality. In the model, her approach can be situated in the execution period of a business model innovation. A comparative learning process is depicted for a certain situation by Sosna, Trevinyo-Rodríguez and Velamuri (2010). The business model re-evaluation proposed by Voelpel, Leibold and Tekie (2004), enables administrators to detect change drivers from the external environement, being associated to the start phase. Girotra and Netessine (2011) support the ideation stage by showing how risk approaching can lead an organization towards a creative business model.

Business model and business model innovation are still rather early fields of research which are portrayed by misty discernments and a general absence of applicable observational information. This is especially valid for the crossing point of the two fields, which depicts the way toward utilizing transparency in advancing the business model of set up firms. Following the idea according to which the examination should deliver pertinent and valuable outcomes (Ulrich, 1984; Hevner, et al., 2004), the general objective of this chapter is to provide information which might help managers in developing their own business model.

Considering company X, an innovation analysis of its business model, focused on outlining its influencing internal and external factors and on describing the effects of change forces on prevailing company conditions, revealed the following:

- Consumers:
    - The digital transformation empowers consumers through better access and product knowledge. Online reviews are crucial in the decision-making process when purchasing home appliances.
    - Consumers expect a personalized, seamless, convenient shopping, and interactive product experience across all touch points.

  - Europe's ageing population will lead to the growth of customers that will want simple access and customer service. Therefore, offline commerce may still dominate.
- Customer
  - The customer market is still consolidating. The increase in negotiating power is threatening the company's product margins.
  - Customers advance their multi-sales channel capabilities. The combination of physical locations vs. digital platforms for a customer presence are emerging. Online sales share is expected to reach approximately 27% by 2020. New business formats like online market platforms may appear (Teece, 2010).
  - Customer requirements are further rising. They expect a seamless process integration, individualized product information to enhance their PoS, and value-added services.
- Competitors
  - The home appliance market in Europe is characterized by low growth rate forecasts and uncertainty. Continued consolidation, strategic pricing attacks, cost savings, potential disruptive mergers and acquisitions or joint ventures activities will be the main threats.
  - Company's Region Europe markets are very heterogeneous in terms of size, market volume, customer group structure and consumer purchasing power.
  - D2C emergence is moderate (4% in 2025). However, various forms are starting to appear more frequently in other regions of the world. Uncertainty prevails.
- Company
  - To reach the company's ambitious 2025 targets, growth in all product price classes is necessary. Operational excellence will be key to remain competitive. In particular, sales cost growth shall be proportionally to turnover growth.
  - The company has to develop an integrated, connected ecosystem to justify a premium price and combat price erosions.
  - Big data analytics capabilities have to be developed. Company needs an enhanced content management system to address new formats and customer requirements.

Based on the results of the project phase process assessment, measures for process improvement were derived. (Figure 43)

Criteria for the development of measures

	Redundancy	Heterogeneity	Commodities	Not-harmonized processes	Not-automated processes	Dezentralized processes
Potential	Processes or activities, which are executed at different locations the same way.	The same processes or activities are executed differently at multiple locations.	Processes or activities with low priority according strategic perspective and Company X set-up.	Processes or activities, which are redundant and heterogeneous at the same time.	Processes or activities with high manual effort and frequent repetition.	The same or similar processes or activities, which are set-up at different locations.
Measures	**Elimination** Redundancies are eliminated and re-located to a single location.	**Standardization** Processes are designed homogeneously.	**Simplification** Reduction of complexity and set-up of a homogeneous and streamlined process design.	**Consolidation** Elimination of redundancies and standardization of process design might be possible.	**Automation** Process steps with insufficient degree of automation might be harmonized and increasingly supported via IT functionalities.	**Bundling** Central pooling of the process under a central responsibility.

Figure 43: Process evaluation: criteria for the development of measures

Source: Own representation

Furthermore, the following processes have been considered for the shared service evaluation of customer accounting, credit management, and customer master data tasks. Their customization on Company X is reflected in the following figures. Figure below presents the shared service evaluation of customer accounting, credit management and CMD–CU (Customer Master Data).

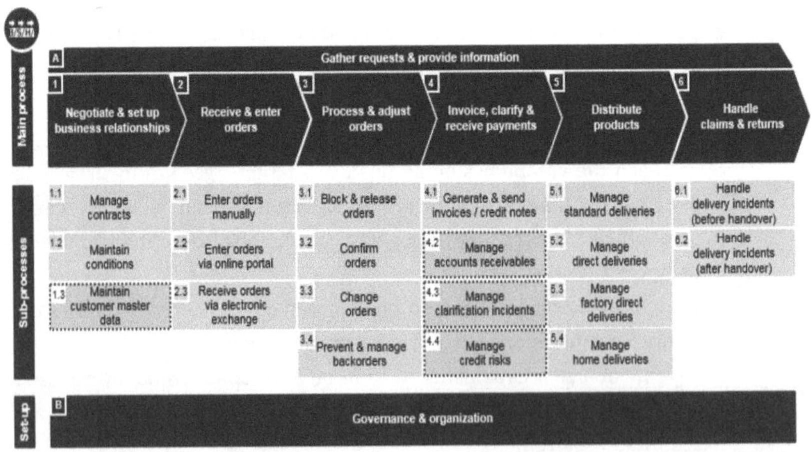

Figure 44: Shared service evaluation: customer accounting, credit management, Customer Master Data

Source: Own representation

Figure below illustrates the process evaluation to further show the description of measures of the collected data.

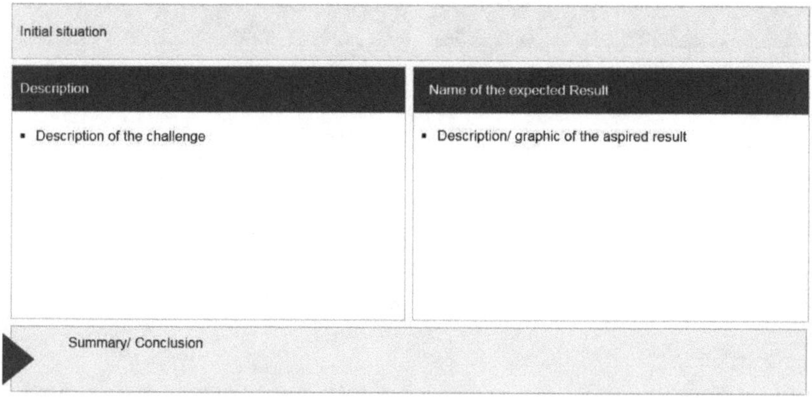

Figure 45: Process evaluation: description of measures

Source: Own representation

Figure 46 emphasises the overview measures of process evaluation of the collected data.

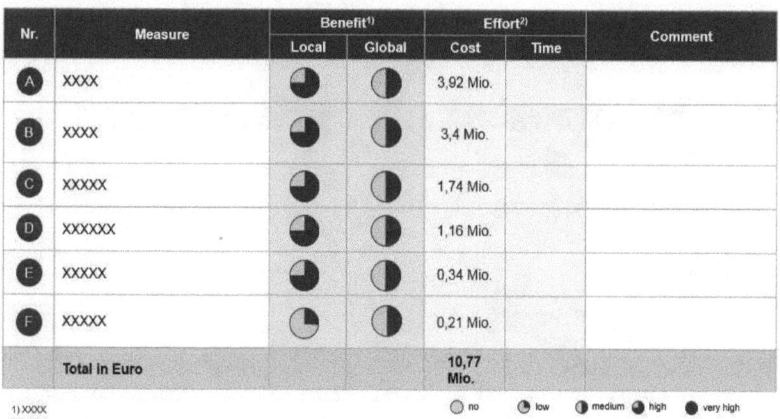

Figure 46: Process evaluation: measures overview

Source: Own representation

Figure 47 presents the portfolio of the process evaluation, as resulted from the collected information.

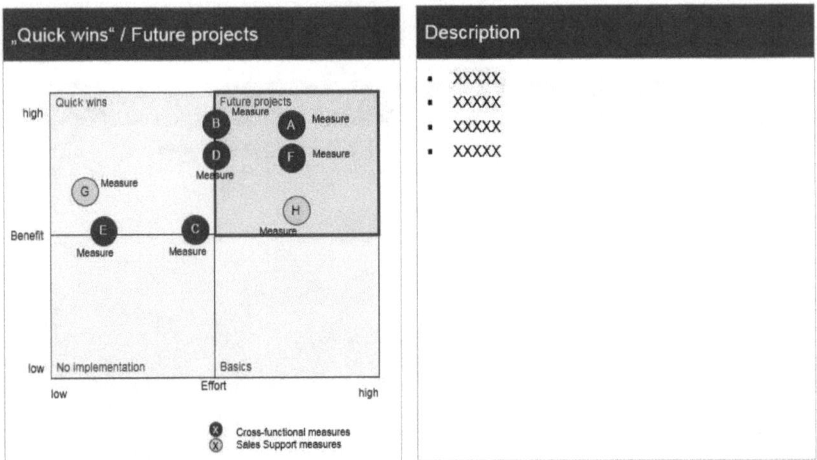

Figure 47: Process evaluation: portfolio of measures

Source: Own representation

Figure 48 outlines the scorecard of the process evaluation as resulted from the analysed information within the case study framework.

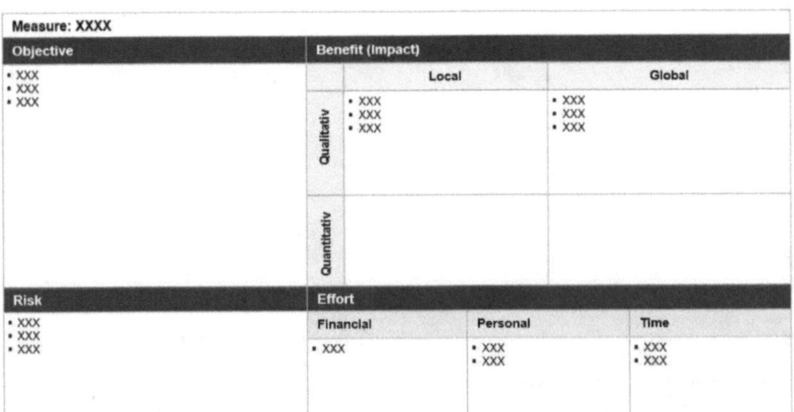

Figure 48: Process evaluation: scorecard of measures

Source: Own representation

Figure 49 reflects the work results of the process evaluation.

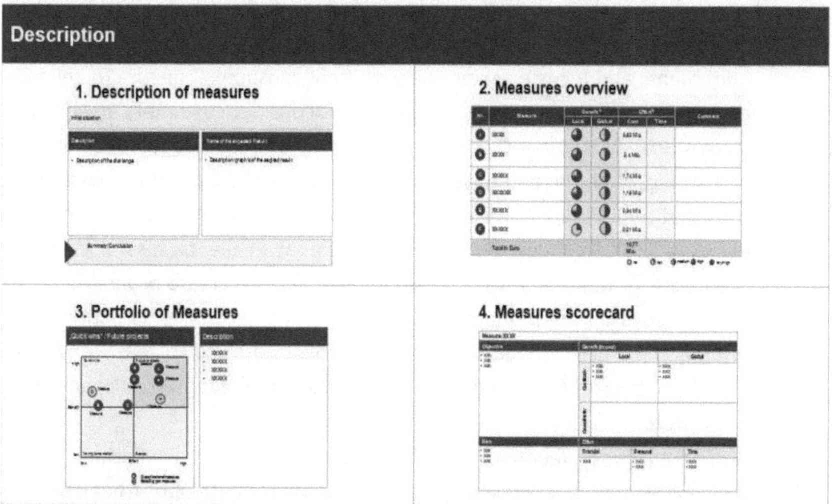

Figure 49: Process evaluation: work results

Source: Own representation

Further on, the chapter focuses on deriving reference processes and corresponding management systems. The applied approach, consisting of five steps, is illustrated in the figure below.

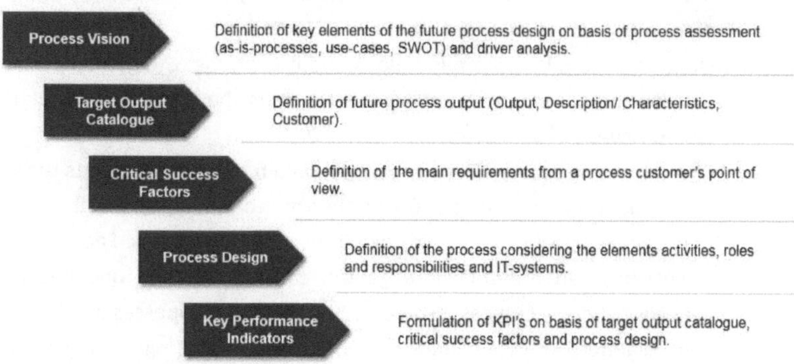

Figure 50: Development of reference processes

Source: Own representation

Within the case study the conducted analysis to *Driving Forces* has given relevant insights to the changing environment and future requirements for Company X. To gain general findings, these have been corroborated with scientific studies. The main cornerstones regarding the future process design resulted from the driving forces analysis are:

- *Customer-oriented*: The processes should sufficiently consider customer requirements and focus on their ability to fulfil consumers' needs. To keep clients coming back, businesses should always consider customers' needs in all their processes. From a trade point of view, inability to address remarkable requesting, invoicing and payment needs, for instance, can make customers confused about the company's products and its image. This can prompt a decrease in clients' devotion and an increment in clients' loss. Focuses on clients are continually advancing, and it is difficult to create programming to suit all needs on the primary attempt. The way to keep clients faithful is by offering them new products/services able to address and solve their necessities. This should effectively be possible through an adaptable, cloud-based framework.
- *Gather customer feedback*: The most direct approach to decide client's greatest needs is to ask them. Organizations can request input from clients in both off and online ways:
  - Client input portals: The company should provide an immediate line to client groups through a client criticism entryway. This is a direct and simple approach to reveal basic issues.
  - Guide evaluations: The company should ask its clients to rate it and its products/services, by offering assessment guides with alternatives alongside each component. While the client criticism entrances enable clients to submit recommendations about anything, the guide appraisals give the company an approach that limits the input to particularly aimed issues.
  - Client warning boards: The company should meet with its clients to talk about their needs, perception about the company, about its products/services, focusing on both strengths and weaknesses. Face-to-face discussions can prompt more gainful conclusions than one-way advanced criticism choices. However, numerous businesses neglect to have real, face-to-face discussions with clients about what they like or dislike.
- *Finish*: Customer input is futile if the company does not follow an activity plan. Instantly following up on client criticism is a key activity for ensuring the company's success in terms of its relationship with its customers. Approaching clients as the core of the business is the way to long haul achievement. Showing that the business is tuning in to the requirements of

purchasers by reliably following up on input will help drive more noteworthy reliability and value.

- *Digitalization*: The processes ought to use IT possibilities to change current activities. Organizations throughout the world lower their working costs, increment their IT abilities, and enhance their own particular business models by developing better products and services at lower costs. The procedure of digitization quickened the pattern toward bigger scale commoditization, as merchandise that had once been considered extravagant nowadays is perceived as common, being available to mass market, by utilizing digitized configuration, assembling, and dispersion frameworks. Digitization additionally impacts humans, business and the society in its entirety, and it's significant to how products are produced, marketed, sold, and distributed. (Veit, et al 2014).
- *Commoditization*: The driving factor for costs descending, keeps on being a considerable focused force. In current circumstances, this may be outlined from multiple points of view, from the globalization of the companies' network and the going with outsourcing of assembling to Asia, to change in the retail basic supply business, to the outsourcing of IT services to India, to the sharp drop in the cost of processing power.
- *Social mediatization throughout the society*: Computerized innovation turns out to be dynamically biger as it's connected to an ever-increasing number of elements of life, businesses, and society. Nowadays, businesses cannot be perceived without the web and all the programming devices provided by technology advancement. Furthermore, countless individuals are utilizing online social networking platforms like Facebook, MySpace, Twitter, and LinkedIn to interact with each other, which constitutes a pattern with huge energy, and, maybe, tremendous significance.
- *Globalization*: Globalization has drawn each country into a solitary financial framework, and through online networking, a considerable number of persons are currently taking part in a global social frame. Subsequently, every organization's technique must address a globalized advertise in which expanding quantities of individuals are taking an interest in social and business groups that rise above national limits. The power and effect of globalization implies that it is mandatory for each organization to: comprehend the present and future effects of overall patterns on activities; build up a globalization system to advance learning openings through introduction to different markets all over the world; to expand its range of products to reach new cli-

ents. As client groups are likewise worldwide, no extensive organization can trust work effectively without tending to worldwide markets.

- *Products/Services Offered*: The company meets a fundamental and continuing need in the commercial centre by offering a constrained range of products and services. It tries to enter new markets with distinctive demographic, geographic, or technological features, aiming the development through the augmentation of business sectors or the production of totally new ones. Its key feature lays in the advantages that are incorporated with its products or services.
- *Markets/Needs Served*: The company aims to offer a range of products and services to a developing market. It seeks after development by offering an expanding number of products and services. Its competitive advantage is based on the quality of its connections and relationships and its image.
- *Generation Capability or Cost Advantage*: Company X tries to obtain competitive advantages by creating and providing products and services of higher quality and at lower prices, compared to its competitors. Every key capacity is identified with creation or activity processes, abilities, and interest in hardware and related services.
- *Selling techniques*: Company X decides upon the products and services it produces and provides, the markets it enters, and the geographical area where it's going to be active, usually based on the abilities and constraints of its essential sales force and strategy. At the end of the day, they offer what they can through their picked technique. Every single other ability, especially selling techniques, will be developed to achieve the goals established in the strategy. Company's key advantage is the comfort it provides to its customers.
- *Distribution Methods*: Company X decides upon the products and services it produces and provides and its clients, based on those types of products and services and clients that can be dealt with through its set up distribution channels. The company is an organization driven by the requirements of its working systems.

Contextual investigation underpins the requirement for adaptability by upgrading selling bolster, chose deals and client related bookkeeping processes. An organization's director needs to connect with the right individuals and assign them their required tasks and expectations. Each organization has its own motivation or extreme goal – the task accomplishment. With this aim, organizations' directors need to deal with the undertaking from the earliest starting point to the end. When a task is allocated, the director has an obligation to comprehend the final objective of the undertaking. This is a vital aspect, as the director should be able to know what type of employees are needed for accomplishing the task, how many are necessary, when how should they be approached for developing the task, etc. Employees would need to comprehend the idea of the undertaking and what parts they will play in the achievement of the final goal. Therefore, it is important to make an exhaustive assessment of the venture that would incorporate the following processes:

- *Open Project Plan Number or ID*: Immediately after endorsement of the undertaking, the appointed task supervisor will start or open a venture design number. By commenting on the task design number or ID beside the undertaking title, this turns into a reference in the information store of all activities. It is essential to have an undertaking design number for various purposes. Each correspondence, including meeting solicitations, ought to incorporate the task ID number regarding the matter header.
- *Beginning Introduction*: The task administrator dives into what the undertaking needs; it is important to contact the people that will help with the venture. The task chief is in charge with contacting the employees and managers of the company for setting up a first meeting; phone calls or e-mails may be used. It is important to explain to each employee/manager what his/her tasks will be and what the general aims of the company are. Thus, employees/managers will know exactly what they will have to expect, and they will have the opportunity to prepare themselves for the venture.
- *Commence Meeting to Determine the Project's Phases*: up to 14 days after the underlying telephone or email presentation, the task supervisor plans a task commence meeting. Here, each venture member will get the opportunity to meet with each other and will take in the terms of their engagement on the task. Regardless of how much the venture supervisor prepares and tries to welcome the perfect individuals to the commence meeting, there might be other important gatherings that will emerge upon introductory exchanges amid the commence meeting. This is an extraordinary chance to check every member's contribution and to establish if other additional members are necessary to achieve the allotted tasks. During this gathering, the task administrator will clarify the extent of the undertaking and afterward allocate a deadline for fulfilment. The task supervisor will then demand to each member to give his/her reasonable course of events to finish the tasks. This gathering is a great opportunity to meet all members face to face, as well as to conceptualize on the most proficient method to continue with the task.
- *Initiating Project Sizing*: The task director's subsequent stage amid the organization start stage is to begin the estimations concerning the final monetary

amount necessary to accomplish the task. Venture measuring incorporates the cost of hardware, for instance, new servers, circuits, switches and so forth. It might likewise incorporate the cost of any vital programming. Furthermore, costs specific to each workforce, either employee or director, should also be considered. It is important to incorporate any office supplies utilized, dispatching and taking care of expenses, and different miscellaneous items.

- *Finish of Project Initiation*: The venture start stage closes when a task administrator can get together all the underlying data to commence the task. A smooth execution of the task is vital.

Within the process assessment project phase, a detailed analysis of the process landscape was conducted and main differences between the selected subsidiaries were identified. This area is organized along the four non-specific periods of innovation processes: start, ideation, mix, and execution. For each stage, the correct significance in a business model innovation setting was investigated. Furthermore, the key difficulties related with a single stage are outlined. Toward the finish of the segment, the straight versus iterative approach of the procedure is applied, before the discoveries are incorporated into an integrative system. The developed 4I-system of business model innovation depicts the general structure of the business model innovation process. It incorporates the stages, and their arrangement, and abridges the key difficulties of each stage.

The internal process needs to be designed according to the external customer process. (Figure 51)

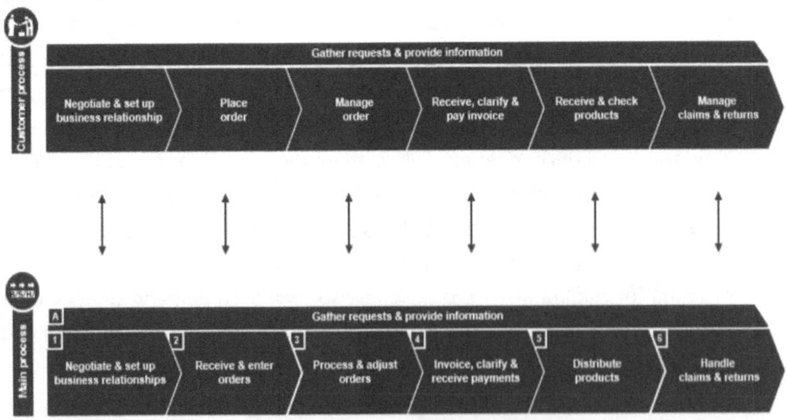

Figure 51: Interaction between external and internal processes

Source: Own representation

The customer should be the starting point and the centre element in identifying potentials for process improvement. An important pre-condition is the consideration of the corresponding customer process and the critical success factors from customer perspective.

Based on the corresponding customer process, the following internal process landscape can be derived. (Figure 52)

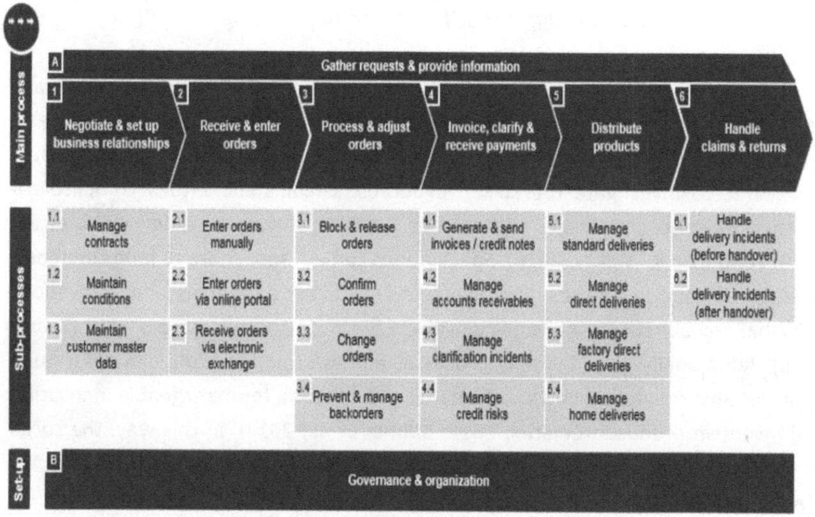

Figure 52: Internal process landscape as a result from process assessment

Source: Own representation

Important internal processes might also be considered in terms of the customer accounting, credit management, customer master data, and sales support activities, as follows:

- Customer accounting, credit management, and customer master data (CMD-CU) tasks can be separated into two clusters:
    - Recurring back-office tasks with significant staff involvement are concluded to bear shared service potential.
    - High degree of local expertise and intensive external customer contact with negative impact, if administered through shared service centre.

  Within project case study future potentials have been identified that would significantly improve customer accounting, credit management, and customer master data processing e.g. fostering standardization, realizing automation potentials, rolling out best practice solutions to REU subsidiaries. However, these potentials have not been considered in this shared service evaluation.

- Sales support: Sales support-related activities should remain locally, as they are typically characterized by direct or indirect customer contact and a high integration into the local sales and logistics processes. Local back-office concepts can generate value for specific tasks. Within project case study potentials have been identified to improve sales support processes e.g. by standardization and automation, reduction of communication and processing steps, and outsourcing of specific tasks to the customer

Related to the selling process, implicitly logistics as part of the process, many researchers in the area of supply chain management have considered social aspects in their approaches (Dyer & Singh,1998) and related asset speculations as an intriguing idea to investigate the social favourable circumstances to accomplice co-creation of important assets and abilities (Vachon & Klassen, 2008; Gold, et al., 2010; Touboulic & Walker, 2015). Speculations can advance more to help community social innovation and research, to create sustainable products and innovations (Marshall, et al., 2015), indicating positive effects on the purchasers' side (Busse, 2016). Additionally, joint learning processes and information trade can assist build up firms' absorptive capacity to acclimatize outside data for manageable innovation and inventive products (Chiarini, 2012; Blome, et al., 2014). In this way, the social view has been perceived as an approach that examines the sustainability of all activities developed inside the organization (Chen & Paulraj, 2004; Vachon & Klassen, 2008). For example, the regular principal components grounded in both the social view and the sustainable supply chain management (SSCM) approaches allude to joint effort and coordination. (Figure 53)

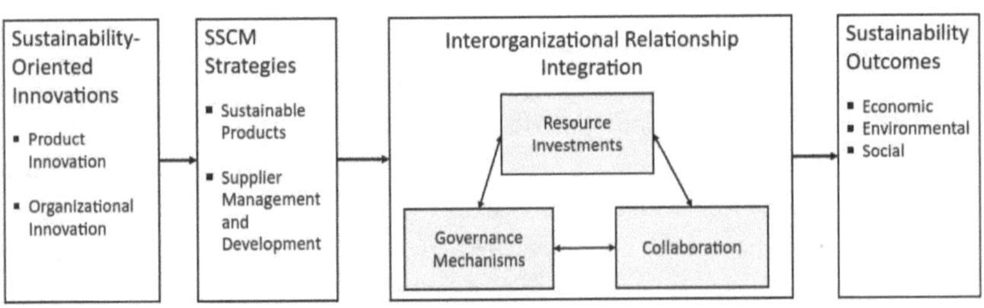

Figure 53: Integrating sustainability-oriented innovation

Source: Chen & Paulral, 2015

Focusing on the selling activity, in the particular case of the Company X, sustainable business processes might refer to the ones illustrated in figures 54 and 55.

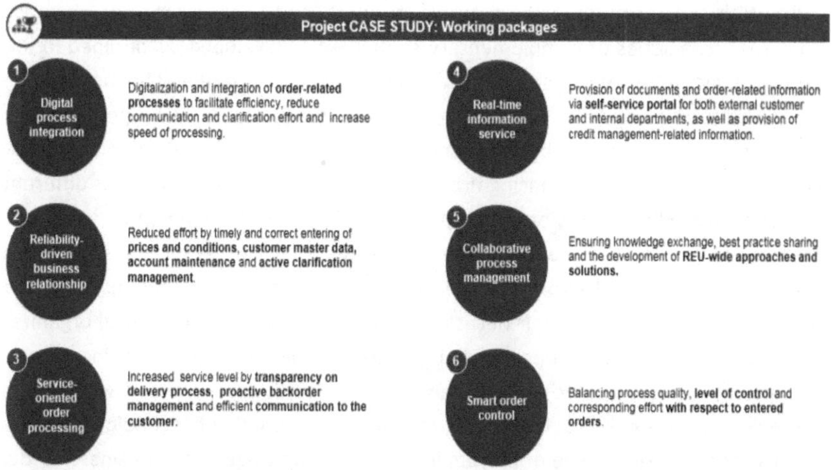

Figure 54: Sustainable business processes in sales aiming to improve operational excellence

Source: own representation

The following six working packages describe the main focus of the case study. Each working package consists of modules which contain a set of detailed measures.

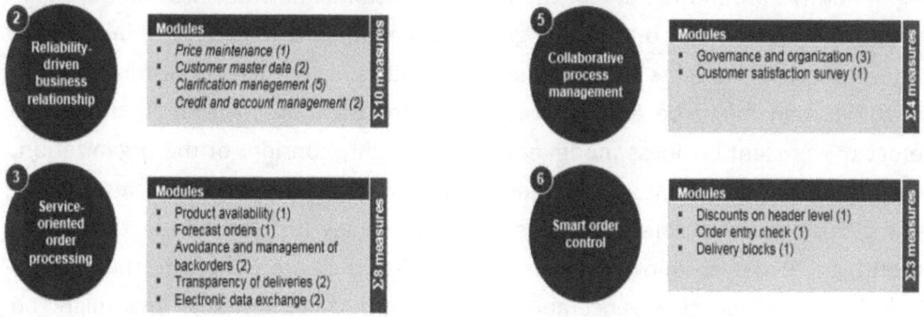

Figure 55: Structuring of measures for sustainable business processes in sales

Source: own representation

With the main aim to test, prove, support, and even, strengthen the case study results, a series of complementary studies were developed, as outlined in the methodology section of this chapter. Their results are briefly outlined further on.

The start stage in business model innovation processes can be portrayed by exercises which centre around the comprehension and checking of the encompassing centre system of the advancing firm. The external environment includes different players such as clients, providers, competitors, colleges, or governments and quickly impacts the activities of the central firm. Two main challenges were distinguished inside the start stage. The principal challenge alludes to the comprehension of the necessities of the players. Their necessities and actions impact the central organization and frequently set the beginning stage, making the difference in business models. Accordingly, it is vital to screen them intently. In this case, contacts with clients or providers, denote the beginning stage of the innovation. Chief Technology Officers (CTO) stress the significance of players in the beginning stage of the business model innovation. Important business model innovation in organizations might be activated by clients as they want to get something extraordinary.

A challenging moment inside the start stage is the distinguishing proof of progress drivers, which can likewise determine business model changes. Innovation changes; digitisation and services changes represent important facts that set off the re-examination of the business model. Current changes in nature or in innovation happen so quickly that it is extremely hard to stay aware of them, yet this is a key precondition for effective business model innovations and a key achievement factor for organizations.

Ideation, the second stage in the nonexclusive innovation process, additionally has its importance and particular difficulties in the business model innovation setting. It centres around the age of thoughts for potential new business models. Furthermore, it focuses also on the change of chances which are recognized in the start stage, into solid thoughts for new business models. There are three fundamental difficulties that might be encountered during the ideation stage: first, trouble to defeat the present business model and to thoroughly consider of the organization, as groups are included into the present business model and industry features. Defeating the present business model is the principal key test for the ideation stage. Second, challenges to think in business models, as they are utilized to think exclusively in new products advancements when approaching an issue. This might be considered the business model reasoning state of mind that is absent. Third, there are no efficient instruments to grow new business model thoughts. As opposed to these logical methodologies, organizations have to apply more imaginative conceptualizing and pitching workshop configurations to fundament new business model thoughts. Outside specialists and thoughts are brought into the ideation procedure which aims at solving an important portion of the distinguished difficulties. However, there is not one best strategy to intentionally develop thoughts on new business models.

The third stage – reconciliation – assumes its part and role in the business model innovation. The exercises inside this stage centre around the improvement of another business model in view of promising thoughts distinguished in the ideation stage. They should be changed into a total and feasible business model. The use of the four measurements (who, what, how, why) of a business model as the focal point revels a fascinating understanding: regularly, the initial thought decides the 'What' and additionally 'Who' segments, without any business model related bounds, though the income model ('Why') and the value chain model ('How') are included amid the reconciliation stage. Two noteworthy difficulties might be faced in this stage. The principal challenge is that organizations battle to incorporate all parts of their new business model. This viewpoint isn't adequately considered by the fund-driven methodologies, to be a specific business case and (to a lesser degree) business design, which are normally utilized. An absence of joining of the business model measurements can prompt troubles or even disappointment in the usage of the new business model. The current worldwide selling associations ought to be utilized to advertise an alternate line of products. The second test for the coordination of the business model is the inclusion and management of partners. As the new business model should be adjusted and incorporated with the partners' business models, multi-sided quality emerges that requires a great deal of vitality and capacity to persuade. The test distinguished here is not quite the same as the one recognized amid the start stage, albeit both allude to partners' cooperation. Amid the start stage, the test is to comprehend the requirements, driving forces, and openings in the association's external environment with a specific end goal to recognize a beginning stage for another business model. Here, amid the reconciliation stage, the distinguished test alludes to the incorporation of partners into the development of new, solid business models. The new models will work if every included partner bolster them and modify their business models accordingly. Subsequently, firms need to effectively deal with their partners.

The last bland innovation process stage – usage – is obviously a pivotal point in time for business model innovations, excessively. Once completely outlined and incorporated, the new business model can be actualized. Usually, this includes immense speculations to be made and risks to be taken by the central firm. Rather than item innovation, where early models can be shared and assessed with clients amid their advancement, another business model frequently should be completely updated before it can be tried. The execution of another business model can be the hardest task of all. The most difficult thing with business model innovation is to effectively update the new business model. Generally, people are reluctant to change because they fear about new circumstance or because they simply don't see motivation to change, as the old business model is still perfectly functionable. Fundamentally, overseeing hierarchical change isn't a simple task, and the all-encompassing extent of the business model that expects changes to a wide range of territories inside the firm makes it significantly harder. In this stage, it is essential to act in a transparent manner and to clarify how the new business model can help the organization.

An important challenge, which was accounted for all through the study was to deal with the picked execution approach. Commonly, pilot and experimental tests are utilized to alleviate chance in the usage procedure. Enormous blast approaches are seldom utilized when another business model is actualized. Or, maybe, firms take after a careful technique of stepping toward the acknowledgment of the business model. The basic test is to guarantee that learnings from these activities are then used to tweak the business model or to perform bigger changes, if required. However, the approach of experimentation learning pays off. In accordance with the recognized progression shrewd approach, new business models are regularly taken off by nation. This is by far the most used approach and furthermore permits to make particular changes, considering each nation's premises.

Throughout the case investigation, five main antecedents that lead firms to open up their business models, were revealed. These are thoroughly presented below.

Antecedent 1: Business model inconsistency

Business model consistency happens when the segments of a business model – for example, the client incentive, the processes, and the income model – are orchestrated as an intelligible and fortifying framework (Mitchell & Coles, 2003; Morris, et al., 2005; Demil & Lecocq, 2010; Teece, 2010; Casadesus-Masanell & Ricart, 2011). Organizations with a conflicting business model in the beginning – few components are missing or are not outlined in a fitting way – are probably going to open their business model keeping in mind the end goal to incorporate the missing assets and capacities of partners. In the 3M Services case, for instance, the organization centres around product development, selling and post-selling support services. This needs capacities for benefit provisioning, for example, film application. The partners' business model, interestingly, centres around this particular procedure which pleasantly supplements the business model of 3M. Accomplishing complementarity makes the organization fascinating for the two gatherings – the central firm and the partner – in light of the fact that both can benefit from each other, by interfacing their business models as a re-upholding framework.

Business model consistency may be perceived as an essential driver for business model execution (Demil & Lecocq, 2010). There are three purposes behind this aspect. First, it reduces the risk of set-back in the underlying phase of usage after a period of time. Second, it assumes an urgent part in avoiding circumstances where the accomplished value disappears from the central firm to different players. Third, the consistency of a business model is valuable for obtaining competitive advantages since "it is harder for a competitor to coordinate a variety of interlocked exercises than it is just to emulate a specific sales force approach, coordinate a procedure innovation, or copy a range of products" (Porter, 1996). On the off chance that consistency can't be accomplished inside, outside associations are a decent method to adjust for the weaknesses. Specialists in the field outline the beneficial outcome of the complementarity of assets and abilities between the union partners (Ahuja, 2000; Douma, et al., 2000; Bierly & Gallagher, 2007).

Antecedent 2: The need to create and capture new value

The second recognized predecessor for outlining open business models is the need to make and capture new value. Firms are progressively under strain to maintain their execution and advantages. Expanded competition, falling costs, commoditization, and higher expenses are just few reasons why firms need to always enhance their business model (Amit & Zott, 2012). This prompts another value creation and capture model which is expected to remain aggressive. For example, to effectively contend with key player on the pharmaceutical market, Shire couldn't develop its business by using a similar business model to the one implemented by its competitors, as this would have required colossal investments in vast R&D capacities with high risk of disappointment. Opening their business model was a key move to quickly develop, considering its restricted assets, and to deliver a wide range of innovative products. Shire's mergers and acquisitions are conclusive in acquiring new thoughts, know-how, and innovation. For Buehler, it was the development impediments of its old business model that drove the firm to explore different avenues regarding an open business model for developing markets. On the other hand, for Hilti, it was the market passage of lower-valued contenders that set off the look for another business model in various ventures.

For new pursuits, Zott & Amit (2013) contend that the objective to create and capture new value is a noteworthy precursor of business model design. Different business model researchers have discovered that organizations will probably enhance their business model if their old model does not properly work any longer (Markides, 2006; Chesbrough, 2007, 2010; Demil & Lecocq, 2010). Adopting an open business model is widely embraced by entrepreneurs as an adequate method for creating value (Chesbrough & Crowther, 2006; IBM Global Business Services, 2012). One impact is that outside partners can accelerate the innovation procedure. Even more critically, in any case, receptiveness acquires new thoughts and information, which enable the central firm to defeat its overwhelming model; a noteworthy boundary to business model innovation (Bouchikhi & Kimberly, 2003; Sandulli & Chesbrough, 2009; Chesbrough, 2010; Frankenberger, et al., 2013).

Antecedent 3: Past involvement in cooperation

Firms with a vast experience in cooperating with other firms will probably open their business model and vice versa. For example, an absence of a partnership with a non-car partner, drove BMW to seek after a reinforcement venture with a set up provider and to assume control advancement. The joint effort abilities with a non-car partner must be first developed and they need to gradually expand. Conversely, organizations with an abnormal state of understanding through existing associations with partners, for example, SAP, demonstrate that the inclusion of partners can progress toward becoming "normal" to the association.

Firms learn and develop the abilities required to work together after a period of time (Möller & Svahn, 2003; Chesbrough & Schwartz, 2007). Researchers have contended that earlier joint effort encounter prompts powerful coordinated efforts and enhances cooperation results (Simonin, 1997; Anand & Khanna, 2000; Sampson, 2005), as experienced firms are more capable to recognize potential associates, arrange and oversee assertions and know when to end joint efforts (Simonin, 1997). Likewise, researchers have contended that organizations with coordinated effort encounter will probably go for new associations (Powell, Koput & Smith-Doerr, 1996).

Antecedent 4: Business model patterns

A main trigger for businesses to open their business model lay in other effective open business models. Usually, businesses analyse other businesses and if the open business model results in an important value generator, such an approach is immediately imitated and implemented. For example, the exchange of the Procter&Gamble business model (Osterwalder & Pigneur, 2010) happened from the pharmaceutical and IT industry, where Eli Lily and IBM had effectively spearheaded receptiveness of their R&D exercises. Correspondingly, at 3M Services, management had examined product benefit frameworks in more settings when choosing to incorporate remotely sourced services into their own particular business model. Also, the organization had various encounters with a multinational organization which resulted in a similar change process.

Different researchers have featured the likelihood of 'receiving', 'duplicating' or 'imitating' a business that has demonstrated to work before, keeping in mind the end goal to accomplish business model innovation (Doganova & Eyquem-Renault, 2009; Baden-Fuller & Morgan, 2010; Teece, 2010; Casadesus-Masanell & Zhu, 2013; Zott & Amit, 2013). Teece (2010), for instance, contends that effective business models can be exchanged starting with one setting then onto the next, determining this way the development of a fruitful business model. Doganova & Eyquem-Renault (2009) outline that business models act both inside and crosswise over firm limits, which thus empowers their replication (intra-firm setting) and impersonation (between firm setting). Baden-Fuller & Morgan (2010) contend that business models may likewise be approached as formulas, which independent from each other, and open for variety and innovation. Casadesus-Masanell & Zhu (2013) demonstrate that directors need to choose whether they remain with their own particular business model or the analyse the business model of other players, keeping in mind the end goal to protect their position in the market.

Antecedent 5: Industry meeting

Characterized as "the obscuring of limits between enterprises" (Bröring, Cloutier & Leker, 2006), industry meeting triggers open business models in two courses, through innovation union, fundamentally influencing R&D, and through the energy of new market participants, requiring more extensive business model changes. For example, in BMW's situation, clients progressively put their attention on consistent in-auto diversion, correspondence and convenience. A superb auto design and a powerful motor are implicitly associated with the brand, though electronic highlights are also important features when clients assess the product. Thus, outside abilities and advancements from cutting-edge hardware businesses were required. Likewise, Nespresso teamed up with family unit machine and designing organizations to build up its Nespresso framework. Its parent organization, Nestlé, could just give its handling knowledge, yet abilities to build up the equipment part of the framework were absent. Shire managed the passage from the pharmaceutical industry to the biotechnology business. It was just through its expounded management of outside assets and speed in authorizing and acquisitions that the organization could remain autonomous and quickly develop.

The quick pace of industry union in numerous enterprises, makes it troublesome for the organizations to secure the skills all alone. Opening the business model in organizations encourages the learning of new abilities (Lei, 2000; Bröring, et al., 2006). Small firms need to collaborate with other players, small or big, to face the organizations that are recently entering the market (Hacklin, et al., 2010). Hence, industry merging urges firms to open their business model to gain aptitudes and advances and to develop in size and power.

There are numerous advancements in the present economy which challenge existing business models and may, accordingly, prompt the appropriation of more transparency in firms. One of them is the expanding digitization and IT enablement of the business world, which facilitates joint effort amongst firms and the development of promising novel business models (Arend, 2013; Rai & Tang, 2014; Sandulli, Rodríguez-Duarte & Sánchez-Fernández, 2014; Veit, et al., 2014). These advancements, along with a general history of business model receptiveness, are extremely evident in the product and cutting-edge enterprises. In such enterprises, environment management represents a committed capacity which drives and incorporates coordinated effort with partners along the whole value chain. However, business model receptiveness is in no way, shape or form bound to the ICT business. Researchers have discovered receptiveness to shape novel business models in novel areas, for example, electric vehicles (Weiller & Neely, 2013; Massa & Tucci, 2014) or 3D printing (Cautela, Pisano & Pironti, 2014). In the more traditionalist industries, such as aviation and safeguard, Ritala et al. (2013) found that "the entire business (counting the main firm) is changing towards open community-oriented structures".

In the new universe of expanded coordinated effort, firm systems and business environments lose their illustrative power. Thus, new investigative gadgets are required, and past discoveries should be surveyed in the light of the new business reality. Clearly, this audit procedure does not stop at investigative gadgets, but rather incorporates apparatuses which examine what has already delivered for administrative practice. A similar manner by which open innovation has tested the closed innovation model and prompted a move in innovation management, business model transparency requires new models to comprehend and oversee collective methods for value creation. Popular management apparatuses, such as Porter's five forces and the value chain, require improvement or substitution.

5.3 Main Concluding Remarks, Limits And Further Research Directions

The introduction of learning to infer further bits of knowledge into business models is a promising theme for future research. There is not one generally accepted sustainable business model, yet there are different approaches to the idea itself. A more exact phrasing, thinking about the two prevailing perspectives, appears to be prudent to anticipate a break down in the area.

In present times, managers are very much aware of the significance of business model innovation and realize that open business models regularly prompt unrivalled execution. In such a context, they need to acquire knowledge about when to adjust their business model and if presenting more transparency is a valuable action in their specific case.

The research findings provide significant insights for specialists in their process of developing sustainable open business models for their businesses. Considering all the information outlined in this chapter, especially focusing on the highlighted antecedents, directors ought to effectively consider opening their business models. This is of high pertinence since, as often as possible, business model pioneers enter from outside the business. Directors need to frequently check these points, always concentrating on achieving the final objective, respectively gaining supremacy on the market. In many areas, conventional key instruments, for example, Porter's five forces, joined with a canvas model (Kim & Mauborgne, 2005) or business guide (Gassmann, Frankenberger & Csik, 2013), will expand the examination and bolster the basic leadership procedure in case the opening of the business model is additionally necessary.

The research results support other studies' findings promoted in the scientific literature, bringing in the same time an innovative perspective on the investigated issue. This enables the profound examination and thinking about information in an explorative way and makes possible to give significant outcomes to common-sense issues. This is an attractive finishing of the research results, outlining a promising course for future research. The acknowledgment of innovations is quantifiable with innovation acknowledgment models and speculations. Just non-existent innovations that bring issues to light through a long improvement process are intelligible for acknowledgment estimating with existent models and hypotheses. These models and hypotheses however require minor alterations if there should be an occurrence of utilization to innovations.

Information from rising economies related to sustainable management research are not so abundant. While this is halfway a constraint of the carried-out research, it additionally adds to the information hole and is an endeavour towards widening the experimental premise of the contextual investigation. This provides an adequate framework for developing future investigations to widen the experimental extension.

As a general recommendation, the change of existing models and hypotheses, specifically in view of the contextual investigation, is made. This mainly refers to the above sketched out components, to consider an application and check for non-existent innovations. Model confirmations can be directed by operationalization of the separate factors and assessment of relationships through basic condition modelling. Also, the subjective assessment on the explained models and hypotheses is confirmed by subjective research.

A surprising outcome for organizations that execute a great operational system is the special relationship between the judgments of the business danger of the New Product Development process.

The significance of understanding the consumer-related business processes in an organization and its aggressive condition to accomplish a compelling review is outstanding, especially for assessors. The company's objectives and systems and those business-related risks that may sensibly be relied upon to bring about dangers of material error are of high importance for directors. Additionally, a legitimate approach is important for developing a proper research methodology and to provide viable declarations from managers' part. For essentially new staff evaluators, the outcomes reveal previously unreported level of comprehension of process-situated business dangers.

This research represents an attempt to investigate the topic of sustainable business practices and further research is required to gain more in-depth insights. The study gave predefined statements about the sustainable business practices implemented and further studies might analyse the intensity and the effectiveness of the taken actions. Also, the attitudes of the employees and their opinion towards benefits and barriers in the implementation of the practices might be a valuable field of research. The detailed study about the perception of managers and their willingness to include sustainability criteria in the decision-making process could reveal interesting results and might also represent an area worth exploring.

Conclusions

The concept of sustainability is an ancient and widespread principle of human thought and action. Ever since ancient times humans have guided themselves by this principle and have lived in harmony with nature, in a way in which resources were preserved. The term "sustainability" was first used in this context at the beginning of the 18th century in forestry and, since then, it has been subject to constant changes.

In companies, when entrepreneurs understood their impact on the environment, and the responsibility they have towards it and the communities they belong to, sustainability became a major issue. Furthermore, since its direct correlation with profitability became indisputable, it turned into a subject of high importance on the entrepreneurs' agendas. This process has been going on for decades. The concept of business sustainability is the striving for industry self-regulation, that increasingly tends to implement sustainable business practices. The motives and the attitudes of managers are likely to be influenced by factors such as size, ownership or location of the business.

Lately, sustainability has faced and still faces an increasing significance and consideration in the professional workplace. The main determinants may be related to social viewpoints, administrative perspectives, client prerequisites, among others. Numerous organizations are embracing sustainability in all their hierarchical levels, activities and business forms overall. However, there are many organizations that have not yet achieved the sustainability level as targeted in the initiation phase of their company. One cause may be the fact that most sustainability-related activities are focused on one particular division, or territory of the association, instead of approaching them in a more holistic manner. The organization, in its entirety, should focus on the same goal, respectively achieving a high level of sustainability through its activities. In such a context, a more refined examination is necessary, and this should consider the entire communication procedure to assess the full status of the sustainability execution.

The present thesis has aimed to investigate the development of sustainable business processes in global companies, in a challenging environment.

In order to achieve its goal, it has been structured into two main parts, comprising five main chapters. The first part outlined the current status of research in the area of sustainability, while the second emphasised the main personal contributions and studies developed in the research area.

The first chapter approached a series of theoretical aspects regarding business processes and project management. It aimed to feature the similarity and impact of

V. Just, *Sustainable Business Processes in Global Companies*,
Sustainable Management, Wertschöpfung und Effizienz,
https://doi.org/10.1007/978-3-658-28196-0

business process administration and sustainability, taking into consideration various kinds of organization forms, economic sustainability and sustainability for business association and procedures. In such a framework, the chapter proved, supported and promoted the idea that sustainability in business process administration enhances the company's success in all areas.

The chapter started with general aspects about the business process, an aspect that exists in every company and in all of its departments. Business processes are crucial for the success of any organization. After presenting a thorough analysis of different approaches to business processes, the definition used in the present thesis was emphasized. Respectively, business processes are referred to as a sequence of steps developed in a logical order, having a well-defined starting and finishing point, which leads to a desired result.

Afterwards, a clear distinction between primary processes and supportive processes in organizations and their classification was accomplished. Porter's value chain model, which forms on a division of primary and secondary activities, bears direct relation to business processes. In accordance with the highly acknowledged value chain model, a classification of business processes can be determined. Generally, it can be stated that primary processes in the value chain are those directly involved in value creation, by producing goods or services, respectively logistics, marketing and sales. The remaining processes – supportive processes – have a supportive function and they may refer to procuring, controlling and human resources, for example. Other classification of business processes may be accomplished based on their degree of formality, process-oriented thinking and on an analytical approach, among other aspects.

Business processes and process management can be approached as important elements for achieving the companies' goals. Closely related to these aspects, project management is thoroughly approached further on in chapter one, emphasising its importance for business process improvement. Project management implies starting, arranging, executing, controlling, and achieving a particular objective in a predetermined time. Strategic company plans are regularly realised in the projects procedure. In business practice, objectives are increasingly planned and accomplished in project programs. Referring only to the assessment of strategic projects – and their impact to the planned business goals – project portfolio management is a fresh approach for a lot of businesses. However, other means of assessment of the business performance might include, among others, the project scorecard and the balanced scorecard. All these assessment tools were detailed in chapter one.

The second chapter of the thesis closed the first part by approaching interesting theoretical aspects related to sustainability in business processes, risk and risk management.

Firstly, the chapter approached sustainability issues, especially in relation to economic development and business performance. In an extremely dynamic and changing environment, businesses have to quickly react and adapt, in order to ensure their survival and success on the market. Due to the cumulative impact of social and environmental issues on business success, companies are more oriented towards sustainability, which is generally based on economic, ecological and social pillars. In such a context, the requirements for sustainable business processes have increased tremendously. Processes are part of the infrastructure of every company and are an essential component in the analysis of corporate performance when it comes to business sustainability. Therefore, process modelling is essential for an organization. Various types of process modelling, such as the Value Chain Diagram, Event-Oriented Process Chain, Event-based Process Chain in Column Form, Swim Lane Process Mapping Diagram, Term-based Models, Business Process Modelling Notation (BPMN), were debated in the chapter.

Further on, the second chapter outlined important information related to sustainability in business processes, focusing on the importance of process management and risk management when acting in complex environments.

All aspects of process management influence sustainability. A high level of process orientation is an important element to gain sustainability, too. Process orientation implies the support of the company's vision and derived strategies, as well as emphasizing the core competences. It also strengthens the customer orientation within the company and leads to continuous improvement of processes and performance.

Sustainability for process management is an important factor for corporate success; sustainability cannot be generalized but gained by matching the company's individual process needs with generally accepted aspects specific to process management. In order to create a sustainable process, all specific characteristics must be clearly defined and marked, all steps of the process management must be documented and shared with all involved parties, and all risks related to the process must be identified and analysed. Sustainability should also be incorporated in management, risk methods and practices. Sustainability covers the political, monetary and social aspects, whereas sustainability-related risks should be a key element in investigating the risks of an organization, especially when considering their potential budgetary effects.

Long-term sustainable business processes require efficient sustainability management and regular monitoring of the defined sustainability goals. Sustainability performance measurement offers many advantages to the company, such as satisfying the information needs of stakeholders.

When assessing the performance of an organization, the obtained profit and the return of investment are the key metrics taken into consideration by shareholders. However, the social responsibility and the environmental factors should also play a decisive role when considering a sustainable development of the company.

Companies increasingly align their products and processes to the idea of sustainable development. Measurement represents an essential precondition for improved sustainability. The appropriate key performance indicators to make the sustainability performance of companies quantifiable and controllable, should be measured, monitored and adjusted, in order to achieve sustainable development and processes. Indicators are an important means for measuring, predicting, planning, and managing, playing a key role in the determination of the achievement of targets and the identification of needs for optimization.

The second part of the thesis outlined the main personal contributions and studies developed in the research area, all well-structured into three chapters.

The third chapter approached the influence of the risk management and the project management on business performance, taking into consideration sustainability issues.

The chapter started with highlighting important aspects about risk management and project management, as these represent essential elements that need to be considered when assessing the business performance, especially when sustainability aspects are approached.

Project management influences the success and development of a company. In order to ensure successful business processes, project management needs to have controlling methods and indices aiming to comprehensively plan, steer, supervise, evaluate, and control the projects. Indices for project management control can be established from quantitative, as well as qualitative criteria. Quantitative criteria compare costs, time, earnings and yield returns, while qualitative criteria refer to the potential or the attractiveness of a project. Quantitative indices may refer to Cash flow, Rate of return, Return on Investment (ROI), Cash Flow ROI (CFROI), Amortisation duration (Ad), or the Expected Commercial Value (ECV). On the other hand, qualitative indices may include strategic contributions, interdependencies, target achievement, etc.

Besides project management, risk management is also vital for achieving business goals.

Characterized as any occasion or condition that could unfavourably influence the accomplishment of business goals, within the chapter, risk was approached from the perspective of the risk management system and of the Enterprise Risk Management (ERM). A risk management system comprises of hierarchical segments to actualize and execute risk management. The risk management process itself guarantees the treatment of risks, as distinguishing, assessment, observing, and detailing. Risk management is a continuous process. ERM incorporates various procedures and strategies, representing a coordinated way to deal with the risks of organizations. Due to the expansion in ecological complexity, an institutionalized approach of managing risks and openings isn't just helpful, but also significant for business continuation. The way associations manage such risks is the key part for progress and can be found in the organization's general performance.

Further on, the third chapter focused on assessing risk management in the context of business performance. Risks may be assessed using both quantitative (monetary) and qualitative (subjective) techniques. Quantitative techniques are, generally, centred around the calculation of certain monetary factors and their connection (e.g. affectability examination, situation investigation), while subjective techniques regularly accentuate the information of risk proprietors or risk takers (e.g. interviews, cross-useful workshops).

In the ERM assessment process, the singularity of each organization must be considered. Approaching ERM as a proper way to deal with the different risks an association might face (counting risks with regards to sustainability), it appears to be legitimate to assess the result in monetary figures as well as from other perspectives. Therefore, along with quantitative methodologies, subjective ones are expected to comprehend the importance of ERM for each organization. In this way, the usage of key performance indicators (KPIs), as well as vital objectives, the association and every connected procedure as to the sustainability point, is pertinent. Besides, in order to assess the viability of other ERM methods, KPIs can also be employed. These refer to an improved version of the Balanced Scorecard technique and the Economic Value Added (EVA), which were thoroughly presented in the chapter.

However, the chapter focuses on KPIs. Companies usually measure their sustainability performance using special indicators, so-called KPIs, since their use is seen as a promising method for measuring the sustainability of business processes. A large number of key figures can be accessed from different sources, which are more or less suitable, depending on the sector and company. KPIs can provide companies with information on the sustainability of their business processes and support the optimization of sustainability performance, with the help of defined targets. Due to the high importance of the economic activity in an organization, economical KPIs were the core of the analysis outlined further on in the chapter. Social or ecological KPIs were not particularly addressed. There are numerous economical KPIs, such as: revenue, operating costs, salaries, donations, taxes, financial consequences of climate change, corporate social benefits, public financial inflows (subsidies), local personnel, operating result, net value added, sales growth, equity ratio, return on equity, return on debt, development of fixed assets, return on investment (ROI), development of working capital (WC), etc. However, the focus of the chapter was only on sales growth, operating result (EBIT), equity ratio, and return on equity.

As sustainability and business performance are strongly related to quality, chapter three ended up by outlining a series of aspects specific to the implementation of EFQM and the Project Excellence Model in project management. The Project Excellence Model affects the achievement of business goals. Accordingly, an organization that tries to be effective ought to apply the Project Excellence Model or EFQM in the task administration process. Consequently, it can be disputed that EFQM and the Project Excellence Model cohere concerning sustainable business success.

To somehow translate various theoretical aspects into practice, chapter four outlined an innovative approach to performant business models in a sustainable context, focusing on the transport industry and promoting the idea of car-sharing, especially car-sharing with self-driving cars, in the particular case of Germany. After the assessment of present and future transport modes, car-sharing with self-driving cars was promoted as a sustainable business model in the transport industry. In the end, the chapter outlined a series of future directions and challenges specific to the investigated topic. Furthermore, an innovative analysis focused on three main directions has been developed in chapter four. This related to the mid-2012 until mid-2017 time span, and aimed at: analysing the level of data/information on self-driving vehicles (in view of Google Trends); estimating the subjective evaluation of the recognized pinnacles (occasions) that prompt an expansion of required data (therefore an increment of the hunt list); comparing the normal evaluation with consequences for the share trading system. The analysis revealed that the most researched term was the one equivalent to "self-driving vehicles", while the pattern analysis of financial markets demonstrated a reasonable connection of subjective evaluation and stock cost for the investigated cases.

Different social, economic, demographic, political etc. changes that societies face nowadays, are highly impacting the current characteristics of mobility. Investigating the case of Germany, such particular challenges may be translated to: urbanization, aging population, reduction in the number of persons per household, reduction in the consumption of resources, limited financial resources for infrastructure, increase in demand for multimodality, higher demand for flexibility in regard to mobility. Considering these changes, in order to face them in the most effective and efficient manner, a series of requirements can be identified for developing an innovative and sustainable future urban mobility system in Germany, which was the aim of the chapter. To determine these requirements, the modal split in Germany represented the starting point in the analysis outlined the chapter.

Mobility itself does not portray a thought process, but is utilized rather to physically achieve another objective: development. The choice of transport depends on various criteria, especially on individual conditions. These criteria can be derived from the marketing mix. The weaknesses of each transport mode become obvious, requiring their improvement using innovative approaches, especially in order to meet the public needs regarding the product, price, place, and promotion. However, due to its insignificance, the last component of the marketing mix (promotion) was not thoroughly approached.

Socio-demographic changes and an increased demand for mobility require a paradigm shift in the establishment of mobility services. After analysing the most well-known methods of transport, it was revealed that many of the current transport modes can't satisfy Germans' wants and needs. In such a context, innovative solutions should be developed by both existing companies and start-ups acting in the transport industry. Implementing a self-driving car-sharing model in Germany would shift the existing mobility towards a more sustainable, future-oriented one. The self-driving car-sharing model could be given by the state (open transport) or by private mobility suppliers, such as automotive manufacturers or software provides such as Google, for example. If such a model could be widely implemented, this could respond to socio-demographic changes, as well as to a considerable number of other important current issues in the mobility area.

Assisted driving systems have been including various functionalities, nowadays achieving the status of semi-automated driving. This advancement depends on different worldwide megatrends specific to the most recent decades, among which digitization has been the most pronounced. Furthermore, a series of prerequisites to future mobility systems are directly connected with demographic, legislative, economical, social, and innovative related issues.

As the automobile (as an item) gets an impressive extent of a client's normal wage and since the usage rate is, or may be low, customers become especially interested in sharing solutions. Car sharing may be approached in two particular ways – free-coasting and perpetual station car-sharing models – that are depicted by their (versatile) get and drop-off zone. Various factors supporting the development of such a model may refer to cost savings, environmental friendliness, administrational effort reduction, and fun, among other aspects. However, the most representative, especially in attracting clients, are low costs and car availability.

Companies acting in the automotive industry are concentrating their efforts towards understanding how customers use and benefit their services. Some manufacturers offer value-adding services to the car-sharing experience itself, such as app development. However, the best business model could be represented by providing fully autonomous vehicles to car-sharing service providers. These are just a few examples of how car manufactures can change their business model and switch from car production alone to implementing and providing additional services.

The idea of self-driving cars in a car-sharing model is based on the classical model of taxi companies, which is characterized by flexible places of return. With many of these providers, customers have the opportunity to order a vehicle via a smartphone to their site or to locate a vehicle in the vicinity, while the payment of the service can be carried out directly via an app. Unlike the current system with drivers, the idea of a model with self-driving vehicles could incorporate a much higher flexibility: vehicles are distributed automatically according to the transport flow analysis throughout the city centre, in order to reduce waiting time for customers as much as possible. At the same time, the function of a smart carpooling solution may be integrated, due to customers' demands. This would mean that customers will take a small detour to reduce their own travel costs while automatically being shared through the system with other customers in the vehicle.

Car sharing, as part of individual motorized transportation, currently faces various issues. One of the most important is related to the distance from door to car-sharing station or car location. If this distance could be minimized, more people would use this transport mode. Comparing the car-sharing offer with the use of a private car, it requires less effort in terms of maintenance as this is usually done through the car-sharing provider. Factors against car-sharing may refer to uncertainty about availability, the discomfort of driving someone else's car, the effort and complexity of renting and the lack of car-sharing offers close-by.

However, some of these issues may be solved through focusing on the "positioning" component of the marketing mix when considering the possibility of self-driving cars in the development of a car-sharing model. Positioning is characterized by the product (self-driving cars in a car-sharing model), its distinct features in contrast to present transport modes, and the characteristics of the customer. Positioning relates to flexibility, costs, availability, accessibility, total travel time, reliability, low complexity of using, no or low maintenance, comfort. In terms of the distinctive features of positioning, products become accessible to everyone, there is little complexity but a high level of comfort. In terms of customers' satisfaction, positioning leads to an increase in demand for flexibility. Self-driving cars can be provided from the place of departure to the final destination (door-to-door mobility). An app can support the booking of a car, in order to provide the car at the desired place. Cars are provided by a third party, and there is no need for registration, maintenance etc. It also saves time, as there will be no waiting time for public transport, and no time related to searching for parking space. It allows for ecological friendliness as the car arrives when called at any time of day, and a broader group can be reached than in the case of a private car or public transport: e.g. elderly people who don't want to drive anymore or children, blind people etc.

In addition, self-driving vehicles in a car-sharing model simultaneously bear several challenges and obstacles, which could lead to problems or even failure of such a business model. These challenges include technical, operational, political, and social aspects. While the social challenge is minimized to the factor of acceptance, the technical challenge refers to the vehicles themselves and less to the car-sharing model. Technology acceptance is understood as a psychological process that starts with pure interest in an innovation and leads toward the regular use of this innovation. Consequently, acceptance can be defined as a collection of evaluation and effects. Acceptance represents a critical success factor when dealing with innovations. Self-driving cars in a car-sharing model represent a sustainable mobility concept that takes the changing environment into account and implements most motives from a customer perspective in regard to the choice of transportation. The political challenge is currently strongly determined by legislation, which must be adjusted according to the technology and the possibilities of autonomous cars, in order to allow a large-scale deployment and expansion. Ultimately, the challenge lies in the operation and maintenance of self-driving vehicles in a car sharing model and the associated services, for example app development, generally for smartphones.

The last chapter of the thesis focused on a comprehensive and complex case study research which aimed to reveal insight into the structure and difficulties related to the development of sustainable business processe, keeping in mind the end goal of generating a system for supporting directors in enhancing their business models.

Focusing on a contemporary phenomenon outlined in its real-life context, the main research method implied was the exploratory and descriptive case study research. Aiming to answer the main research question, referring to the way business processes can be improved in global companies in a sustainable context, a single-case study was developed, based on a holistic approach. However, some other small pieces of research were carried out mainly for strengthening the case study results.

The additional pieces of research consisted in analysing various articles, news etc. about other global companies, important players in their field of activity.

The chapter was centred on a case study to increase process efficiency, quality and agility in business processes, by taking the example of sales support processes in various countries. The overall aim of the case study was to ensure quick adaptability of processes through standardization and further automation that shall support the sustainability of processes.

The case study research was based on a comprehensive literature review process and on a complex analysis of a company's internal records and documents. Furthermore, qualitative pieces of research were also carried out to expand the methods of data collection and to bring new insights to the investigated issues. Onsite visits were accomplished, unstructured interviews were carried out and video conferences were held. Following an inductive approach, all the research outcomes were interpreted and complemented with the authors' extensive knowledge and expertise in global companies; their synthesis is outlined further on.

An activity developed since ancient times – commerce, more precisely selling – was chosen as the main topic of interest in terms of business processes in the case study framework. In present times, the selling system faces important challenges and changes, especially due to the technological advancement. The increasing digitalisation of the world comes with many advantages, but also responsibilities for companies. In such a context, many tasks have to be mastered in a modern sales organisation. Some examples may refer to adapting modern and efficient sales strategies, developing new sales and marketing channels and customer behaviour, being always one step ahead of the customer and addressing customer problems individually instead of offering standard solutions. This underlines the importance of pure (sales) competencies, processes and strategic partnerships. All business processes are becoming more transparent for the customer. In order to ensure success in such a process-oriented, competitive industry, trends must be identified and exploited at an early stage, especially in sales organizations. Sales have already undergone an enormous change – but the real revolution is still to come. Before a company's sales organization can be planned, the actual strategic orientation must be thoroughly worked out and thought through. The sales strategy is regarded as a long-term orientation of all sales activities of a company, which are adapted to customer and market requirements. For the sales management, this means recognizing market changes and changes in customer needs at an early stage, considering all possible dangers. If this advanced planning fails, no reasonable sales strategy can be derived; this way, the continued existence of the entire company is in danger in the long term. At the same time, a well-designed sales strategy enables the anticipation of the market potential that might be exploited to achieve long-term and sustainable corporate success through competitive advantages and to minimize risks. In addition to the specific markets and products, the core content of a sales strategy is the selection of the company's target customer groups and the proper sales channels. Other elements of a sales strategy include sales volumes, prices, resources, profit contributions, risks, and revenue streams. In order to define these strategy contents and parameters in a meaningful way, the sales management has to have an accurate, realistic image of the current status, but also of future developments. One appropriate approach for the development of the strategy is the 7C model. The starting point in this model is the strategic core of the company, which consists of the range of services, the customer segments and the markets relevant to the company. The following six factors are derived from this core, considering both the current and the future/target status and refer to: customer perception, customer interface, internal value chain, cooperation, concepts for the future, and human capital.

In order to make certain that the company's customers are efficiently served, especially in accordance with their individual needs, the sales management must also define and design a sales organization structure. Usually, this determines which customers are served by which employees, in which markets. This organisation can be classically regulated according to function, territory/region, products or product lines, customers or a mixture of these alternatives.

In addition to the strategic orientation and organization of sales, sales controlling is the third dimension in the management of sales organizations. As part of the management and measurement of sales activities, various concepts are developed to measure the overall corporate success factors, such as the key performance indicators. Some of the most relevant key performance indicators that companies might take into consideration when assessing their selling activity are turnover, revenue, gross profit, customer satisfaction, incoming orders, etc. On the other hand, other performance indicators may refer to market and customer potential, volume of contracts, number of complaints, etc. The key performance indicators play the most important role in a serious planning process. They are clearly related to the performance of the company and serve as a guide for management and as comparative or control values. The key performance indicators are defined by the performance indicators which serve for detailed and targeted control and the thorough control of smaller factors.

The company analysis deals with internal factors of the company and compares possible specific strengths and weaknesses of the organisation with other market players in a sector. The analysis focuses on the company's strategic goal, its trained competencies and their impact on future business development. In addition to the analysis of internal strengths, weaknesses, risks and opportunities, the company's environment is also examined and analysed in more detail during the strategic planning process. As the term 'corporate environmental analysis' shows, the corporate environmental analysis is always placed in the context of the corporate environment. Porter has developed a suitable method for determining the business environment, which defines and analyses the five competitive forces ("five forces") of an industry. These competitive forces include suppliers, customers, replacement products, the company's potential market supporters and existing industry competition. Porter's model is based on the company's relative position to the industry as a whole and how competitive forces are handled. The analysis focuses on direct competitors, customers and the company itself. The aim of this method and the measures derived from it try to achieve the best possible position in the industry and, implicitly generate higher income. On this basis, other instruments of a company analysis can be built up, such as competition analysis, SWOT analysis or the analysis of internal and external factors of a company.

A classical tool for determining the external factors is the PESTEL analysis, which examines the political, economic, social, technological, environmental/ecological and legal dimensions of a company. As is the case of most company or environment analyses, it is of great importance to regularly and conscientiously carry out the PESTEL analysis, as the above-mentioned dimensions of the analysis can constantly evolve and change. It is important to determine the relevance of the factors for the company in order to evaluate the analyses. Not every factor is actually important for the company or the industry. It is therefore advisable to determine which dimensions are particularly essential and should be thoroughly examined before the analysis is carried out. The analysis of the internal and external factors can be accomplished for the entire industry, the company or just one organizational unit. The influencing factors particularly addressing the selling activity may be divided in: external factors (high demand, intense competition, market dynamics, number of customers, etc.) and internal factors (number of internal projects, low resources, variety of offered products and services, new acquired skills, etc.). Lewin's model can be used to document certain management decisions and thus make changes more acceptable, in the organization or workforce. Within the case study research frame, driving forces were used to understand future environmental changes in sales and sales support processes, following the scheme: Current sales and sales support processes ➔ Driving forces ➔ Current sales and sales support processes ➔ Transformation process – Implementation of measures ➔ Future sales and sales support processes. All future driving forces were considered for the definition of upcoming measures on sales and sales support processes. Driving forces are parameters, which will influence a defined object in the future. Within the case study, the conducted analysis of driving forces has given relevant insights to the changing environment and future requirements for Company X. To gain general findings, these have been corroborated with scientific studies. The main cornerstones regarding the future process design, resulted from the driving forces analysis, were related to: becoming more customer-oriented; gathering customer feedback; digitalization; commoditization; social mediatization throughout the society, especially in social media platforms; globalization; offered products/services; markets/needs served; generating capability or cost advantage; selling techniques; distribution methods.

The internal process landscape, as a result of process assessment, might include the following steps: negotiate and set up business relationships; receive and enter orders; process and adjust orders, invoice, clarify and receive payments; distribute products; handle claims and returns. However, in a more particular case, important internal processes might also be considered in terms of the customer accounting, credit management, customer master data, and sales support activities. Focusing on the selling activity, in the particular case of the Company X, sustainable business processes might refer to: digital process integration; reliability-driven business relationships; service-oriented order processing; real-time information service; collaborative process management; smart order control.

The way highly competitive and challenging environment businesses are acting currently, model innovation is recognized as an important lever to achieve competitive advantage; this subject was thoroughly approached in the chapter. Business models and business model innovation are still rather nascent fields of research, characterized by unclear perceptions and a general lack of relevant empirical knowledge. This is particularly true for the intersection of both fields, which describes the process of using openness in innovating the business model of established firms.

After an exhaustive presentation of various approaches on business models, the chapter outlined important information specific to the company included in the case study, which can be easily replicated to other global companies, too.

Considering company X, an innovation analysis of its business model, focused on outlining its internal and external influencing factors and on describing the effects of change forces in prevailing company conditions, revealed the following:

- Consumers: the digital transformation empowers consumers through better access and product knowledge; online reviews are crucial in the decision-making process when purchasing home appliances; consumers expect a personalized, seamless, convenient shopping, and interactive product experience across all touch points; Europe's ageing population will lead to the growth of customers that will want simple access and customer service; offline commerce may still dominate, although online sales are expected to expand.

- Customer: the customer market is still consolidating; the increase in negotiating power is threatening the Company's product margins; customers develop their multi-sales channel capabilities; the combination of physical locations vs. digital platforms for a customer presence are emerging; customer requirements are further rising.
- Competitors: the home appliance market in Europe is characterized by low growth rate, forecasts and uncertainty; continued consolidation, strategic pricing attacks, cost savings, potential disruptive mergers and acquisitions or joint ventures activities will be the main threats; company's Region Europe markets are very heterogeneous in terms of size, market volume, customer group structure and consumer purchasing power.
- Company: in order to reach the Company's ambitious 2025 targets, growth in all product price ranges is necessary; operational excellence will be key to remain competitive; in particular, sales cost growth shall be proportional to turnover growth; the company has to develop an integrated, connected ecosystem to justify a premium price and combat price erosions; big data analytics capabilities have to be developed; the company needs an enhanced content management system to address new formats and customer requirements.

Throughout the case investigation, various stages in business model invocation were revealed. The starting stage in business model innovation processes can be portrayed by exercises which focus on the comprehension and checking of the encompassing centre system of the advancing firm. The external environment includes different players such as clients, providers, competitors, colleges, or governments and quickly impacts the activities of the central firm. Ideation, the second stage in the nonexclusive innovation process, additionally has its importance and particular difficulties in the business model innovation setting. It centres around the age of thoughts for potential new business models. The third stage – reconciliation – assumes its part and role in the business model innovation. The exercises inside this stage centre around the improvement of another business model in view of promising thoughts distinguished in the ideation stage. They should be changed into a total and feasible business model. As the new business model should be adjusted and incorporated within the partners' business models, multi-sided quality emerges that requires a great deal of vitality and capacity to persuade. The test distinguished here is not quite the same as the one recognized amid the start stage, albeit both allude to the cooperation between partners. Amid the start stage, the test is to comprehend the requirements, driving forces, and openings in the association's external environment, with the specific end goal to recognize a beginning stage for another business model. Here, amid the reconciliation stage, the distinguished test alludes to the incorporation of partners into the development of new, solid business models. The new models will work if every included partner bolster them and modify their business models accordingly. Subsequently, firms need to effectively deal with their partners. The last innovation process stage – usage – is obviously a pivotal point in time for business model innovations, excessively. Once completely outlined and incorporated, the new business model can be updated. Usually, this includes immense speculations to be made and risks to be taken by the central firm. Rather than item innovation, where early models can be shared and assessed with clients amid their advancement, another business model should be completely and frequently updated before it can be tried. The execution of another business model can be the hardest task of all. The most difficult thing with business model innovation is to effectively update the new business model. Generally, people are reluctant to change because they fear about new circumstance or because they simply don't see any motivation to change, as the old business model is still perfectly functionable. Fundamentally, overseeing hierarchical change isn't a simple task, and the all-encompassing extent of the business model that expects changes to a wide range of territories inside the firm makes it significantly harder. At this stage, it is essential to act in a transparent manner and to clarify how the new business model can help the organization.

A powerful procedure for reasonable advancement requires great management. It must give coordination, initiative, organization, and money related control, outfitting aptitudes and limits and guaranteeing adherence to timetables. The parts, duties, and connection dispatches between the distinctive key members in procedure processes must be unmistakably characterized and comprehended.

Transition Management enables associations to advance toward their desired state. Switching from the actual business model to the desired one is not an easy task. To do this, inner change operators are named to lead the usage of particular parts of the transition procedure. The general procedure is completely customer driven and encouraged through a point by point change management system. Key Performance Indicators are explored as a feature of a progressing change activity. A key differentiator to the transition procedure is a cross-utilitarian and interdisciplinary structure. This structure guarantees that vital activities are tended to as a piece of the transition, notwithstanding those identified with strategic usage. The way to update an effective transition is to limit interruption to existing services, at the beginning and all through the transition procedure. Transition work streams and an itemised transition plan including points of reference, all movement and information required from the customer give a system to every territory of administration conveyance. Transition plans incorporate key dates and tasks, notices, interdependencies, and points of reference.

Furthermore, as the open business model was revealed as the most efficient and effective one, the case revealed five main precedents that lead firms to open up their business models, respectively: business model inconsistency, the need to create and capture new value, past involvement in cooperation, business model patterns, and industry meeting. Organizations with conflicting business model in the beginning – few components are missing or are not outlined in a fitting way – are probably going to open their business model keeping in mind the end goal to incorporate the missing assets and capacities of partners. The second recognized predecessor for opening business models is the need to create and capture new value. Firms are progressively under strain to maintain their execution and advantages. Organizations will probably enhance their business model if their old model does not work properly any longer. Adopting an open business model is widely embraced by entrepreneurs as an adequate method for creating and capturing value. Firms with a vast experience in cooperating with other firms will probably open their business model and vice versa. Firms learn and develop the abilities required to work together after a period of time; earlier joint effort encounter prompt and powerful coordinated efforts and enhances cooperation results. A main trigger for businesses to open their business model lay in other effective open business models, too. Usually, businesses analyse other businesses and if the open business model results in an important value generator, such an approach is immediately imitated and implemented. Furthermore, industry meeting triggers open business models in two courses, through innovation union, influencing fundamentally R&D, and through the energy of new market participants, requiring more extensive business model changes. Scholars have broadly perceived that industry union rethinks the structure and the aggressive forces in an industry. Innovative advancements trigger the making of new progressive firms which, thusly, challenge industry limits and the incentives of industry pioneers. As a result, firms need to obtain the necessary abilities to approach their market position in a more extensive way. Furthermore, they have to reconsider their business model of significant value creation and capture, to react to the new circumstance – henceforth they have to alter their business model.

Innovation changes; digitisation and service changes represent important factors that set off the re-examination of the business model. In present times, managers are very much aware of the significance of business model innovation and realize that open business models regularly prompt unrivalled execution. In such a context, they need to acquire knowledge about when to adjust their business model and whether presenting more transparency is a valuable action in their specific case.

The research findings provided significant insights for specialists in their process of developing sustainable open business models for their businesses. Considering all the information outlined in the last chapter, especially focusing on the highlighted precedents, directors ought to effectively consider opening their business models. This is of high pertinence since, as often as possible, business model pioneers enter from outside the business. Directors need to frequently check these points, always concentrating on achieving the final objective, respectively gaining supremacy on the market.

Even if the case study research was based only on a single case, its results may be easily considered as a best practice guide and can be replicated to other global companies, too, especially with the main aim to improve their business model performance.

The research results support other studies' findings promoted in the scientific literature, bringing at the same time an innovative perspective on the investigated issue. This enables the profound examination of information in an explorative way and allows significant outcomes to common-sense issues. This is an attractive conclusion of the research results, outlining a promising course for future research. The acknowledgment of innovations is quantifiable with innovation acknowledgment models and speculations. Non-existent innovations that bring issues to light through a long improvement process are intelligible for acknowledgment estimating with existent models and hypotheses. However, these models and hypotheses require minor alterations if there should be an occurrence of utilization to innovations.

This research, implicitly the present thesis, represents an attempt to investigate the topic of sustainable business practices and further research is required to gain more in-depth insights. The study gave predefined statements about the sustainable business practices implemented and further studies might analyse the intensity and the effectiveness of the taken actions. Also, the attitudes of the employees and their opinion towards benefits and barriers in the implementation of the practices might be a valuable field of research. The detailed study about the perception of managers and their willingness to include sustainability criteria in the decision-making process could reveal interesting results and might also represent an area worth exploring.

Bibliography

Abdelkafi, N., & Täuscher, K. (2016). *Business models for sustainability from a system dynamics perspective*. Organization & Environment, 29(1), 74-96.

Agudo-Valiente, J. M., Garcés-Ayerbe, C., & Salvador-Figueras, M. (2015). *Corporate social performance and stakeholder dialogue management*. Corporate Social Responsibility and Environmental Management, 22(1), 13-31.

Akrivou, K., & Bradbury-Huang, H. (2015). *Educating integrated catalysts: Transforming business schools toward ethics and sustainability*. Academy of Management Learning & Education, 14(2), 222-240.

Amidi, S. (2016). Neue Geschäftsmodelle. Automobilwoche. http://www.automobilwoche.de/article/20160715/AGENTURMELDUNGEN/307149901/autokonzerne-suchen-nahe-zu-start-ups [Accessed July 20, 2016].

Anderson, Dan. R. (2005), *Corporate Survival: The Critical Importance of Sustainability Risk Management*, IUniverse, Lincoln. No. 10, pp. 21-22

Arnold, C.; Klee, C. (2015): *Akzeptanz von Produktinnovationen: Eine Einführung:* Springer Fachmedien Wiesbaden. https://books.google.de/books?id=NZ4vCwAAQBAJ.

Baccarini, David., *The concept of project complexity–a review. "In International Journal of Project Management", 14 Nr. 4, 201–204. Elsevier, 1996.*

Bahn A. G (2013) *Facts and Figures, about Sustainability 2013, for people*. For markets. For tomorrow. http://www.dbschenker.ch/file/log-ch-de/8643002/vmpwVeJu7jMIznTdC8QIljH66zo/8375298/data/facts_and_figures_2013.pdf, Einsicht: 06.04.2017

Bai, C., Sarkis, J., & Dou, Y. (2015). *Corporate sustainability development in China: review and analysis.* Industrial Management & Data Systems, 115(1), 5-40.

Bardt, H. (2011) *Indikatoren ökonomischer Nachhaltigkeit,* Forschungsberichte aus dem Institut der deutschen Wirtschaft, Köln 2011

Bartels, A., Just, V., Kompalla, A., Schmid, J. (2017) - *Forces And Effects In The Privatisation Process: An Empirical Study Of Telecommunications Companies In Germany And Romania.* Ecoforum, vol. 6, no. 1, pg. 1-8.

Bartels, A., Plesea, D.A., Studeny, M., Just,V. (201)6 *"Amfiteatru Economic"* The Interdependence Of Competition Policy, Consumer Policy and Regulation in Intro-

V. Just, *Sustainable Business Processes in Global Companies*,
Sustainable Management, Wertschöpfung und Effizienz,
https://doi.org/10.1007/978-3-658-28196-0

ducing and Safeguarding Effective Competition in the Eu Telecommunications Market Vol.19, No.45, p.367-380.

Bastian, H und Gleich. R (2011) *Komplexität in Beratungsprojekten*. European Business School, 15 (3): 193-196.

Bastian, H und Wald. A, Bibliometric, B (2011). *View on the Use of Contingency Theory in Project Management Research*. European Business School, Vol. 1, No. 1, pp. 230-261

Baumgartner, R. J., & Rauter, R. (2017). *Strategic perspectives of corporate sustainability management to develop a sustainable organization*. Journal of Cleaner Production, 140, 81-92.

Bayer, P. (2010)., *Was ist Komplexität?"* wandelweb.de. 11. April 2010. p=1039 (Zugriff am 22. Februar 2017). http://www.wandelweb.de/blog/?

Beasley, M, S.; Chen, A; Karen, N; Lorraine,W (2006). *Working Hand IN Hand:* Balanced Scorecards and Enterprise Risk Management, Strategic Finance; Vol. 87 Issue 9, p49

Becker, C., Betz, S., Chitchyan, R., Duboc, L., Easterbrook, S. M., Penzenstadler, B., & Venters, C. C. (2016). *Requirements: The key to sustainability. IEEE Software, 33*(1), 56-65.

Becker, J., (1995). *Grundsätze ordnungsmäßiger Modellierung*. Wirtschaftsinformatik. Management Science 35(8), 982–1003.

Becker, J.; Kugeler, M. and Rosemann, M., (2015). *Prozessmanagement Ein Leitfaden zur prozessorientierten Organisationsgestaltung*. Berlin: Springer. 23(4), 234-275

Behringer, S. (2014) *Konzerncontrolling*, 2. Auflage, Springer Gabler Verlag, Heidelberg. Business Strategy and the Environment, Vol. 11, 34-117

Bejinariu, R. M., Buchmüller, M. and Just, V., *Research on key factors impacting process sustainability global companies*, International Journal of Research in Computer Application and Management Vol. 4(11), p.22-31

Bejinariu, R. M., Just, V. (2016). *Research on Key Factors Impacting Process Sustainability Global Companies. 2nd International Conference BASIQ- New Trends in Sustainable Business and Consumption* - The Association for Innovation and Quality in Sustainable Business, The Faculty of Business and Tourism and The Allensbach University, 2-3 June 2016, Konstanz, Germany. Available from: http://www.conference.ase.ro/guide.html [Accessed 19 November 2017].

Berylls Strategy Advisors, (2016). *Gründe gegen die Nutzung von Carsharing in Deutschland im Jahr 2014 Statista, 2016*. http://de.statista.com/statistik/daten/studie/169936/umfrage/gruende-gegen-die-nutzung-von-carsharing-in-deutschland/ [Accessed on 14th Feb 2016].

Binckebanck, L., Elste, R. (Hrsg.) (2016): *Digitalisierung im Vertrieb, Strategien zum Einsatz neuer Technologien in Vertriebsorganisationen,* Springer Fachmedien, Wiesbaden, *Vol. 37 Iss: 8,* 1094 - 1110.

Blewitt, J., (2008). *Understanding Sustainable Development*. Journal of Marketing. Vol. 15(4): 335–343

BMVI, (2015). *Strategie automatisiertes und vernetztes Fahren.* , p.32.Bosch (Hrsg.) (2017) Reporting und Daten, Bosch Global https://www.bosch.com/de/nachhaltigkeit/reporting-und-daten/, Einsicht: 20.03.2017

Braulio-Gonzalo, M., Bovea, M. D., & Ruá, M. J. (2015*). Sustainability on the urban scale: Proposal of a structure of indicators for the Spanish context*. Environmental Impact Assessment Review, 53, 16-30.

Brocke, J., and Rosemann, M., (2014). *Handbook on business process management 2* - Strategic Alignement, Governance, People and Culture. 5 (7), S. 419–457

Brown, J. (2004). *Does Privatization Raise Productivity?* Evidence from Comprehensive Panel Data on Manufacturing Firms in Hungary, Romania, Russia, and Ukraine, Upjohn Institute Working Paper. no. 04-107, pp. 1-53.

Brucks, M (1986*),"A Typology of Consumer Knowledge Content*", in NA - Advances in Consumer Research. Association for Consumer Research Volume 13(8), Pages: 58-63.

Brünger, C (2009). Erfolgreiches Risikomanagement mit COSO ERM. Empfehlungen für die Gestaltung und Umsetzung in der Praxis. New York: Free Press. Vol. 19: 123-166.

Buchholz, D., Guodys, D., and Tietjen, S., (2015). *Methoden der Geschäftsprozessmodellierung im Vergleich. Study work. Hochschule für Ökonomie und Management Bremen*. Pp 75-83.

Buhr, A. (2011): *Vertrieb geht heute anders, Wie Sie den Kunden 3.0 begeistern*, GABAL Verlag, Offenbach. Vol.6, p. 16-72

Buhr, S., (2016). *Uber and Toyota confirm strategic investment and auto leasing deal.* https://techcrunch.com/2016/05/24/uber-and-toyota-confirm-strategic-deal/ [Accessed July 26, 2016].

Bundesamt, S (2016) *Verbraucherpreise, Preisindex für Telekommunikationsdienstleistungen, Destatis*, https://www.destatis.de/ DE/ ZahlenFakten/ GesamtwirtschaftUmwelt /Preise/ Verbraucherpreisindizes/ Tabellen_/Telekommunikationspreise.html, accessed September 22, 2016.

Bundesamt, S (Hrsg.) (2017). *Nachhaltige Entwicklung in Deutschland, Indikatorenbericht 2016*, Nachhaltigkeitsstrategie für Deutschland, Statistisches Bundesamt (Destatis), 2017

Bundesverband CarSharing e.V., (2015). *Carsharing-Balance 2015*: Further growth and adjustment in the German carsharing-market. http://www.carsharing.de/presse/pressemitteilungen/carsharing-balance-2015-further-growth-and-adjustment-the-german [Accessed July 27, 2016].

Buob, M. (2010): *Verkaufskomplexität im Außendienst, Konzeption, Erfolgsauswirkungen, Möglichkeiten im Umgang.* Ecological Economics 15 (3): 193-196.

Burlton, R. T., (2001). *Business Process Management: Profiting From Process. Indianapolis*: Sams Publishing.

Burlton, R.T. ,(2017). *Business Process Management: Profiting From Process. Indianapolis*: Journal of Marketing Intelligence & Planning, vol. 19 (5): 161-172.

Burns, T, und Stalker. G.M. (1961) *The Management of Innovation.* Educational Technology & Society, vol. 3 (3): 45-48.

BusinessDictionary (2017): *Online Definitionen und Wörterbuch* (Internetquelle) http://www.businessdictionary.com/definition/driving-forces.html,Einsichtnahme: 24.03.2017

Buttigieg, E., (2015). *Consumer and competition policies:* synergy needed. Consumer Policy Review, 15(5), pp.192-197.

Calvo-Mora, A., Navarro-García, A., & Periañez-Cristobal, R. (2015). *Project to improve knowledge management and key business results through the EFQM excellence model.* International Journal of Project Management, 33(8), 1638-1651.

Calvo-Mora, A., Navarro-García, A., Rey-Moreno, M., & Perianez-Cristobal, R. (2016). *Excellence management practices, knowledge management and key business re-*

sults in large organisations and SMEs: A multi-group analysis. European Management Journal, 34(6), 661-673.

Camilleri, M. A. (2015). *Valuing stakeholder engagement and sustainability reporting*. Corporate Reputation Review, 18(3), 210-222.

Campana, Christophe/Schott, Eric (2005): *Strategisches Projektmanagement,* Journal of American Academy of Business, p. 115-124

Carayannis, E. G., Sindakis, S., & Walter, C. (2015). *Business model innovation as lever of organizational sustainability*. The Journal of Technology Transfer, 40(1), 85-104.

Change-Management-Coach (2008): *Force Field Analysis:* Practical Application Tool, www.change-management-coach.com/force-field-analysis.html, Einsichtnahme: 08.02.2017.

Christensen, C. M., Raynor, M. E. and McDonald, R., (2015). *What Is Disruptive Innovation.* https://hbr.org/2015/12/what-is-disruptive-innovation [Accessed 12.12.2016].

Christian, K (2007), *Strategisches Multiprojektmanagement – Konzeption, Methoden und Strukturen, 2nd edition, Becker, Wolfgang (Hrsg.);* Weber, Jürgen (Hrsg.), Wiesbaden 2013, ISBN-13: 978-3835009158, p. 72-85.

Cilliers, P. (1998). *Complexity and Postmodernism*: Understanding Complex Systems. Journal of Applied Management & Entrepreneurship. Vol. 33, 403-522.

Clifton, J. (2003). *Privatisation in the European Union. Public Enterprises and Integration.* Academy of Management Review, 25(3), pp. 581-590.

Costanza, R. and Patten, B.C., (2015). *Defining and predicting sustainability*, Ecological Economics 15 (3): 193-196.

Crane, A., & Matten, D. (2016). *Business ethics: Managing corporate citizenship and sustainability in the age of globalization*. United Kingdom. *Oxford University Press.* Vol 5(2), pp. 70-80

Cuervo, A., and Villalonga, B., (2000). *Explaining the Variance in the Performance Effects of Privatization*. Academy of Management Review.

Cusumano, M., Kahl, S. & Suarez, F., (2006). *Product, process, and service: a new industry lifecycle model.* Journal of Service Management, 24(3), 245-267.

Dan, W (2017), *"The Simplicity Cycle."* ChangeThis. 26. April 2006. http://changethis.com/ manifesto/show/22. SimplicityCycle (Zugriff am 21. Februar 2017).

Dave. S (2010), "*The Origins of Cynefin*." Cognitive Edge. 24. August 2010. http://cognitive-edge.com/articles/summary-article-on-cynefin-origins/ (Zugriff am 21. Februar 2017).

David M, P., Peter J. T (2012). *ERM Determinants, Use, and Effects on the Firm,* American Risk and Insurance Association Annual Meeting, Minneapolis, MN, August 2012. 4(3), pp.13-25.

Davies, A., (2016). Maven, GM's Car-Sharing Scheme, *Is REally About Driverless Future*. Wired. Available at: https://www.wired.com/2016/01/maven-gms-car-sharing-scheme-is-really-about-a-driverless-future/ [Accessed July 29, 2016].

DeBord, M., (2016). *Self-driving cars make all the difference. Business Insider Deutschland*. Available at: http://www.businessinsider.de/musk-tesla-car-sharing-2016-7?r=US&IR=T [Accessed July 29, 2016].

Deepa, M., Barua, A und Whinston, A (2010) "*An Empirical Analysis of the Impact of Information Capabilities Design on Business Process Outsourcing Performance*." MIS Quarterly Vol. 34, No. 1, März 2010: 39-62.

Deloitte, T (2015). *Industry 4.0. Challenges and solutions for the digital transformation and use of exponential technologies*. Deloitte, pp.1–30.

Denning, S., (2016). *Can new disruption research suggest defenses against threats and opportunities for innovators?.* Strategy & Leadership, [e-journal] 44(3), pp.3-8. http://dx.doi.org/10.1108/SL-04-2016-0024.

Deutschland, V (Ed), (2016). *Auto nutzen statt besitzen*. Available at: https://www.vcd.org/themen/auto-umwelt/carsharing/ [Accessed on 13th Feb 2016].

Dharwadkar, R., George, G., & Brandes, P. (2000) *Privatization in emerging economies*: An agency theory perspective, Academy of Management Review, 25(3), July 2000, pp. 650-669.

Diamandis, P., (2015). *12 Industries Disrupted by Tech Companies Expanding Into New Markets.* https://singularityhub.com/2015/10/26/12-industries-disrupted-by-tech-companies-expanding-into-new-markets [Accessed 5.01.2017].

Diehlmann, J. & Häcker, J., (2013). *Automotive Management: Navigating the next decade of auto industry transformation,* De Gruyter. Volume 22, Number 6, pp. 703-804

Dietz, W., 2016. Neue Geschäftsmodelle. Automobilwoche: http://www.automobilwoche.de/article/20160715/AGENTURMELDUNGEN/307149901/autokonzerne-suchen-nahe-zu-start-ups [Accessed July 20, 2016].

Doppelt, B. (2017). *Leading change toward sustainability: A change-management guide for business, government and civil society*. Routledge. Vol. 3(8). Pp 205-302

Dürr, M. (2011). *Bioenergie und Nachhaltigkeit*: Ein Bewertungsmodell für Bionenergieprojekte und dem Aspekt der Nachhaltigkeit, in: Reihe Nachhaltigkeit, Band 42, Diplomica Verlag GmbH, Hamburg 2011

EFQM: *Implementing the EFQM Model* 2010, http://www.dgq.de/dateien/EFQMModel.pdf, last called 02..09.09.2015

Engert, S., Rauter, R., & Baumgartner, R. J. (2016). *Exploring the integration of corporate sustainability into strategic management: a literature review*. Journal of cleaner production, 112, 2833-2850.

Ernst, G & Young, K (2012). *Connected Car – das Auto der Zukunft*. [pdf] Available at: http://www.ey.com/Publication/vwLUAssets/Connected_Car_-_das_Auto_der_Zukunft_2012/$FILE/Connected%20Car%202012.pdf [Accessed on 20th Feb 2016].

Escrig, A. B., & de Menezes, L. M. (2015). *What characterizes leading companies within business excellence models? An analysis of "EFQM Recognized for Excellence"* recipients in Spain. International Journal of Production Economics, 169, 362-375.

Esi, M. C. (2013). *Performance and Excellence in Defining, Asserting and Concretizing the Mission of Business Organization.* Procedia-Social and Behavioral Sciences, 92, 323-327.

European Commission, (2016). *National Regulatory Authorities.* [online] https://ec.europa.eu/digital-single-market/en/national-regulatory-authorities [Accessed 19 December 2016].

European Parliament, (2015). *Challenges for Competition Policy in a Digitalised Economy.* [pdf] Brussels: European Parliament. Available at: http://www.europarl.europa.eu/studies [Accessed 5 December 2016].

Fazel, L. (2014): *Akzeptanz von Elektromobilität*: Entwicklung und Validierung eines Modells unter Berücksichtigung der Nutzungsform des Carsharing, Springer.

Fellnhofer, K. (2017). *Drivers of innovation success in sustainable businesses.* Journal of Cleaner Production, 167, 1534-1545.

Fichter, K. & Schneidewind, U. (Hrsg.) (2013). *Umweltschutz im globalen Wettbewerb*: Neue Spielregeln für das grenzenlose Unternehmen, Springer Verlag, Berlin Heidelberg: vol. 2 (3), pp 312-332

Figge, F., (2001*). Keine Nachhaltigkeit ohne ökonomischen Erfolg*. Kein ökonomischer Erfolg ohne Nachhaltigkeit, in: PriceWaterhouseCoopers, Wertschaffendes Umweltmanagement 28-37

Fischer, H., et al., (2006). *Geschäftsprozesse Realisieren:* Ein Praxisorientierter Leitfaden von der Strategie bis zur Implementierung. Wiesbaden: Springer Verlag. Pp 55-67

Fleig, Dr. J. (o.J.a): (2017) *Ziele und Aufgaben für den Außendienst,* Managementhandbuch, http://www.business-wissen.de/hb/ziele-und-aufgaben-fuer-den-aussendienst-1, Einsichtnahme: pp 204-207.

Fredendal, L, Lawrence D., Janet B. Craig, P, J., Fowler, und Damali, U (2009) *„Barriers to Swift, Even Flow in the Internal Supply Chain of Perioperative Surgical Services Department*: A Case Study." Decision Sciences Vol. 40, Issue 2, Mai 2009: 327-349.

Frederic. V (2015), *Die Kunst vernetzt zu denken, Ideen und Werkzeuge für einen neuen Umgang mit Komplexität, 10*. Auflage. München: deutscher Taschenbuch Verlag. *Harvard Business Review 76(4)*, 1998: 36-49.

Frigo, M, L; Anderson, R, J. (2011). *What Is Strategic Risk Management?,* Strategic Finance -Montvale- 92, No. 10, pp. 21-22

Fuschi, D. (2016). *A network based business partnership model for SMEs management.* Entrepreneurship and sustainability issues, 3(3), 282-289.

Gallotta, B., Garza-Reyes, J. A., Anosike, A., Lim, M. K., & Roberts, I. (2016). *A conceptual framework for the implementation of sustainability business processes.* Proceedings of the 27th Production and Operations Management Society (POMS).

Gandy, D. L. (2015). *Small business strategies for company profitability and sustainability* (Doctoral dissertation, Walden University).

Gates, S., Nicolas, J.-L.,Walker, P., (2012), *Enterprise risk management: A process for enhanced management and improved performance*, Management Accounting Quarterly, 13 (3), pp.28-38

Geldmacher, W.; Just, V.; Kopia, J.; Kompalla, A. (2017): *"Development of a modified technology acceptance model for an innovative car sharing concept with self-*

driving cars" in BASIQ International Conference: New Trends in Sustainable Business and Consumption - 2017, edited by Rodica Pamfilie, Vasile Dinu, Laurenţiu Tăchiciu, Doru Pleşea, Cristinel Vasiliu, Proceedings of BASIQ Vol. 01.

Geldmacher, W.; Plesea, D.A. Just, V. (2016): *"SWOT Analysis and Evaluation of a Driverless Carsharing Model"* in Proceedings of The 11th European Conference on Innovation and Entrepreneurship 2016; edited by Minna Tunkkari Eskelinen, Iiris Aaltio, Proceedings of ECIE, p. 921-928.

Geldmacher,W., Just, V., Bussian,A., Kopia,J., 2016 *Requirements towards sustainable future urban mobility in Germany*, ISSN: 2457-483X, p116-123

Gibert, M. G. (2004): The Meaning of Technology. Readings from American Sources, 204-253

Giulietti, M., Price, C.W. and Waterson, M., (2005). *Consumer choice and competition policy: a study of UK energy markets*. The Economic Journal, 115(506), pp.949-968.

Global Corporate & Specialty SE, (2016). *Top10 Global Business Risks for 2016*, München, Germany. 15(56), pp.94-96

Godlevskaja, O., Van I, J. & Van der W, T., (2011). *Moving from product-based to service-based business strategies: Services categorisation schemes for the automotive industry*. International Journal of Quality & Reliability Management, 28(1), pp.62–94.

Greenblatt, J.B.; Shaheen, S. (2015): *Automated Vehicles, On-Demand Mobility, and Environmental Impacts*, in: Current Sustainable/Renewable Energy Reports. Pp 7-16

GRI (2006) *Leitfaden zur Nachhaltigkeitsberichterstattung*, Version 3.0, https://www.globalreporting.org/resourcelibrary/GRI-G3-German-Reporting-Guidelines.pdf, Einsicht: 19.04.2017.

Guidi, M., (2015). *The Impact of Independence on Regulatory Outcomes*: the Case of EU Competition Policy. JCMS: Journal of Common Market Studies, 53(6), pp.1195-1213.

Gunner, L., (2011). *Unternehmen und Nachhaltigkeit, Analyse und Weiterentwicklung aus der Perspektive der wissensbasierten Theorie der Unternehmung, Dissertation Universität Stuttgart, Springer Fachmedien*, Wiesbaden. pp.15-23

Hachicha, M., Fahad, M., Moalla, N., & Ouzrout, Y. (2016). *Data & Knowledge Engineering*, 105, 73-89.

Hahn, T., & Aragón-Correa, J. A. (2015). *Toward cognitive plurality on corporate sustainability in organizations:* The role of organizational factors. Vol. 1, No. 1, pp. 230-261

Hahn, T., Pinkse, J., Preuss, L., & Figge, F. (2015). *Tensions in corporate sustainability: Towards an integrative framework*. Journal of Business Ethics, 127(2), 297-316.

Hammer, M, (2014), *What is Business Process Management?,* In: Brocke, J.v.; Rosemann, M., 2014, Handbook on business process management 1 - Introduction, Methods and Information Systems, page 3 – 16.

Harper, L (2016). Collins Dictionary, [online] Glasgow: Harper Collins Publishers. https://www.collinsdictionary.com/dictionary/english-thesaurus/

Harry, P; Guhlich, A., (2016). *Wir wollen bei der Digitalisierung ganz vorne mitspielen*. Stuttgarter Zeitung. Available at: http://www.stuttgarter-zeitung.de/inhalt.interview-mit-porsche-chef-blume-wir-wollen-bei-der-digitalisierung-ganz-vorne-mitspielen.a93510fa-61d4-4a5b-9131-0acc7e49c545.html [Accessed July 29, 2016].

Harvard Business School, (2010). *Improving Business Processes (Pocket Mentor)*. Harvard: Harvard Business Press.

Harvard Computing Group Inc., (2017). *Process Mapping- The Swimlane diagram* http://images.google.de/imgres?imgurl=http://taskmap.com/wordpress/wp-

Hassani, H., Silva, E. S., & Al Kaabi, A. M. (2017). *The role of innovation and technology in sustaining the petroleum and petrochemical industry*. Technological Forecasting and Social Change, 119, 1-17.

Haubrock, M., and Schär, W., (2002). *Bertriebswirtschaft und Management im Krankenhaus*. Bern: Hans Huber. Vol. 7 No. 2, p.1

Hauff, V. M., and Kleine, A., (2014). *Nachhaltige Entwicklung: Grundlagen und Umsetzung,* 2. Auflage, Oldenbourg Wissenschaftsverlag, München. Vol. 1, No. 1, pp. 230-261

Henkel AG & Co. KgaA (2017) Kennzahlen & Fortschritt, http://www.henkel.de/ nachhaltigkeit/ reporting-center/ kennzahlen-und-fortschritt, Einsicht: 13.04.2017

Henning, D (2016). *Multi projekt management* - Studie): www.multiprojektmanagement.org: Ergebnisbericht Multi projekt management - Studie 2004-2006, http://www.multiprojektmanagement.org/ downloads/ 2007 - 09 01_ Ergebnisbericht_ v02.pdf, last called 09.01.2016.

Henning, D., Georg G, H. (2006). *Organisatorische Einflussfaktoren des Multiprojektmanagements,* Projektmanagement aktuell 3/2006,Nürnberg, S. 12–19.

Henning, D., Georg, G, H., Eric, S (2005).*Die gelebte Projektorganisation:* Das Management von Projektelandschaften: Zeitschrift projektMANAGEMENT aktuell, Ausgabe 2/2005, http://www.multiprojektmanagement.org/ downloads/ dammer_ etal_05. pdf , last called 12.12.2015.

Henri, B und Pinsonneault, A. (2005),. *A Model of Organizational Integration, Implementation Effort, and Performance.* " Organization Science 16(2), April 2005: 165-179.

Henry, M (1979.). *The Structuring of Organizations*. Englewood Cliffs, NJ, USA: Prentice-Hall, 4(5*)*, pp. 52–57

Hillman, J. R., (2005). *Understanding Sustainable Development, in Experimental Agriculture*. J. Blewitt, vol. 47, no. 3, pp. 8 – 21,

Hölscher, J. and Stephan, J., (2014). *Competition Policy in Central Eastern Europe in the Light of EU Accession.* JCMS: Journal of Common Market Studies, [e-journal] 42(2), pp.321–345. http://dx.doi.org/10.1111/j.1468-5965.2004.00490.x.

Horton, G., (2014). Beispiele für Disruptive Innovation. http://www. zephram.de/blog/innovation/disruptive-innovation-beispiele> [Accessed 19.12.2016].

Horvath, P., and Gleich, R., (1998). Prozess-Benchmarking in der Maschinenbaubranche. . ZwF, 93, 1998,7-8, pp. 325-329.

Howarth, D., (2015). *Internal Policies: The Commission Defends the EU Consumer*. JCMS: Journal of Common Market Studies, 46(s1), pp.91-107.

Huber, E., Kuster, J., Lippmann, R,. Schmid, A. (2011), *Handbuch Projektmanagement*, 3rd edition, Berlin (u. a.), ISBN-13: 978-3642212420

Hungenberg, H. (2004): *Strategischen Management in Unternehmen*, 3. Auflage, Wiesbaden. pp.76-99.

Huth, C., Kieckhäfer, K. & Spengler, T.S., (2015). *Make-or-buy strategies for electric vehicle batteries—a simulation-based analysis.* Technological Forecasting and Social Change, 99, pp.22–34.

IHK Nürnberg für Mittelfranken (Hrsg.) (2015). *Lexikon der Nachhaltigkeit, Wirtschaft: Sustainable Value Ansatz, Industrie- und Handelskammer Nürnberg für*

Mittelfranken,https://www.nachhaltigkeit.info/artikel/sustainable_value_ansatz_1142.htm, Einsicht: 06.04.2017

Institut für Mobilitätsforschung (Ed.), *2015. Die Zukunft der Mobilität, Szenarien für Deutschland in 2035.* [pdf] Munich. Available at: http://www.ifmo.de/tl_files/publications_content/2015/ifmo_2015_Zukunft_der_Mobilitaet_Szenarien_2035_de.pdf [Accessed on 16th Feb 2016].

Institute of Risk Management, (2006). About Risk Management, https://www.theirm.org/about/risk-management/, 15.03.2016, London

International Transport Forum / OECD, (2015). *Automated and Autonomous Driving.* Regulation under uncertainty. , pp.1–32.

Isaksson, R. B., Garvare, R., & Johnson, M. (2015*). The crippled bottom line–measuring and managing sustainability*. International Journal of Productivity and Performance Management, 64(3), 334-355

Jäger, S. (2008): *Möglichkeiten der Unternehmensanalyse im Rahmen der strategischen Unternehmensplanung*, 1. Auflage 2008, GRIN Verlag.

Jahangir,K., Somers, T, M und Bhattacherjee, A (2007) *„The Impact of ERP Implementation on Business Process Outcomes: A Factor-Based Study.“* Journal of Management Information Systems Vol. 24, No. 1, 101-134.

Jan, K., Just V, (2016), Performance and enterprise risk management, ASE Bucharest. The Bucharest University of Economic Studies vol. 6(8), pp.325–378

Jankal, R. (2014). *The role of innovation in the assessment of the excellence of enterprise subjects*. Procedia-Social and Behavioral Sciences, 109, 541-545.

Jankalová, M. (2014). *Methodical basis of the Business Excellence status assessment*. Procedia-Social and Behavioral Sciences, 109, 546-551.

Joann, M., (2015). *GM fights back in talent war with 1 biln. Dollar investment. Forbes*. Available at: http://www.forbes.com/sites/joannmuller/2015/05/14/gm-fights-back-in-talent-war-with-1-billion-investment-in-rd-tech-center/#5c2abe606870 [Accessed June 20, 2007].

Jockisch, M., (2010). *Das Technologieakzeptanzmodell. In: Das ist gar kein Modell*, Bandow/Holzmüller. Wiesbaden: Springer.

John. P (1995), *“Management of multiple simultaneous projects: a state-of-the-art review.”* In International Journal of Project Management, 13 Nr. 3, 163-168. Elsevier.

Johnson, M. P. (2015). *Sustainability management and small and medium-sized enterprises: Managers' awareness and implementation of innovative tools*. Corporate Social Responsibility and Environmental Management, 22(5), 271-285.

Joseph, H M., und Johnson. M. E (2009) „*When Should a Process Be Art, Not Science?*" Harvard Business Review 87(3), März 2009: 58-65.

Just, V, (2016), *Project Manager, Forschungsgebiet Business Processes and sustainability.* M.Sc. no. 2, pg. 37-41,

Just, V, (2016). *Research in Sustainable Business Process Management.* Journal of Interdisciplinary Economic Research. Vol.1. pp 14-27

Just, V., Buchmüller, M. und Sarbu, A., 2016. *Research in sustainable business process management Editor European Society of Interdisciplinary Economic Research* "Journal of interdisciplinary economic research" Vol.1, 2016, p.14-.27.

Kandachar, P., & Halme, M. (Eds.). (2017). *Sustainability challenges and solutions at the base of the pyramid:* Business, technology and the poor. Routledge.

Karavul, B., (2015). *Prozessmanagement.* http://www.projekt managementhandbuch.de / add-on/prozessmanagement/ [Accessed 19 November 2017].

Kates, R. Parris, T. and Leiserowitz, A. (2016) *"What is Sustainable Development? Goals, Indicators, Values, and practice,"* in Environment, vol. 47, no. 3, pp. 8 – 21.

Keller, G., Nuttgens, M. and Scheer, A.-W., (2015). *Semantische Prozessmodellierung auf der Grundlage "Ereignisgesteuerter Prozessketten (EPK)"*. Veröffentlichungen des Instituts für Wirtschaftsinformatik. Heft 89. Hrsg.: A.-W. Scheer. Saarbrucken. kit.edu/downloads/Bericht_MOP_13_14.pdf (Accessed on: 01st November 2017)

Kiehne, J., Olaru, M., Sven, J. I. and Maier, D. (2016). *Does Globalization drive Innovation?.* Intern. Conference on Production Research – Africa, Europe and the Middle East 4th International Conference on Quality and Innovation in Engineering and Management, 250-255. 25-30. July. Cluj-Napoca, Romania. UTPress.

Kompalla, A., Geldmacher, W., Just, V., Lange, S. (2017) - *Tailored automotive business strategies in the context of digitalization and service-oriented models*, Quality Access to Success, vol. 18, no. 156, pg. 77-84.

Kompas, N., (2017). *Indikatoren. Kompass Nachhaltigkeit, ed.*: http://kmu.kompass-nachhaltigkeit.de/ nachhaltige beschaffung /prozessphase ninstrumente/ messen-und-berichten/ indikatoren/ [Accessed 19 November 2017].

Kopia, J Just, V, Geldmacher, W., Bußian, A (2017) *"Organization Performance And Enterprise Risk Management"* , Ecoforum Journal Vol 6, No 1 (2017), ISSN 2344 – 2174, http://www.ecoforumjournal.ro/index.php/eco/article/view/573

Kralisch, D., Ott, D., Lapkin, A. A., Yaseneva, P., De Soete, W., Jones, M., & Finkbeiner, M. (2018). *The need for innovation management and decision guidance in sustainable process design.* Journal of Cleaner Production, 172, 2374-2388.

Kraus, V., Lehner, O.M., (2013), *The nexus of enterprise risk management and value creation*: Connecting the Dots and Finding the Blind Spots, Journal of Finance and Risk Perspectives, Vol. 1, No. 1, pp. 230-261

Kütz, M.: Effizienz steigern mit PMO, in: B. Sandrino-Arndt, R. L. Thomas, L. Becker (Hrsg.) (2010): *Handbuch Project Management Office*, Düsseldorf 2010, S. 269 – 298.

Lacoste, S. (2016). *Sustainable value co-creation in business networks.* Industrial Marketing Management, 52, 151-162.

Laier, R. (2011). *Value Reporting, Analyse von Relevanz und Qualität der wertorientierten Berichterstattung von DAX-30 Unternehmen*, 1. Auflage, Dissertation Technische Universität Darmstadt, Springer Fachmedien, Wiesbaden pp 201 - 227

Laudien, S. M., & Daxböck, B. (2016). *The influence of the industrial internet of things on business model design:* A qualitative-empirical analysis. International Journal of Innovation Management, 20(08), 164--214.

Lemmer, R., (2012). *Management & Erfolg - Personal - Internationale Insel.* Wirtschaftswoche, 05 November, Issue 45, pp. 80-84.

Levina, O., (2015). *Exploring the Role of Business Process Management in Sustainability Initiatives. MCIS 2015 Proceedings.* http://aisel.aisnet.org/cgi/viewcontent.cgi?article=1002&context=mcis2015 [Accessed 3 June 2018].

Lexikon der Nachhaltigkeit, (2015). *Indikatoren. Industrie und Handelskammer Nürnberg, ed.* https://www.nachhaltigkeit.info/ artikel/indikatoren_1385.htm. [Accessed 19 November 2017].

Lianos, I., (2013). *Some Reflections on the Question of the Goals of EU Competition Law.* CLES Working Paper Series, [e-journal] 3(January 2013), pp.1-65. http://dx.doi.org/10.2139/ssrn.2235875.

Liese, S. & Zapke, A. (2011) *Kennzahlen der Nachhaltigkeit: Bewertung und Beurteilung der Zertifizierungskriterien des DGNB unter Benchmark-Aspekten, Hochschule für Technik und Wirtschaft*, Berlin 2011. Environment 4(13):58-69.

Loorbach, D., & Shiroyama, H. (2016). *Governance of urban sustainability transitions.* Berlin: Springer. 26(4), pp.641-658

LoveToKnow, (2016). *Your Dictionary*. Burlingame: LoveToKnow Corp. Available at: http://thesaurus.yourdictionary.com/disruption [Accessed 12.12.2016].

Lozano, R. (2015). *A holistic perspective on corporate sustainability drivers.* Corporate Social Responsibility and Environmental Management, 22(1), 32-44.

Ludovic-Alexandre, V und Marle, F (2008), *Understanding project complexity: implications on project management".* In Kybernetes, Emerald Group Publishing.Vol. 37 Iss: 8, 1094 - 1110.

Luthra, S., Garg, D., & Haleem, A. (2015). *An analysis of interactions among critical success factors to implement green supply chain management towards sustainability:* An Indian perspective. Resources Policy, 46, 37-50.

Luthra, S., Garg, D., & Haleem, A. (2015). *Critical success factors of green supply chain management for achieving sustainability in Indian automobile industry*. Production Planning & Control, 26(5), 339-362.

Maas, K., Schaltegger, S., & Crutzen, N. (2016). *Advancing the integration of corporate sustainability measurement, management and reporting.* Journal of cleaner production, 133, 859-862.

Maas, K., Schaltegger, S., & Crutzen, N. (2016). *Integrating corporate sustainability assessment, management accounting, control, and reporting*. Journal of Cleaner Production, 136, 237-248.

Mahalingam, T., Nagarajan, S. K., & Chaudhri, A. (2018). *Impact Factor*: 3.029 Peer Reviewed & Indexed Journal. 15(4): 335–343

Manager Magazin, (2016). *Porsche stellt 1600 Tesla-Fighter* ein. http://www.manager-magazin.de/unternehmen/autoindustrie/porsche-1500-jobs-fuer-mission-e-und-gegen-tesla-a-1104843.html [Accessed July 29, 2016].

Manfred Rauch, Diplom.-Ing., Managing Director, Forschungsgebiet Projektmanagement. management in a modern developed economy – like the UK, www.apmgroup.co.uk, 2011-12-20

Mani, V., Agrawal, R., & Sharma, V. (2015). *Social sustainability in the supply chain: Analysis of enablers*. Management Research Review, 38(9), 1016-1042.

Maria. P (2005) *Die Komplexitäts-Falle*: Wie sich Komplexität auf den Menschen auswirkt: vom Informationsmangel bis zum Zusammenbruch. Norderstedt: Books on Demand. in Group & Organization Management, vol. 37, no. 5, pp. 655 – 685,

Markus, S., Rosenkranz, C und Holten. R (2012) *"Der Einfluss der Komplexität auf die Standardisierung von Geschäftsprozessen."* Wirtschaftsinformatik , 2012: 251-261.

Marquardt, K., (2017). *Smart Services – Characteristics, Challenges, Opportunities and Business Models. The 11th International Conference on Business Excellence:* Strategy, Complexity and Energy in changing times. Bucharest, Romania, 30-31.

Martens, M. L., & Carvalho, M. M. (2017). *Key factors of sustainability in project management context:* A survey exploring the project managers' perspective. International Journal of Project Management, 35(6), 1084-1102.

Martin. P (2013) *"Komplex ist mehr als kompliziert."* wirtschaft + weiterbildung, Juni: 42-43.

Mason, Richard O. (1978) *„Measuring information output: A communication systems approach."* Information & Management 1(5): 219-234.

Massa, L., Farneti, F., & Scappini, B. (2015). *Developing a sustainability report in a small to medium enterprise: process and consequences*. Meditari Accountancy Research, 23(1), 62-91.

Mateescu R. (2015). *The Role of Process Interactions Management In Ensuring Business Sustainability*. Volume 5, Number 2, pp. 70-80

McKinsey & StanfordUniversity, (2016). *Automotive revolution – perspective towards 2030*. Stanford University, PEEC Sustainable Transportation Seminar, (January 1st). Volume 11, Number 4, pp. 113-128

Meck, G. and Weiguny, B., (2015). *Disruption, Baby*, Disruption!. http://www.faz.net/aktuell/wirtschaft/wirtschaftswissen/das-wirtschaftswort-des-jahres-disruption-baby-disruption-13985491.html [Accessed 19.12.2016].

Meyer, J., and Teuteberg, F., (2012). *Nachhaltiges Geschäftsprozessmanagement – Status Quo und Forschungsagenda.* In: Multikonferenz Wirtschaftsinformatik 2012, Institut für Wirtschaftsinformatik, Braunschweig. 2, pp. 42-49.

Michael S, MSc, MBA, BA, Managing Director,(2016). Forschungsgebiet Management. 37. pp. 80-88.

Michael. G (2014). *Kompetenzbasiertes Projektmanagement* (PM3): *Handbuch für die Projektarbeit, Qualifizierung und Zertifizierung auf Basis der IPMA Competence*

Baseline Version 3.0, Auflage 7. GPM Deutsche Gesellschaft für Projektmanagement, 2014.

Mocan, B., Fulea, M., Olaru, M. and Buchmueller, M., (2015). *Paradigm shift in robotic systems programming for increasing business sustainability.* The international Conference BASIQ– New Trends in Sustainable Business and Consumption, Bucharest, Rumania, 18-19 June 2015, Bucharest: Amfiteatru Economic. 24(5*)*, pp. 503–520

Moeller, S. & Wittkowski, K., (2010). *The burdens of ownership: reasons for preferring renting.* Managing Service Quality: An International Journal, 20(2), pp.176–191.

Monti, G., (2007). *EC Competition Law.* Cambridge: Cambridge University Press.

Müller, T., (2011). *Zukunftsthema Geschäftsprozessmanagement.* Eine Studie zum Status quo des Geschäftsprozessmanagements in deutschen und österreichischen Unternehmen. Frankfurt a, Main: PricewaterhouseCoopers AG Wirtschaftsprüfungsgesellschaft. Vol. 1, No. 2(4), pp. 14- 24

Nappi, V., & Rozenfeld, H. (2015). *The incorporation of sustainability indicators into a performance measurement system.* Procedia CIRP, 26, 7-12.

Neubauer, F., & Lank, A. G. (2016). *The family business: Its governance for sustainability.* Springer. 36, pp. 499-514.

Nielsen, S., (2012). *Top Management Team Diversity: A Review of Theories and Methodologies.* International Journal of Management, pp. 301-316.

Nigel, M und Ramirez. R (2008) *„Information technology innovation diffusion: an information requirements paradigm."* Information Systems Journal 18(3): 247-273.

Nina, G., Just, V. (2017). *Approach for Measuring Sustainable Employability - A Concept for Academic Education.* In Proceedings of 11th annual International Technology, Education and Development Conference Valencia INTED, March 6-8, Valencia, Spain, 11th International Technology, Education and Development Conference. 43, pp. 49-51.

Nina, G; Just, V, Mathias, S., Michael, S., Michael, B; (2017) *Approach for measuring sustainable employability - a concept for academic education In: 2017 Proceedings of 11th annual International Technology, Education and Development Conference Valencia* 11th International Technology, Education and Development Conference, 6th-8th March, 2017, Valencia, Spain

Object Management Group, (2017). *Business Process Model and Notation (BPMN) V1.1.* [online] Available at: <http://www.omg.org/spec/BPMN/1.1/PDF/> [Accessed 21st June 2017].

OECD, (2009). *Competition Law and Policy.* [pdf] OECD. OECD Journal: Available at: <https://www.oecd.org/oecdjournal/38956797.pdf> [Accessed 25 December 2016].

Oehler, A. and Reisch, L.A., (2016). *Behavioral Economics* - eine neue Grundlage für Verbraucherpolitik? [pdf] Berlin: Verbraucherzentrale Bundesverband e.V. Available at: <http://www.vzbv.de/sites/default/files/mediapics/ studie_behavioral_economics_12_ 2008.pdf> [Accessed 8 December 2016].

ÖGUT (Hrsg.) (2017). *Wesentliche ökologische, soziale und ökonomische Aspekte zur Beurteilung von Nachhaltigkeitsberichten, Positionspapier,* Österreichische Gesellschaft für Umwelt und Technik, im Auftrag des Lebensministeriums, http://www.oegut.at/downloads/pdf/nh-berichterstattung-positionspapier.pdf, Einsicht: 13.04.2017

Ole, H Edoardo J, Miria G, und Margunn A. (2006) "*Reflexive Standardization: Side Effects and Complexity in Standard Making.*" Management Information Systems Quarterly 30(2), 2006: 563-581.

Onete, C, B., Dina R and Denisa, E, V. (2013), *Social Media In The Development Of Sustainable Business*. Bucharest Academy of Economic Studies, Romania, Vol. 15(7). Pp 659-670

Onete, C, B., Dina, R., and Negoi, E, R. (2011) *Estimating The Importance Of Social Media In Consumers' Education And Information Using New Techniques.* Academy of Economic Studies, Bucharest, Romania. vol. 8(5), pp 736-745

Oskam, I., Bossink, B., & de Man, A. P. (2017). *The interaction between network ties and business modeling: Case studies of sustainability-oriented innovations*. Journal of Cleaner Production.pp. 49-54.

Oxford, (2016). *Oxford Dictionaries.* [online] Oxford: Oxford University Press. Available at: <https://en.oxforddictionaries.com/thesaurus/disruption> [Accessed 15.12.2016].

Pádua, S. I. D., & Jabbour, C. J. C. (2015). *Promotion and evolution of sustainability performance measurement systems from a perspective of business process management*: From a literature review to a pentagonal proposal. Business Process Management Journal, 21(2), 403-418.

Paeger, J., (2016). *Die Industrielle Revolution.* [online] Available at: <http://www.oekosystem

Paisittanand, S. & Olson, D.L., (2006). *A simulation study of IT outsourcing in the credit card business.* European Journal of Operational Research, 175(2), pp.1248–1261.

Parnes, L.B., (2016). *Competition and consumer protection.* Consumer Policy Review, 16(5), pp.189-192.

Parvaneh, S., Saudah, S., Zaleha, A, S., Abdul, B (2014). *A Proposed Model of the Relationship between Enterprise Risk Management and Firm Performance*, International Journal of Information Processing and Management (IJIPM) Volume 5, Number 2, pp. 70-80

Paul, H (2014), *Fundamentals of Risk Management: Understanding, evaluating and implementing effective risk management*, Kogan Page Limited London, 3rd Edition vol. 3, pp. 100 – 104, 2014.

Paul, L und Liukko, M (2004) *„Standard, routine and non-routine processes in health care. "* International Journal of Health Care Qualitiy Assurance 17(1),: 39-46.

Pepels, W., (2012). *Handbuch des Marketings.* Munich: Oldenburg Verlag..

Perez, C., (2009). *Technological revolutions and techno-economic paradigms.* [pdf] Available at: <http://technologygovernance.eu/files/main.pdf> [Accessed 04.02.2017].

Pernici, B., Aiello, M. and Donnellan, B. (2012). *"What IS Can Do for Environmental Sustainability :* A Report from CAiSE ' 11 Panel on Green and Sustainable IS.", 30 (18).

Perrini, F., (2006). *SMEs and CSR Theory: Evidence and Implications from an Italian Perspective.* Journal of Business Ethics, Issue 67, pp. 305-316.

Peso, K (2016). *Neue Geschäftsmodelle*. Automobilwoche. Available at: http://www.automobilwoche.de/article/20160715/AGENTURMELDUNGEN/307149901/autokonzerne-suchen-nahe-zu-start-ups [Accessed July 20, 2016].

Phillips, J.J., Bothell T.W., Snead G.L. (2015 *The Project Management Scorecard*, Burlington, 53-62.

PMI (2010). *A Guide to the Project Management Body of Knowledge* p.27-35

Porter, M. E., (2015). *Wettbewerbsstrategie:* Methoden zur Analyse von Branchen und Konkurrenten. Frankfurt/Main, New York: Campus.Vol.7, pp 235

Posselt, G. (2014) *Mitarbeiter führen mit Kennzahlen* – Attention Leadership, Der Weg zum unternehmerischen Erfolg mit zufriedenen Mitarbeitern, Springer Fachmedien, Wiesbaden 2014

Pufahl, M (2015): *Sales Performance Management*, Exzellenz im Vertrieb mit ganzheitlichen Steuerungskonzepten. Springer Fachmedien, Wiesbaden 2. pp. 23-38

Puls Marktforschung, (2013). *Autos kaufen oder teilen*?, Nürnberg. *Journal of Purchasing*, 8(1), pp.63–80.

Quarshie, A. M., Salmi, A., & Leuschner, R. (2016). *Sustainability and corporate social responsibility in supply chains: The state of research in supply chain management and business ethics journals*. Journal of Purchasing and Supply Management, 22(2), 82-97.

Qureshi, M. I., Rasli, A. M., Jusoh, A., & Kowang, T. O. (2015). *Sustainability: A new manufacturing paradigm*. Journal Teknologi, 77(22), 47-53.

Rantala, T., Ukko, J., Saunila, M., & Havukainen, J. (2018). T*he effect of sustainability in the adoption of technological, service, and business model innovations.* Journal of Cleaner Production, 172, 46-55.

Reichl .M. (2015) *Corporate Governance ohne Paragrafen*, Linde Verlag, Wien.State Street Corporate Responsibility Report 2013, Available: http://www.statestreet.com/ content/dam/statestreet/ documents/values/2013_CR_Report.pdf.

Reidel, M., (2016). *So will Volkswagen die Mobilität der Zukunft prägen.* Horizont. Available at: http://www.horizont.net/marketing/nachrichten/Strategie-2025-So-will-Volkswagen-die-Mobilitaet-der-Zukunft-praegen-140799 [Accessed July 20, 2016].

Rezaee, Z. (2016). *Business sustainability research: A theoretical and integrated perspective*. Journal of Accounting Literature, 36, 48-64.

Rogall. H., (2013). *Nachhaltige Ökonomie,* in: Volkswirtschaftslehre für Sozialwissenschaftler: Einführung in eine zukunftsfähige Wirtschaftslehre, S.123-143, 2.

Roome, N., & Louche, C. (2016). *Journeying toward business models for sustainability: A conceptual model found inside the black box of organisational transformation*. Organization & Environment, 29(1), 11-35.

Rosemann, M. and Schwegmann, A., (2015). *Vorbereitung der Prozessmodellierung.* In: Becker, J., Kugler, M. and Rosemann, M. (eds.). Prozessmanagement. Ein Leitfaden zur prozessorientierten Organisationsgestaltung. Muenster: Springer, p. 67.

Sabrina, L (2015) *Komplexität im Projektmanagement. Zühlke, Schlieren, Schweiz:* Soringer Fachmedien Wiesbaden. Vol. 16(9), pp.344-373

Sánchez, M. A. (2015). *Integrating sustainability issues into project management.* Journal of Cleaner Production, 96, 319-330.

Sarbu, A., Mateescu, R., Buchmüller, M. and Just, V., (2016) *Governance as a key factor for ensuring the sustainability of outsourcing model,* 4th International Conference on Management, Leadership and Governance – ICMLG, 14-15 April 2016, St. Petersburg, Russia, indexed Thomson Reuters ISI Web of Science, http://www.academic-conferences.org/conferences/icmlg/ . ISSN: 2049-6818, p.466 -474

Sari, K., Oktay, F. & Tevfik, A.T., (2010). *A simulation model for managing outsourcing decisions.* International Journal of Management and Enterprise Development, 9(2), pp.132–146.

Schaltegger, S., & Wagner, M. (Eds.). (2017). *Managing the business case for sustainability: The integration of social, environmental and economic performance.* Routledge. *Organization Science 16(2),* April: 165-179.

Schaltegger, S., Burritt, R., & Petersen, H. (2017). *An introduction to corporate environmental management: Striving for sustainability.* Routledge. *7(2),* 65-73.

Schaltegger, S., Hansen, E. G., & Lüdeke-Freund, F. (2016). *Business models for sustainability:* Origins, present research, and future avenues. Routledge. *11(9),* 235-239.

Scheer, A-W.. (2011). *ARIS - Modellierungsmethoden, Metamodelle, Anwendungen.* Springer. Vol. 3,pp 32-40

Scheiblich, M., Just, V., Rauch, M., Studeny, M, (2016). *Key performance indicators for process of project prioritisation management,* Editor European Society of Interdisciplinary Economic Research, issue 2, pages "Journal of interdisciplinary economic research" Vol.2, 2016 103-108M ISSN: 2196-4688

Scheiblich, M., Just, V., Rauch, M., Studeny, M, (2016). *Key performance indicators for process of project prioritisation management,* 2016, issue 2, pages 103-108M ISSN: 2196-4688

Schendler, A., (2009), *Getting Green DONE.* New York: PublicAffairs. Vol. 19(12), p 34-37

Schewe, G., (2015). *Workflow*. Available from: http://wirtschaftslexikon.gabler.de/Definition/workflow.html [Accessed 19 2017].

Schmechel, D. u. A. (2013) *Von Säulen, Dimensionen und Kompetenzen, Bayerische Landesanstalt für Wald und Forstwirtschaft*, LWF-Wissen 72, 2013

Schmelzer, H. J. & Sesselmann, W. (2013). *Geschäftsprozessmanagement in der Praxis*: Kunden zufrieden stellen – Produktivität steigern – Wert erhöhen, 8. Auflage, Hanser Verlag, München 2013

Schmid, J., Just, V, (2016) *A Study of The Impact of Corporate Governance of the Upper Echelon on the Value of The Firm – A Focus on the Gender of the Board and Supervisory Board* 28th International Business Information Management Association Conference - Vision 2020: Innovation Management, Development Sustainability, and Competitive Economic Growth - International Business Information Management Association , 9-10 November 2016 Seville, Spain

Schneider, A. (2015). *Reflexivity in sustainability accounting and management: Transcending the economic focus of corporate sustainability.* Journal of Business Ethics, 127(3), 525-536.

Schnobrich, S.; Barz, M. (2013): *Die Business AG* — Aktiengesellschaft für den Mittelstand: Ein Praxisleitfaden zur Kleinen AG, Springer. Vol. 10(5). Pp 108-117

Schuler, H., Haller, S. (2008): *Der neue Innendienst, Mehr Vertriebsproduktivität durch die interne Service-Firma (ISF)*, 1. Auflage 2008, Gabler Verlag, Wiesbaden 2008.

Sebastian, N (2007). *The Definitive Guide to Project Management*. 2nd Ed.n. London (Financial Times / Prentice Hall): 2007. ISBN 978-0-273-71097-4

Shin-Wie, L (2012). *Does ERM (Enterprise Risk Management) Help Firm's Performance in Times of Crisis?,* University of Amsterdam, Amsterdam Business School, Master in International Finance.28-47.

Siemens (Hrsg.) (2015). *Siemens Value Map*, Unser Beitrag zur nachhaltigen Entwicklung Deutschlands, http://www.siemens.com/entry/de/de/ingenuity-for-life/content/pdf/Siemens_Value_Map_Business_to_Society.pdf, Einsicht: 20.03.2017

Silberg, G. et al., (2012). *Self-driving cars: The next revolution.* White paper, KPMG LLP & Center of Automotive Research., 9(2), pp.132–146.

Silvestre, B. S. (2015). *Sustainable supply chain management in emerging economies: Environmental turbulence, institutional voids and sustainability trajectories.* International Journal of Production Economics, 167, 156-169.

Slawinski, N., & Bansal, P. (2015). *Short on time: Intertemporal tensions in business sustainability*. Organization Science, 26(2), 531-549.

Song, Y. W., and Choi, J. K., (2011). *Sustainable Business Process Management for Construction Companies.* In: Journal of Construction Engineering and Project Management, Volume 2, Issue 2.pp 33

Spain,S., Studeny, M., Bartels,A., Rauch, M., Scheiblich, M., Just, V and Buchmüller, M (2016). *Measuring Innovation and Predicting Firm Performance (Part 2).* International Business Information Management Association (IBIMA, ISBN: 978-0-9860419-8-3, page 365 - 374), 9-10 November 2016

Springer, V. S., (2013). *Dimensionen und Kompetenzen, Bayerische Landesanstalt für Wald und Forstwirtschaft.* Journal of Management and Enterprise Development, Vol. 9(2), pp.132–146.

SRC, (2014). *What are waves of innovation.* Available from: http://www.src.sk.ca/node/377 [Accessed 03.03.2018].

Srebotnjak, T., (2011). *Nachhaltigkeit messen – Konzeptionelle Grundlagen und Indikatoren.* Available from: http://ecologic.eu/sites/files/ presentation /2013/TSR_ 112011_ Kompaktseminar_Final.pdf.

State Street Corporate Responsibility Report (2013) [Online], Available: http://www.statestreet.com/content/dam/statestreet/documents/values/2013_CR_Report.pdf

Statista, D (2015a). *Overview Drivers License in Germany.* http://de.statista.com/statistik/daten/studie/257867/umfrage/carsharing--interesse-und-nutzung-in-deutschland/ [Accessed July 27, 2016].

Statista, D (2015b). *Utilization and interest for CarSharing.* Available at: http://de.statista.com/statistik/daten/studie/257867/umfrage/carsharing--interesse-und-nutzung-in-deutschland/ [Accessed July 27, 2016].

Steinke, K. H., (2014). *Green Controlling*: Leitfaden für die erfolgreiche Integration ökologischer Zielsetzungen in Unternehmensplanung und -steuerung, Internationaler Controler Verein.

Stiehl, V., (2017). *Vermittler zwischen den Welten.* [online] Available at: <http://it-republik.de/jaxenter/artikel/BPMN---Vermittler-zwischen-den-Welten-2531.html> [Accessed 21st June 2017].

Sun, J., Wu, S., & Yang, K. (2018). *An ecosystemic framework for business sustainability.* Business Horizons, 61(1), 59-72.

Svensson, G., & Wagner, B. (2015). *Implementing and managing economic, social and environmental efforts of business sustainability: Propositions for measurement and structural models.* Management of Environmental Quality: An International Journal, 26(2), 195-213.

t3N, (2016). *Upcoming visions of Tesla CEO Musk.* Available at: http://t3n.de/news/tesla-masterplan-carsharing-solar-727887/ [Accessed July 29, 2016].

Tachkov, P. (2011). *Nachhaltigkeitsmanagement bei deutschen Unternehmen: empirische Ergebnisse zu Nutzung von Key Performance Indikatoren und Durchführung von Nachhaltigkeitsaktivitäten, Kompetenzzentrum für Innovation und nachhaltiges Management,* Arbeitsbericht Nr. 32a, Ludwigshafen 2011

Tachkov, P., (2011). *Nachhaltigkeitsmanagement bei deutschen Unternehmen: empirische Ergebnisse zu Nutzung von Key Performance Indikatoren und Durchführung von Nachhaltigkeitsaktivitäten, Kompetenzzentrum für Innovation und nachhaltiges Management,* Arbeitsbericht Nr. 32a, Ludwigshafen. Available from: http://www.uni-kl.de/universitaet/verwaltung/zentrale-dienste/qualitaetsmanagement-und-personalentwicklung/prozessmanagement/die-phasen-des-prozessmanagements-im-ueberblick/ [Accessed 19 2017].

Takehiko, N., Barnaby, D (2006),"*Integrating BSC and COSO ERM Frameworks,*" Cost Management, 44, pp. 201–206.

Tarikere T, N., Saxena, K, C und Bharadwaj. S, S (2007) *"Process-oriented taxonomy of BPOs: an exploratory study."* Business Process Management Journal, Vol. 13 Issue: 4,: 588-606.

Technische Universität Kaiserslautern, (2015), *Die Phasen des Prozessmanagements im Überblick.* [online] Available at: < http://www.uni-kl.de/universitaet/verwaltung/zentrale-dienste/qualitaetsmanagement-und-personalentwicklung/prozessmanagement/die-phasen-des-prozessmanagements-im-ueberblick/> [Accessed 27th October 2015].

Thomas, B., Just, V., Kersten, W., Christian, M. (2005) *"Development of an Approach for Analyzing Supply Chain Complexity."* In Mass Customization. Concepts - Tools - Realisation, von Thomas Blecker und Gerhard Friedrich, Amfiteatru Economic, vol. 14(7), p 47-59, ISSN 1582-9146.

Thor, M (2009): *Projektmanagementerfolg*. In Gessler, Michael (Hrsg.). Kompetenzb asiertes Projektmanagement (PM3) Issue 1. Nürnberg: GPM Deutsche Gesellschaft für Pro jektmanagement, Vol. 11, No. 2(14), pp. 143- 148

Tiffert, A. (Hrsg.) et al. (2013): *Führung von Vertriebsorganisationen, Strategie, Koordination, Umsetzung*. Springer Fachmedien, Wiesbaden 2013., 7(5), pp.133–141.

Trkman, P., Budler, M., & Groznik, A. (2015). *A business model approach to supply chain management. Supply Chain Management:* An International Journal, 20(6), 587-602.

Tseng, M., Lim, M., & Wong, W. P. (2015). *Sustainable supply chain management: A closed-loop network hierarchical approach.* Industrial Management & Data Systems, 115(3), 436-461.

Tukker, A., & Tischner, U. (Eds.). (2017). *New business for old Europe: product-service development, competitiveness and sustainability*. Routledge. *Harvard business review*, 77(5), pp.133–141.

Vahs, D. & Schäfer-Kunz, J. (2012), *Einführung in die Betriebswirtschaftslehre*, 6. Überarbeitete Auflage, Schäffer-Poeschel Verlag, Stuttgart 2012 *Journal of Purchasing*, 8(1), pp.63–80.

Valente, M. (2015). *Business sustainability embeddedness as a strategic imperative: A process framework.* Business & Society, 54(1), 126-142.

Vartiak, L., & Jankalova, M. (2017). *The Business Excellence Assessment*. Procedia engineering, 192, 917-922.

VCD (2014a): *Welches sind die Gründe für Ihre Verkehrsmittelwahl?*, Statista, Available at: http://de.statista.com/statistik/daten/studie/372765/umfrage/gruende-fuer-die-wahl-von-verkehrsmitteln/ (Accessed on: 29th June 2016).

Vertrauen, L, N. (2014): Ein Mechanismus der Reduktion sozialer Komplexität, 5. Auflage. Stuttgart: UTB. 23(4), pp.55-63

Vickers, J., (2016). *Healthy competition and its consumer wins*. Consumer Policy Review, 12(4), pp.142-147. Tactics and Techniques, pp. 23-38

Viereckl, R., (2015). *Racing ahead with autonomous cars and digital innovation, Strategy. Journal of Operational Research*, 175(2), pp.1248–1261.

Vogt, A., (2016). *Ride Sharing Investments*. Automobilwoche. Available at: http://www.automobilwoche.de/article/20160525/NACHRICHTEN/305259995/hersteller-beteiligen-sich-an-fahrdiensten-toyota-und-uber,-vw-und-gett,-gm-und-lyft.

Volkswagen Press Release, (2016). *Volkswagen Strategie Together*. Available at: http://www.volkswagenag.com/content/vwcorp/content/de/investor_relations.bin.html/superteaser/tabs/tab/teaserlists/link_1/file/Presse_deutsch_NICHTanimiert_Version_24.pdf [Accessed July 15, 2016].

Vom Brocke, J., & Sonnenberg, C. (2015). *Value-orientation in business process management*. In *Handbook on Business Process Management 2* Springer, Berlin, Heidelberg. (pp. 101-132).

Weber, T., (2016). *Neue Geschäftsmodelle.* Automobilwoche. Available at: http://www.automobilwoche.de/article/20160715/AGENTURMELDUNGEN/307149901/autokonzerne-suchen-nahe-zu-start-ups [Accessed July 20, 2016].

Weis,B. X., (2014). *Praxishandbuch Innovation.* [e-book] Wiesbaden: Gabler Verlag. http://dx.doi.org/10.1007/978-3-8349-4638-6_2.

Wilkens, S., (2007). *Effizientes Nachhaltigkeitsmanagement, Betriebswirtschaftliche Forschung zur Unternehmensführung*, Dissertation Universität Hamburg, GWV Fachverlag GmbH, Wiesbaden, , S. 242-248

Wirtschaftslexikon24, (2015). *Prozessmanagement.* Available from: http://www.wirtschaftslexikon24.com/d/prozessmanagement/prozessmanagement.htm [Accessed 19 2017].

Wise, M., (2017). Competition Law and Policy in the European Union (2005). *OECD Journal of Competition Law and Policy,* 9(1), pp.7-80.

Wittmayer, J. M., Van Steenbergen, F., Rok, A., & Roorda, C. (2016). *Governing sustainability: a dialogue between Local Agenda 21 and transition management. Local Environment*, 21(8), 939-955.

Wolter, M. I., Mönnig, A., Hummel, M., Schneemann, C., Weber, E., Zika, G., Helmrich, R., Maier, T. and Neuber-Pohl, C., (2015). *Industrie 4.0 und die Folgen für Arbeitsmarkt und Wirtschaft.* [pdf] Available at: <http://doku.iab.de/forschungsbericht/2015/fb0815.pdf> [Accessed 20.12.2016].

Woods, M. (2007). *Linking Risk Management to Strategic Controls*: A Case Study of Tesco plc. International Journal of Risk Assessment and Management 7(8): 1074–1088.

World Commission on Environment and Development, (1987) *Our common future*. Oxford: Oxford University Press.

Wright, W. F. (2016). *Client business models, process business risks and the risk of material misstatement of revenue.* Accounting, Organizations and Society, 48, 43-55.

Yin, R.K., 2003. *Case Study Research: Design and Methods*. 3rd ed. Thousand Oaks, California, London, New Delhi: Sage.

Zu, L (2013). *Sustainability Risk Management*, In: Idowu, S.O., Capaldi, N., Zu, L., Das Gupta, A. (Eds.), 2013, Encyclopedia of Corporate Social Responsibility, Springer-Verlag, Berlin. Environment 47(3): 8-21.

Zu, L. (2013), *Sustainability Risk Management, in: Encyclopedia of Corporate Social Responsibility*, Berlin: Springer. pp. 2395 – 2407

Kolibri 360 GmbH
Ferdinand-Jühlke-Straße 7
99095 Erfurt, Deutschland
produktsicherheit@kolibri360.de